Wilson, Maxwell

Joe Haines's book about Wilson anecdote, much of it unknown, illuminating insight into the character of these two men he knew so well. This is history written by one who was there when it was happening and knew the key figures' thought. Joe draws a fascinating analogy between Maxwell and Trump, both men who loved the limelight but dreaded boredom.

Peter Jay, former UK ambassador to the United States of America and one-time Chief of Staff to Robert Maxwell.

An eye-witness, first-hand account of one of the most fascinating periods of modern British history, written by one of the keenest and most intelligent political minds of the era. It is a masterpiece, of equal value to the general reader and the scholar.

Peter Oborne, political writer and broadcaster.

Joe Haines comes to this memoir from a unique position. Growing up among London's poorest working people, he acquired a valuable sense of British Labour public opinion and values. He then progressed to work for much of his life at the top of journalism and politics and close to two remarkable men: Harold Wilson, one of Britain's most successful post-war prime ministers, and Robert Maxwell, one of its most charismatic and notorious characters. Each, as I observed, greatly valued his political judgment and trusted his honesty and integrity. Haines writes vividly and with wit about people and an age now seeming long past, yet which shaped the society now crumbling around us.

Lord Donoughue, Chief Policy Adviser to Harold Wilson (1974-76) and James Callaghan (1976-79).

KICK 'EM BACK
Wilson, Maxwell and Me

Joe Haines

Grosvenor House
Publishing Limited

This book is published by
Grosvenor House Publishing Ltd
Link House
140 The Broadway, Tolworth, Surrey, KT6 7HT.
www.grosvenorhousepublishing.co.uk

A CIP record for this book
is available from the British Library

ISBN 978-1-78623-442-1

Dedication

For my wife, Irene, who has had to put up with a lot.

Preface

All the main characters in this book are more than men of yesterday, they are men of yester-decade. Hardly contemporary, barely historical yet. Harold Wilson, had he lived, would be more than 100 now, and his wife, Mary, died in 2018 aged 102, a lonely end though in truth she had lived a lonely life since Alzheimer's remorselessly destroyed her husband's once-fine intellect; he was Prime Minister in another age, remembered by the elderly but his importance insufficiently recognised today. Robert Maxwell reached the peak of his perennial notoriety when he died in 1991 in mid-Atlantic - but not by drowning, for no sea-water was found in his lungs. His death, typically, on November 5, was explosive and occurred in mystery and controversy, much as he lived, though a heart attack was its most probable cause. And I, who worked with them each of them for a period of seven years, retired on a pension from full-time, paid employment in 1990.

So why do I bother to write about us now? I suppose because despite the millions of words written about both of them, they were words written, in the main, by those who never knew them, knew of them second-hand at best, or hated them while knowing little about them. There are still brush strokes to complete and round off their portraits.

Wilson will be a growing and eventually, I believe, a substantial figure in British political history, even more so as his successors diminish in stature. Where is his like today? They will still write about, and misunderstand, him in 100 years time whereas most of his successors will merely be footnotes. I wish I had been able to write about him in more glowing terms than I do at times and predict an even greater place in history for him but I hope this memoir will help to reduce those misunderstandings. It is rare for biographers to know their subjects intimately; usually, they can only deal with the written record, sometimes objectively, sometimes subjectively and sometimes plainly wrong.

I was fortunate with both Wilson and Maxwell, because I knew them so well. They were both profoundly insecure men, both believing in dark forces working to bring them down. I knew Wilson better because my work was for him alone and I was consulted on almost everything he did. With Maxwell, I was more detached. When I offered, many years ago, the opinion about biographers who did not personally know their subject, one of Wilson's professional biographers, Philip Ziegler, gave me an abusive answer when I thought I was being uncontroversial and only proved my point.

To give a simple explanation of what I mean. I went with Wilson when he delivered the Ernest Bevin Memorial lecture, in which he highly praised the former Foreign Secretary in Clement Attlee's Government. I said to him when he came off the platform, "I didn't know that you thought so much of him." "Joe," he replied, "the only good news I ever heard about Bevin was when they told me he was dead." What is the professional historian of the future to write of the governmental relationship between the two men – one anti-Israeli, the other very much pro - if he only knows the written or public record? Even private diaries are often written with the hope of eventual publication and can be an uncertain guide.

I have tried here to relate what conditions were like in his office and his government when I joined him on January 1, 1969, and what they were like when I left him, without suggesting that all or any changes, good or bad, were down to me, though my predecessor at No. 10 blamed me for the loss of the 1970 general election, which demonstrated a green eye rather than a perspicacious one. As Machiavelli said, "place the saddle on the right horse." I have also sought to examine the relationships between him and his leading colleagues, opposing politicians like Ted Heath and Jeremy Thorpe and, as ever, his notorious secretary, Lady Falkender, and glance at the amazing coincidence that both Thorpe and she were involved in murder plots at around the same time, one as an instigator and the other as the intended target..

What I have not done, in any substantial way, is to write a history of his governments. I have written extensively in the past, and so has he, and so have his biographers, official and unofficial. What I am attempting to do, without repeating myself inordinately, is to show the pressures he was under, how he responded, and what a genuinely funny, warm man he was, totally lacking in pomposity and, on the better days, someone it was a joy to work for and with. To do that, I have to deal with much that is part of his political history that is on the written record, but also much that isn't. I have looked at the suspicion in which he was held by his own colleagues as well as MI 5 and how he fuelled them, perhaps unnecessarily so.

The same applies to the lengthy section on Maxwell. I have tried to set out the culture of the *Daily Mirror* when I first joined it, fatalistic about its own future, shackled hand and foot by corrupt unions and plodding on into a feared and unknown digital destiny in the dissemination of the news. I was at the *Mirror* for seven years before Maxwell came and for seven years afterwards. The most virulent writings about him came from people who knew him little or not at all. To some extent they were right. He was as amoral and dictatorial as Donald Trump. He could be appalling; he was a bully, boastful, a cutter of legal corners and in the end, a massive thief and the consequences of his actions lived on, and still live, long after his burial in the Mount of Olives in Jerusalem. But there was another side to him which was none of those things.

I have tried, too, to describe how powerful people, men, mainly, reacted to him, from the rebellious to the craven, from those with whom one would willingly serve in the trenches to those always ready with a white flag. They should have learned from his wartime record: those who waved a white flag in front of him ran the risk of being shot. But just as no person is good all the way through, short of those who are officially so and sanctified, few are totally rotten; Maxwell, without fuss or publicity, paid for an operation which saved the sight of a *Mirror* reporter's daughter. He never told me that. The reporter did. He could sometimes do good by stealth. That was the other Maxwell.

Wilson and Maxwell could hardly have been more different yet they shared one crucial characteristic: they both suffered from chronic insecurity and both were lonely men. I was a friend and companion to Wilson – not my description but one given to me by Lady Falkender in the brief halcyon days of our relationship. Wilson had a genuine sense of humour and could be very amusing, even if waspishly so on occasions. When the Speaker, Sir John Hylton-Foster, suddenly died in 1965, leaving Wilson's Government to replace him out of its thin majority, he lamented privately: "He died as he lived, unhelpful." And I still think as a Commons classic his off-the-cuff description of Sir Bernard Braine, a Conservative MP who interrupted him in a debate, as a "misnomer." That aspect of him was captured beautifully on his retirement by the *Sun's* cartoonist, Stanley Franklin, who portrayed him as Max Miller – the best comedian of my age, "the Cheeky Chappie" - over the caption, "There will never be another like him, lady, there will never be another." The original cartoon hangs on my wall at home.

Maxwell had no friends. He had acolytes, toadies, flatterers and ex-employees. It was those in those categories who were ready to pin their label on me after the crash. I have let them down lightly in this memoir, but not altogether. I say in all modesty that Maxwell sought to make me his friend, no matter how candid, and in that respect he allowed me a licence which few, if any, others enjoyed. There was one ludicrous episode when he asked me to meet him outside the office and took me off towards the Czech embassy where he was having lunch. He got straight to the point. He was upset, he said, and took personally, my repeated refusal to accept an office car from him. I pointed out, as I had before, that I didn't drive. "Your wife does," he said. "I may want her to drive you up to see me. I will buy you a Rolls-Royce." I feebly retorted that I couldn't get it into my garage. He really got upset then and said I could have any car that did fit, though if I'd said a Fiat I don't think his rage would have been containable. "All right," I said. "I'll have a Mercedes." "Good," he said, and stopped the car. "You can go back now." And I went back to my own lunch appointment, 45 minutes late and several miles away. Lord Beaverbrook was apt to act in the same way. It was an example of the same chronic sense of insecurity from which Wilson suffered but he tackled it in a profoundly different way. Where Wilson would try to win over people who resisted him, Maxwell would seek to batter them into submission, buy them off or destroy them.

When Maxwell commented, "Jerusalem wasn't built in a day," it was funny only because he didn't know that the correct quotation was about Rome. Yet he did have a sense of humour. Surprisingly, in later years, he and Wilson got on well and after Wilson's retirement Maxwell gave him the use of a flat in Oxford without fuss or publicity. Wilson never had the contempt for him as he had, say, for Jeffrey Archer, who almost fawned on Maxwell. Perhaps Archer saw in him the successful tycoon he never was.

After I had written *The Politics of Power* revealing the appalling turmoil of what was Wilson, private office, relations between us were understandably strained. But Maxwell ended that when he called me up to his office one day – and Wilson was there. It was as though nothing had happened between us. He was warm and friendly without a word of reproach. Later we had other conversations, but the last was the saddest. We were both attending a dinner at the Café Royal when we met in the cloakroom. We spent 30 minutes in recalling our past days together before moving to our tables. At the end of the evening, we met again in the cloakroom and spent another 30 minutes while he repeated everything he had said to me earlier. He had no memory of meeting me only two hours before.

For both him and Maxwell, I am trying to add a little knowledge which will help historians and general readers to get a better balance. Wilson's human side is well known; Maxwell's is not.

As for me, a minor player and observer in this cast, I have been praised and vilified in equal measure for working for them; sometimes, but not often, by people who did know me. I hope I'm indifferent to both attitudes, or too old to care. But I thought that as someone whose relationship with both men was unique, I ought to tell how a boy from the poorest part of London, whose regular education ended effectively when he was 11, arrived in those positions of influence, in both cases with some reluctance. My background was little different from Maxwell's in its beginning, except in degree. We were both raised in poverty, his extreme. Wilson's was lower middle class; perhaps I had reached that level monetarily by the time we first met, though I don't think that it made the slightest difference to either or us and I would have contested it, anyway. I certainly don't put forward my upbringing as an excuse or defence for my association with these two men, but as a possible explanation. It is for others to make up their minds whether my overall contribution to either or both had a positive or negative effect. For myself, I have no doubt.

Joe Haines, 2018

Kick 'em Back

I was born, long, long ago in one of the poorest districts of South-east London and expect to die, in a rather shorter period, in one of the richest towns of Kent. From a poverty-stricken slum to the affluence of Royal Tunbridge Wells was a giant step for me, if not for mankind. The Rotherhithe of my childhood was shabby, grubby, and disheveled, occasional houses with broken windows, paint peeling from the shopfronts, sawdust strewn on the floor of the local pub, wharves whitened by the dust of millions of bags of flour that had passed through them, principal roads made of wooden blocks covered with black tar, accident-prone whenever a drizzle fell upon them, the façade of insanitary terraced houses and flats blackened by the coal fires of generations and the streets littered with, well, litter. An air of pessimism and chronic unemployment pervaded it between the wars and not much hope immediately after the second one.

Only the green magnificence of Southwark Park and the spirit of the people alleviated an environment little improved since the days of Dickens. It was a community with a proud past, a dismal present and no apparent future. In its heyday, it was a rural village outside London; so healthy was the air that Henry IV went there to be cured of his ailments, reputedly including leprosy. He died a chronic invalid. By my time, he could have arrived healthy and left a very sick monarch.

The streets were narrow and the pathways, one of which was ironically named Sun Alley, because it only briefly saw the sun or moon in its miserable existence. Homeless, dossers, beggars - how so many of the people remained honest is a mystery. For the price to be paid today for a penthouse in a converted warehouse in Rotherhithe Street a speculator could once have bought most of the district.

Nowadays, smart new private apartments (only council tenants live in flats) abound and the fog and dirt of Rotherhithe's Dark Age is all but forgotten except by older former inhabitants like me. The slum housing, as squalid as any south and east of

Westminster, has gone, assisted in large part by the Luftwaffe. The new housing which has replaced it has all the fitments a young couple could desire. My wife and I were born too early. We searched for weeks before our marriage for somewhere to live. Fortunately, a friend of a friend in my wife's office tipped us off about a flat in Deptford that was vacant: one bedroom, kitchen and living room and 57 stairs to climb to reach it. We stayed there for nearly five years. The political lesson was that rent controls don't work. Deptford was no better than Rotherhithe and in some respects worse. But that's getting ahead of my story.

There was no relief from the general poverty of Rotherhithe as I grew up. My run-down primary school, which disappeared decades ago, was painted, long before my time, in standard local authority flaking green and yellow. The classrooms were crowded, the sporting facilities non-existent and the lavatories were outside in the playground. There were no organised games on the premises though the boys competed to see who could pee the highest up the lavatory wall. The teaching staff were kindly, patient and female but taught us no more than the basic three Rs and some geography. Its stone steps dipped in the middle, worn smooth by countless children of several generations scampering up and down them. Free school meals were a luxury we never experienced. It was joked later in life that we were too poor to afford them. I avoided catching the usual childhood diseases of mumps, measles and chicken pox which were widespread, but I got scarlet fever, a rather worse affliction, and spent three weeks in an isolation room at the New Cross Fever Hospital.

The bug-ridden, gaslit slum in which I lived for the first ten years of my life had to be fumigated every year or so, to clear the lath and plaster walls of the infestation. Take me anywhere in the world and if there are bugs there I will know them by their smell, in the same way as I would recognize the odour of Rotherhithe's underground station, a combination of damp, decay and decrepitude, built in the 19th century and showing it, its platform walls green with the slime left by water leaking from the nearby Thames. It was hardly a gateway to rich pastures – not with

Surrey Docks and New Cross stations in one direction and Stepney, Whitechapel and Shoreditch in the other, but it was more than Greenwich and Blackheath had at the time.

The sights and those smells of the past have long since disappeared from Rotherhithe, but not the memories. We played football in the streets, climbed drainpipes of the new blocks of flats that were being built to replace our homes, bought chestnuts in winter from an itinerant with his brazier on wheels, threw penny fireworks at each other, built effigies of Guy Fawkes to wheedle coins from passers-by and stood outside the tobacconists to cadge fag-cards from the smokers. We foraged on the river shore for decent pieces of wood to make scooters or carts and ran errands for those housewives ready to pay a penny or two for our services, mainly buying bags of coke for them at the local gashouse. Opposite our first home at 30 Adams Gardens was a tall gas-lamp. I was always entranced, especially when it was foggy, which was often, to see the gaslighter come each evening to illuminate the street into a bright yellow haze. We were allowed outside to play when darkness fell to an extent which would horrify mothers of today but no one ever got hurt except by another playmate. Anyone who molested children in those days would have suffered street justice if an irate parent caught them at it, though I knew of none who were.

My mother, my sisters and I decamped from our slum terrace in 1938 and moved into a small, new and sturdy block of flats. Ours was the middle of three blocks joined together. On the left-wing, appropriately, lived Dick Barrett the leader of the most militant trade union in Britain. In the right-wing, to become more famous than either of us, lived the Bygraves family, whose eldest son, Wally, after the war ended and he left the RAF, changed his Christian name to Max and became known all over the world as a singer and comedian. Max's parents were always seen together, trotting down to the nearby Bricklayers' Arms every evening. When Max had earned enough to buy them a house in the yearned-after middle-class area of Lewisham, they couldn't break the habit of a lifetime. They would board a 47 bus at night and come back to The Brick.

Poor though it was, Rotherhithe wasn't always like that. The *Fighting Temeraire,* captured at Trafalgar, was broken up there in the first dry dock in Britain. J.M.W. Turner's famous painting of her was when she was off Greenwich, being towed to the dry dock for destruction. Brunel built the first under-river tunnel there to connect it with the north of London.

The *Mayflower* set sail from there for Plymouth in 1620 to pick up the pilgrims making their fateful voyage to America for a new life free from persecution. I was born and grew up about 300 yards from where it left. Most of the crew, including their captain, Christopher Jones, came back and were eventually buried in St Mary's churchyard, no more than 100 yards from the river Thames. A subsequent church built on the site in the early 18th century was where my wife, Irene, and I married in 1955. There is a Mayflower Street nearby and a West Street, probably named after the ship's owner, to arouse the interest of the amateur historian. A public house, called the Spread Eagle in my youth, was renamed the Mayflower by an enterprising new owner and attracts adventuresome U.S tourists who dare to explore British food and London outside the West End and another, evocatively called The Ship, where for two or three years in my late teens I spent the hours before a late lunch on Sunday playing cards for money.

Rotherhithe's most distinctive feature as I was growing up flowed from a landmark Independent Labour Party decision in the early part of the 20th century to plant trees in every street in Bermondsey, into which Rotherhithe was incorporated, a decision which is still evident today despite the ravages of the war and modern architecture. But peacetime had its ravages, too. The increased river trade filled its wharves with grain, which smelled evilly in the summertime, as did the wharf which held imported animal skins. "Don't go near there," my mother warned, "or you'll get anthrax," which sounded as dreadful as catching smallpox or tuberculosis. Factory hooters blared at 8.a.m. calling their workers to a day of miserable work of heavy labour, which was better than nothing. There was a strong work ethic in those days, as the long queues outside the Labour Exchange each day would testify. Needs must. There was no other honest source of income.

The river shore swarmed with rats, seeking to plunder barges beached there. The principal local employers were the master stevedores who controlled the business in the Surrey Docks – now fashionably renamed Surrey Quays without a dock in sight – and it was a hideous, cruel and dangerous, more dangerous than the coal mines, working environment they offered. The stevedores' labourers and the dockers would assemble twice a day, standing on "the stones," a large shed open to the weather, hoping to be called to work by the gangers, or foremen, charged with hiring. For the fortunate ones as well as for the disappointed, always a large number, a pub across the road to the dock entrance opened at 6.30 a.m. My mother hated it; the work was doubly dangerous if a man had a couple of pints inside him before he started.

Our house had two bedrooms, one shared by my mother and my two older sisters and the other occupied by me, a scullery, tiny living room or kitchen, an outside, unlighted lavatory and a yard, not much bigger than its description. My weekly task was to tear up the copies of our only newspaper, *The People,* into rectangles to be used as toilet paper.

My sisters could not have been more different. Emma, eight years older than me, was robust, aggressive, and unafraid of anything but ghosts and had at least one fairly convincing story seeing one. Before the war she worked on the production line of Cross and Blackwell's canned food factory, then when war broke out worked a lathe in a munitions factory and spent her evenings as an air raid warden. She married at the age of 19 in June, 1940, when our world seemed to be crashing around us and the French had scurried to make peace with Hitler. That took some courage. My other sister, Elizabeth, named after my mother, was called Lizzie by us, which she hated, and Betty by her friends. She was thin, scrawny with a persistent cough which marked her out as a potential tuberculosis victim. When the bombing of London started she spent every night in an air raid shelter and eventually escaped her terror by joining the Land Army. It worked a miracle on her, physically. She went from scrawny to brawny, put on a couple of stones and was a picture of glowing health. That's what leaving urban poverty for rural plenty could do for you.

The other occupant of our house was my paternal grandfather who lived, slept, ate and was eventually laid out in the front room when the time came to bury him. He was illiterate. A friend once wrote a signature for him which he laboriously copied and memorised. But he didn't know which way up it went so when he had to use it, it was always upside down. When I was six I sometimes read a newspaper to him, or anything I could find, to his and my delight. I read everything I could lay my hands on. My mother bought me *Champion* each week and I always saw second-hand copies of *Hotspur, Wizard* and *Rover.* I devoured them all, as well as my mother's weekly extravagance, the *Red Star Weekly.*

My grandfather and my mother, as the saying had it, "didn't get on," for reasons unknown to me and probably forgotten by them. I suppose she did his washing, but the only meal I ever saw her supply him with was a daily raw egg beaten inside a cup of hot tea. The street named Adams Gardens was no doubt so called by someone with a sense of humour, though there were two allotments at one end which I suppose partly excused its description.

One end of Adams Gardens was too narrow for the ambulance that came to take Seamus, as grandfather was generally and mystifyingly known – Thomas as he was baptized - to his last bed in St Olave's hospital and he had to walk to it, waving vigorously. Gracie Field's hit song of the period, "Wish me Luck as you Wave me Goodbye" comes to mind each time I remember him. He was born 11 years before Colonel Custer was killed at Little Big Horn and his grandfather would have been alive at the time of Waterloo and Trafalgar. That I knew someone whose grandfather would have existed then brought those events excitingly closer. Seamus died, aged 72, of a heart attack the day he was due to leave hospital having been cured of a carbuncle, a common affliction in those days. My sadness at his death, limited as it was by his permanent unpleasantness to my mother, was exceeded by my disappointment. I had received the best birthday present of my life, a football, that morning on my ninth birthday and I had rushed home from school to play with it, but as

I reached the house I saw that all the curtains had been drawn. In those days that meant only one thing, that death had arrived. My mother may have detested him, but she knew what was right and proper.

As was also the custom, barbaric as I think it now, I was taken into his room to view his body in the open coffin. I must admit, I was curious but unmoved. My lasting memory of that morning was that he needed a shave. I hadn't realized that facial hair continued to grow after a man had died.

Anyway, the football had to stay locked away until the funeral carriage, pulled by two black horses, had safely taken him to Honor Oak Cemetery and a grave which, as far as I know, was never visited by anyone again. There were no tears. Sentiment was an indulgence in those days when there were other things than death to worry about. While my mother was at the cemetery, grandfather's daughter, one of my Aunt Roses (I had several) arranged for someone to enter the house and removed every stick of his belongings. Gratitude for tolerating him for 15 years wasn't much in evidence, either.

It must have been his tenancy originally, however, because he was named as living there at the time of the 1900 census when my mother was a four-year-old living and growing up in Stepney. Why he was called Seamus no one ever told me. The only connection with Ireland that I knew was that he received a box of shamrock on St Patrick's Day every year. He was not a Catholic nor was his funeral service conducted in a Catholic church. Stories about the enmity between him and my mother were handed down to me by my sisters. One, which may or may not have been embroidered by the retelling, stood out. One Saturday evening, it was said, a neighbour told my mother that Seamus was getting drunk at The Bricklayers' Arms. He could be nasty when not sober, so my mother locked the front door, to protect us children rather than herself. Seamus was undaunted, however, and tried to climb through the window of his room. My mother waited until he was teetering on the window sill and then pushed him backwards. He (a 15-stone docker) called the police and she (with a fighting weight of eight-stone) was charged with assault at Tower Bridge

Magistrates' Court and fined five shillings, which was heavy for the time – the equivalent of a week's rent – and bound over not to repeat the offence. Only a 1930s magistrate could have passed such a sentence. Still, Seamus never tried it again.

School was not a burden for me. For a start, we never had homework. We had exams every six months or so and I usually came top, except for one occasion when I was accused by the teacher of copying the arithmetic answers from the girl sitting next to me and demoted to seventh place. That was hurtful, because I was better at "maths", as it is archly called today, than anyone else in the class. I wasn't cheating: my eyes were too weak to see the blackboard and I asked a fellow pupil to read out the sums to me. I then worked out the answer in my head (mental arithmetic was my speciality) and wrote down the answers, without any working out on the page.

The teacher was determined that I wouldn't "cheat" again. At the next exam, she placed Bill, the dunce of the class (who also happened to be the best footballer in the school by far and my best friend at the time) next to me. When the results were announced, she glossed over the fact that I had come top of the class again; instead, she praised my friend for his hard work which had raised him from 23rd to sixth in the rankings. How the blazingly apparent logic of what had happened escaped her, I'll never know. But at the next exam my friend Bill was sitting somewhere else and came bottom again.

Being ahead of the others had its drawbacks. I was nicknamed "professor" which I didn't mind, and also "Bugs-eyes" which I did. I had frequent black eyes from many fights resulting from the name-calling; but there would have been more of them if I hadn't retaliated.

I was also a good footballer for my age. One day I was proudly told by our sports mistress that I had been chosen to play inside right for the senior school, which conveniently happened to be at the bottom of the street where I lived. Any pride on my part was soon shattered. The seniors didn't want a kid playing with them and so I never received a pass throughout the game. It taught me I had to make my own luck.

My biggest gain from primary school was that it gave me a love of epic poetry. When I was 10, a prize was offered (a penknife, would you believe; there would be questions in the Commons if it happened today) for the first pupil who could recite 26 verses of the "Lays of Ancient Rome," with not too many stumbles on the way. It was my first public speaking engagement, but I drew my breath and started at the chosen point in the poem: "The consul's brow was sad and the consul's speech was low..."and got the penknife.

I progressed to the senior school (having failed my grammar school exam perhaps because, once again, I couldn't read the blackboard and was too frightened or too proud to admit it) where discipline was severe. One teacher, mockingly known as "Tarbrush" because of a hairstyle 20 years in advance of his time, was slight of stature but immense in sadism. He would stand on a desk and jump off with a cane in his hand when he was administering punishment. But he was a figure of fun. Others were almost as severe but more fair: one, Mr Chesterton - if he had a Christian name we never knew it and we were too terrified to give him a nickname – once caned a boy because he had seen him jump on the back of a lorry outside school hours. We thought that a bit unfair. We all jumped on lorries or horse and carts to get a free ride. Ginger was unlucky.

I had one holiday in my early life, arranged by the local Labour council for the children of the poor. I spent a fortnight at St Margaret's Bay near Dymchurch, in Kent, and saw the sea and a beach for the first time in my life and a distant blur on the horizon which they said was France. Captivating. Apart from that, I never went on holiday, though there was each year a "busman's holiday" when local busmen took us to Theydon Bois in Essex in coaches or buses hired by the council. My mother never went beyond Southend in her life until she flew to Canada in 1961 to see her younger daughter. Southend was the London working class's Costa Brava, just as the Peckham Rye department store, Jones and Higgins, was their Harrods. We lived in a classless society in that we were all members of the same class. The West End was another country, where the toffs lived and shopped. Only they went abroad for their holidays.

And then, after Dymchurch, the Second World War broke out. In the month before, August, 1939, I sat on the grass at Kennington Oval and watched the last Test Match to be played in England for six years. I remember Learie Constantine bowling and the England captain, Wally Hammond, hitting the ball straight at me, behind the boundary rope. Life wasn't always dreary. But there can't be many still alive who were with us on that day.

I was evacuated on September 1, 1939, to live with an aunt Louise (one of two of that name) in Twickenham, Middlesex, not very far from the centre of London which the experts had confidently forecast would soon be consumed with fire or otherwise destroyed. It is a definition of experts to say that they know the best way to get things wrong. I listened, as did most people, at 11 a.m. on September 3, to the doleful voice of Neville Chamberlain announcing that Adolf Hitler had not responded to our ultimatum to them to leave Poland and thus "we are at war with Germany."

No one realized on that terrible morning that what had happened was to transform our lives, politically, socially, and in every other way that the war-enforced technologies would bring. Nor could I have known that I was one of the last generation of boys who could make their way to a successful career without a higher education. But the age of deference was ending and the despised working classes were needed to fill the ranks of the armed forces and to win the war and their wives, daughters and sisters were recruited to the war factories.

But immediately in September, 1939, it was the bore war, not a bombing war, that happened. In Twickenham, I was with a 14-year-old cousin called George, two healthy young boys with nothing to do, and both unwilling to accept the morning cold bath Aunt Louise imposed upon us (probably more to keep his hormones in check than mine. I was only 11).

That bath was the first point of friction between us and our aunt. The second was that, as she ran a sweet shop, we usually took a handful of sweets on our way out to the riverside. Falling into the Thames as I tried to help a fisherman land an eel was the third and final event that made Aunt Louise say, "Enough!"

We were sent home 10 days after arriving. My mother was prim and proper and probably relieved at my homecoming: my aunt was a scarlet woman, not being married to the man she was living with; she was an ex-journalist, and the impression I got was that you couldn't expect anything else from someone who had worked in a profession of depravity. Apart from an early air raid warning, which turned out to be a false alarm, nothing had occurred in the war on the home front, though *The Royal Oak* had been sunk at Scapa Flow.

The only domestic happening of note while I was away was that my school had been taken over by the Air Raid Precautions (ARP) organisation never to re-open again as a place of learning, and that the headmaster, Cross by name and nature, had absconded with the School Holiday Fund money, never to be seen again. Some of us few pupils still remaining in London entered his abandoned garden and found a huge stack of empty wine and spirit bottles gathered in a corner. I often wondered whether the bombs or the alcohol did for him eventually. But that was the end of my regular schooling, aged eleven and a half.

After France's ignominious collapse, I was compulsorily evacuated again, this time to Lewes in Sussex where I would sit on the hillside and watch the Battle of Britain going on above me. Hardly a safe haven from the war; more like a front seat. At the beginning of September, I was sent home again, this time after a tussle with two brothers who were staying in the same house and who came off much the worse. The trouble was that they were the sons of a policeman and he took me back to my flat. I knocked and Emma opened the door. She saw me, turned her head and called out to my mother: "I told you he would come home." That was on a Wednesday. The blitz on London started the following Saturday.

* * * * * *

I had my hiccups on the way to Fleet Street but I never deviated from my ambition to escape the drudgery and poverty which was Rotherhithe, even though my mother shielded my two older sisters

11

and me from the worst of it. The success I had in life, however success is measured, was largely due to my mother and to Rotherhithe itself. They moulded and shaped me. She encouraged me to find a job which was not in the docks, which, one way or another, caused the deaths of my grandfather, my father and an uncle and which crippled another uncle (a semi-professional boxer, as well, until a crane in the docks tore his leg off) and Rotherhithe gave me the inspiration to leave it.

Losing my mother didn't mean losing her influence. Leaving Rotherhithe didn't mean Rotherhithe left me. It is like my life-long support for Millwall, first seen from the shoulders of my uncle George (one of two) when I was five years old and never forgotten. I can't attend the ground now (The New Den, not the Old Den of my youth) but it is the first result I look for on a Saturday evening. At least the crowd didn't boringly and endlessly chant idiotic slogans or sing over-sentimental songs (What has "Blue Moon" or "We'll never walk alone" got to do with football? Or "Swing Low, Sweet Chariot," a slaves' song, got to do with rugby? At least at Millwall's proceedings were opened with "Shoe-Shine Boy," a song about the moneyless working class).

When I was eleven years old, the other uncle George (a docker, too, he died from tuberculosis in his late 30s) told me: "That temper of yours will get you into trouble one day," a prediction duly fulfilled when, at 14, I got the sack from my first regularly paid job at Associated Press's photo news department for swearing back at the news editor who had sworn at me. At 7.30 in the morning he gave me some photographs to deliver to the *Daily Sketch* at the bottom of Grays Inn Road. I asked for the fare. "Use your own bloody money," he replied. "Take your own bloody pictures," I said and was out of the door in seconds, never to return.

A softer upbringing might have had me saying sorry, yes, sir, but my mother would have been disappointed. That was not how she brought me up. She had her laws for living. "Don't let anyone put on you," she said; she didn't and we didn't. When you are poor, and and we were desperately so, though not so bad as many and better than some in south-east London in the 1920s and 1930s, it is self-respect which holds you together.

That news editor was one of those adults who never understood the frustration of youngsters who knew they were in the right when the grown-ups were wrong. They leave you with no alternative but to retaliate, a lesson drummed into me one day when I was five, arriving home crying. "What's wrong with you? asked my mother. "Harold Shaw kicked me," I sobbed. She grabbed me firmly by the shoulders, turned me around and said, "Go and kick him back." I did, he cried and his mother came calling to complain about me and was dismissed with several fleas in her ear. "Kick 'em back" was my mother's second law of living and allied to the first and one which I usually followed, even when afterwards I hated myself for doing it. She didn't believe in turning the other cheek. But it helped me to become independent of others and didn't prevent my becoming what I always wanted to be, a journalist.

My mother was aggressive in protecting her young. She once told me, in words which seared themselves in my memory, that if she had known the troubles that life was to bring her she would never have married, which was another way of saying I would never have been born. Still, she did and I had been. Apart from my two older sisters, another sister, another Rose, died in infancy; a common event in those days in that area. We were not the worst of her troubles, however. My father died when I was only two, my mother by his bedside. He left nothing except a gold watch which he had acquired when he bought the pawn ticket for it for three pounds ten shillings, from another even more impecunious docker. If ever she was tempted to sell it I don't know. The first time I knew about it was when she gave it to me for my 21st birthday.

My mother was bitter about my father's death. He was only 38. He had been "called on" that morning for work after six months without a job but felt ill and went to his doctor at lunch time. His doctor pronounced that he was a "scrimshanker," someone who was trying to dodge work, and told him to return to his job. He died later that day of pneumonia. The true cause was probably unemployment, malnutrition and the depression of 1930. Labour's Ramsay Macdonald may have been Prime Minister at the time but my mother blamed the Tories for everything.

She was never publicly or privately sentimental. Her first fiancé died in 1917 in France or Belgium during the First World War. She never spoke about him or what might have been had he lived, but frequently sang, "When the poppies bloom again" the first song that I learned. She didn't speak much about my father, either, only about his death. I know nothing about him. Not even why he didn't join the army.

She undoubtedly cared for us but rarely demonstrated it. The only time I saw her in tears was when Emma was said to be dying from pre-clampsia (she wasn't). She was firm with us but unemotional. She never kissed us and we didn't kiss her, except on her death bed. The huggy-feely society didn't exist then. She managed to scrape up enough to give us pocket money each week but only after we had completed our household tasks (mine was to polish all the brass door knobs, the letter box, the door number and the copper hot water tank when we moved in to our new flat. I got sixpence for that).

She had an extraordinary extended family. She was one of three children two girls (the other was yet another Rose) and a boy, named James Effingham after a long-forgotten military notable, and her mother died when she was only 11. She told me that before her mother's death her father had a "fancy woman." Other housewives, knowing his wife was dying, chased the illicit pair into a cul-de-sac one day and literally stoned them. Nevertheless, after my maternal grandmother's death (1907) he married his fancy woman and the pair produced more children until such time during the First World War, drunk, he was signed on by an army recruiting sergeant and found himself enrolled as a private when he recovered the next morning. He died in 1918 in Egypt but the War Graves Commission have no trace of his burial place, so I assume his death wasn't in action.

Anyway, his widow was young and striking enough to marry again, this time a widower with children of his own and she had children by him, too. I had "aunts" and "uncles" and cousins and step-cousins and cousins several times removed living all over Rotherhithe and Deptford and, in one instance, in prison - "Uncle" Charlie, who I never met, being an unsuccessful burglar.

Dishonesty was endemic in this later-acquired family, starting with my mother's step-parents and down through their families. For example, two cousins, both named John, decided to set up business as asphalters. They did so by stealing a lorry, driving it into the premises of a large and successful company, loading the vehicle with the equipment and materials they needed and then driving away before unloading and abandoning the lorry. Their first job was to provide an elderly Jewish small businessman with a new asphalt roof, charging him £100 extra for first removing his old lead roof and disposing of it at a time when lead was selling for little less than the price of gold. I know this because the younger John was captain of the football team I was playing for and he gleefully told us the story one half-time.

A few years earlier, my mother, who was scrupulously honest herself, was horrified when that John's mother, her step-sister, turned up and asked her to look after her three children for an unspecified time as she was expecting to be sent to prison the next day for stealing from the company where she was a cook. To her and everyone else's astonishment, she was found not guilty.

But the worst instance was with yet another uncle who I never met who was arrested in a stolen lorry with a cargo of 25,000 cigarettes. It was a serious enough crime for the case to be heard at the Old Bailey. My mother's step-sister, mentioned above, told us confidently that he would get off as he had bribed the policemen in the case. There was, of course, no doubt about his guilt. I didn't believe what she said; after all, policemen just didn't do that did they?

I was a young sub-editor in *The Glasgow Herald* London office at the time when the case came up. One day, the boy who cleared the Press Association news tapes dropped a few of the pieces of paper in front me, the top one of which said that the judge had stopped the case against Batney (my uncle) and discharged him, free to go. I was sorely worried at the time: I knew, albeit second-hand, that a brazen crime, corruption, had been committed. But how could I possibly prove it if I had the nerve to go to the police and tell them that some of their colleagues had taken a bribe? I couldn't and I didn't. Strictly speaking, it was a moral failing on my part; in practice, nothing would have come of it. Hearsay evidence, twice removed, wouldn't have lasted five minutes before any judge. And I wouldn't have lasted much longer, either.

One criminal I did know and he got what he deserved. He was a genuine cousin and what used to be called a ne'er-do-well. He and a couple of other young dockers stole the wage packets of a large number of their workmates. In the dockworkers' community, that was unforgivable. They were arrested and sentenced to three months' in prison. But the more severe punishment came from their trade union. They had committed the most heinous of crimes, stealing from their comrades. The union took away their union membership card for five years – and without that, they couldn't work. I like to think of it as robust socialism in action.

Knowledge of crimes was commonplace in those days. But no one, but rarely, went to the police and told them. It wasn't done – and, given the case of my uncle who could blame them? There was a highly publicized murder case when a naval officer gallantly tried to stop robbers from Bermondsey escaping by car in an incident near London Bridge. He died and two men in the car, brothers as I recall, were found guilty and hanged. The driver was never caught, though a name of a man I knew by sight was common gossip as the culprit. He was never arrested. The gossip may have been inaccurate, anyway, but he was a popular local footballer and would never have been shopped.

But to return to my mother: she kindled what was to be my lifetime interest in politics. She was an inactive member of the Labour party and her sister was a Labour councillor. She told me how the Tory candidate, Mrs Norah Runge, had captured the Rotherhithe seat from Labour in the party's catastrophic defeat in 1931. "She gave all the (unemployed) men a bag of coal to vote for her," my mother said. As I grew older I wondered why the men didn't take the coal and still vote for the Labour candidate. Perhaps they were too honest. Or disillusioned with Ramsay Macdonald.

By the time the 1935 general election came along, I was ready to play my infinitely small, unwitting and unmeasurable part in the campaign, marching down a street with other children of my age singing in support of the Labour candidate: "Vote, vote for Mr Ben Smith. Chuck old Rungey out the door..." Well, you've got to begin somewhere; I'll bet at the time of writing (2018) there are not many other people who can claim to have participated in any form of electioneering, however minute, that year. Anyway, the memory of losing in 1931 disappeared from the collective Rotherhithe voters' mind in 1935. Their world returned to its proper place and sent Mr Smith to Parliament and eventually to Attlee's Cabinet in 1945, where he was a more than dismal Minister of Food. Mrs Runge, meanwhile, continued to contribute to the national purse by losing her deposit in each further election in which she stood.

The then almost universal poverty of the 1930s thus gave me a practical lesson in geography and economics. Sometimes in the winters of my childhood my mother would announce, "Riga is frozen," a fact about a remote city whose dreadfulness lay in its effect – that ships from the Baltic carrying the timber which was the trade of Surrey Docks were unable to leave harbour and that therefore there was no work here. I knew about Riga before I ever heard of Glasgow.

One day, in about 1938, my mother took me to a political meeting at Millpond Bridge, Rotherhithe's traditional open-air meeting place for a political bust-up. The British Union of Fascist supporters tried to disrupt it and, contrary to general belief nowadays, it was the fascists that the police chased, truncheons aloft and trying to beat out their brains.

During the war that followed, I got a new political mentor, Dick Barrett, who became general secretary of the Amalgamated Union of Stevedores and Dockers, my father's old union, small and militant and dedicated opponent of the dominant dock union, the Transport and General. Dick was a Catholic and a Communist and a noted amateur footballer who would turn out for our boys' team when we were a player short and lived in one wing of our block of flats. He played his football liked he worked in the docks and ran his union, with sustained muscularity and cunning. He taught me more about the guile of the game than anyone else I ever met.

He also taught me about Marx and Engels and the holy St. Stalin of the Soviet Union, whom he worshipped, and how Britain had wickedly suppressed Irish nationalism in the Easter rising (his wife, Kate, a gentle, kind woman, was Irish). He tried to recruit me into the Young Communist League, but it wasn't for me. He had taught me about politics in general but he hadn't convinced me of his in particular. By that time my new best friend was his son, also Dick. Despite his father's persuasion, and bullying in the case of young Dick, we both refused to join up. But he made me ready for the 1945 general election when it eventually came. I last heard from old Dick when he wrote to me from Guy's hospital to congratulate me on my appointment to No. 10. He was proud of me. As blindness overtook him (he was diabetic) he committed suicide rather than be a burden to his family.

When I was 13, my mother told me to go out and get a job, "like all the other children." So I got one - delivering 28lb sacks of coal, which I first had to fill, to flats in a nearby five-storied block known as Swan Lane Buildings. I got sixpence (2 1/2p) an afternoon for that, plus tips. When my mother saw the state I was in when I got home, the job ended. Instead, I got a wonderful occasional job, rowing stevedores' labourers out to the middle of the Thames to unload the raw sugar ships which regularly moored there. My companion was a boy of my age, Albert, and we loved it. The lighterman, who had the contract, kept a careful eye on us from the balcony of the Spread Eagle and when at the end of the day we took his rowing boat home to Wapping Pier he gave us 1s.6d (7 and 1/2p) each. Riches!

Everyone who lived in inner London at that time had their war stories, so I'll largely skip mine, but mention in passing that I never missed an air raid. The small block of flats in which I lived was hit by a reputed 1,000 bomb on May 10, 1941 (the same night as Hitler's deluded deputy, Rudolph Hess, arrived in Scotland on a peace mission) while my mother and I were on its staircase. The noise of the approaching bomb and the sound of it exploding were horrific, and the smell overwhelmingly awful. An old man standing a few yards from me was killed. A baby in the arms of its mother standing next to me was injured. Our flat was one of the lucky ones in the block and only lost its ceilings, windows, water, gas and electricity, and our budgerigar which died of delayed shock three weeks later. Half of the other flats were totally destroyed. We were temporarily homeless and stayed for a short while with my mother's brother, my uncle Jim, for a few days and then returned home. Shortly afterwards Uncle Jim's house was wiped out, too.

Our story was the common fate of scores of thousands of Londoners. The fires that consumed our wharves were replicated for miles along both sides of the Thames and viewed by hundreds of thousands. We were attacked for 57 nights in succession in 1940 but so was everyone else in the capital. Fortunately, the counselling industry which has sprung up in recent years didn't exist to make us relive our experiences and yesterday's events were forgotten when succeeded by the morrows.

One other story, though, I will tell. For nearly 10 years my mother had kept us fed and clothed by scrubbing the floors in St. Olave's hospital from 7 in the morning until 4.30 every evening for a miserly wage of £3.10s a week. In 1944 it was hit by a V1 flying bomb and for months her working days were spent in clearing up the mess. One evening she came home and said, "At last, we've finished and the hospital's clean again." That night I and four friends escorted home two girls who lived in the next street to St Olave's. Apart from our torches, it was, of course, pitch black. As we walked away from the girls' houses having seen them safely indoors (or so we thought) there was a vast explosion nearby and a towering pillar of flame and smoke overshadowed us. It was a V2 rocket and it had just hit the hospital. A large lump of concrete fell next to me. I took off and I ran straight into the arms of policeman. My friends were nowhere to be seen or heard. "Is anyone hurt," he asked. "My friends are down there," I gasped. "I think they're all dead."

They weren't, just lying flat in the (wet) road where they had thrown themselves. The girls were in worse shape: both in hysterics with a large part of a ceiling wrapped around the neck of one of them. When I got home a little later, I said to my mother, affecting to be casual, "Did you say you had finished clearing up in the hospital earlier?" "Yes," she said, "Well......." I began.

I last saw my mother a month after she died in 1963. Don't bother to read that again. You read it correctly the first time. I was at a Labour party conference and I had gone to bed before 11 p.m. to escape the endless drinking and arguing for which most people went there. Suddenly, I awoke and my mother, wearing a pinafore, was standing at the foot of my bed. I sat up, fully awake, and stared at her. Slowly, not abruptly, the image faded. I was not dreaming. A normal dream for me is lost to forgetfulness soon after sleepiness disappears. It certainly doesn't stay in vision when I am awake. I do not draw from this any sweeping inferences about the supernatural or an after-life, nor did I fear at the time or afterwards that I was losing my mind. I do not offer any explanation for what I saw because I don't have one other than that I saw my mother.

I was sober. I was not under any stress. I had found her death, from a brain tumour, more devastating than I imagined it would be. But I was getting over that. I do not claim any special powers which make me see beyond the grave. An "apparition" probably best describes it but I shrink from one definition of that word which is "ghost." But what I do state, firmly and rationally, is that I saw my mother than night and no psychiatrist or any other so-called expert in this field will convince me otherwise. Nor do I need any spiritualist or ghost seekers to offer me support. I've read "Borley Rectory" by Harry Price, the famous fictional account of a haunted rectory falsely presented as the truth, and I think it is a field wide open to the practice of fraudsters. But the memory of what I saw is as vivid today as it was more than 50 years ago and if my assertion sows doubt in the mind of readers about the veracity of the rest of this account, so be it. We live in a cynical world.

This is a convenient point at which to interrupt the discursive chronology of my narrative, because I had an identical experience more than 40 years later when my dearest friend, Kay Carmichael, wife of Professor David Donnison and ex-wife of Neil Carmichael, MP, died after a long illness related to poliomyelitis in her youth.

From the first moment we met during the general election campaign of 1964 we struck up a close relationship. We agreed on almost everything. It was not a sexual accord and could never have been: apart from anything else, she lived in Glasgow and I lived in Kent. But it didn't stop Janey Buchan, the malicious and jealous wife of another Glasgow MP and supposed friend of both of us, from spreading the story that Kay was my mistress, solely because she couldn't understand why Kay, rather than she, was made a member of Bernard Donoughue's Policy Unit at 10 Downing Street. The reason was merit, pure merit. She was a valuable and much respected member of the team and responsible, among other things, for the establishment of a Gaelic radio station. Harold Wilson wanted to make her a peeress but thought it difficult when her husband was an MP. She wouldn't have taken it, anyway.

From the beginning, we spoke frequently, exchanged books or suggested books for each other to read; she would seek my advice and I would seek hers on any topic. She was a prison reformer and took my wife and me on a tour of Barlinnie prison in Glasgow where a novel and successful scheme, for which she was responsible, for the rehabilitation of violent convicts was under way (it was so successful that it was scrapped. Civil servants administering Scottish prisons were not going to accept a programme that effectively proved they had pursued the wrong path during a lifetime of work). She also introduced us to Jimmy Boyle, the Gorbals murderer later to be social reformer and I had no fears when he took my wife on a tour of their part of the prison.

At a busy time in my life, I once went eight months without speaking to Kay. One day, guilt-ridden, I phoned. She was out. I didn't leave a message. I thought I would try again later. Thirty minutes later she called me. She said she had been walking with her dog and suddenly felt impelled to phone me. Fearing something was wrong, she abandoned her walk and dashed home to do so. Thought transference, probably. Coincidence, never.

On Christmas Day, 2009, she phoned for the last time. I said I was planning to call her on New Year's Day. She laughed and said some endearing things to me. When I put the telephone down,; I said to my wife: "I think she was saying goodbye." The next day her husband called in distress to say she had died.

I arranged to go to Glasgow for her funeral but the worst snowfall for a generation caused most flights to be cancelled. In addition, I had a dreadful cold. On the afternoon of her cremation, I fell asleep. This time I saw an apparition of Kay. It was, again, clear, vivid and unforgettable.

The polio in her 'teens had left her with a withered left arm. In this appearance the arm was perfect. Her hair was black, with no grey and she looked about 35, the age she was when I first met her. She was wearing a smart dark blue dress. She walked towards me, we embraced and I could feel her shoulder blades sharply. She said, "It's all right, Joe, I have spoken to David."

Then she slowly evaporated.

Two women to whom I had been very close, my mother and Kay, had died and I saw both of them after death. I never saw any other relative or friend, male or female, not even my sisters, after they had died. Make of it as you will, I have no explanation I want to impose upon you.

* * * * * *

Never willingly to give in, an attitude implanted by my mother, was an incentive and an obstacle. It meant not listening to advice to change when I thought it was wrong and sometimes not listening when it was right. However, I went from being a primary schoolboy whose effective, regular education ended when I was 11 years old to political editor, assistant editor, chief leader writer, columnist and director of *The Daily Mirror*.

On my way I met every Prime Minister from Harold Macmillan to Gordon Brown and observed and listened to Clement Attlee, Winston Churchill, Anthony Eden, Alec Douglas-Home, the always entrancing Aneurin Bevan, David Cameron and Theresa May. I also met countless would-be Prime Ministers, some crooks, a couple of Russian spies, some compulsive self-seeking liars, a few of whom are still in public life, and delightful companions who I might never have otherwise known. I never went to or seriously considered going to or could afford, a university, which, on the whole, benefited me. I learned a lot more doing the most menial tasks ("Get me a cup of tea," "Sweep the floor," "See if the tobacconist has got any cigarettes.") than I would have listening to a lecturer in media studies, had such poseurs existed in my day. I once discussed careers with Lord Bevan, one-time political editor of the *Mirror,* and the legendary Hugh Cudlipp, the most dynamic, aggressive, populist popular editor Fleet Street ever knew. We discovered that between us we did not have a single educational qualification. No doubt academics will say that proves the necessity of their existence; I am old enough to differ.

I was fascinated by politics and writing even before I was a teenager. It sounds nerdy today but I read *Mein Kampf,* published in weekly edition form, when I was 12. It was a book too far at that age. When I briefly returned to school at 14, necessary in order to get a leaving certificate and a job, I was advised by a school careers officer that I should get an office job until I was 18 when I could take up my dead father's union ticket and work as a casual labourer in the Surrey Docks. I had decided to ignore her advice before I had left the room. The trouble with people like her was that working-class children weren't expected to have the ambition or the ability to earn more than a messenger's or a labourer's weekly wage. I wasn't a geographical Cockney (though my mother was), but I spoke like one and Cockneys were looked down upon by non-Cockneys; it was as though we were latter-day cotton pickers, a kind of early white on white racism.

I was 17 when the war against Germany and in Europe ended and dreading the looming call-up which might send me to fight the Japanese. The atomic bombs ended that. But just before they were dropped, party politics resumed again in Britain with the 1945 general election. In Rotherhithe Ben Smith won again and Mrs Runge returned to lose her deposit again. She was a game girl. Much, much more important was, to the general amazement, the sweeping of Churchill out of office and the arrival of a genuine majority Labour Government led by Clement Attlee.

For a former taxi-driver, Smith did well until he was made Minister of Food and introduced bread rationing. That was a ration too far for a country which had been severely restricted in its eating for more than five years. He quickly resigned and made for the political sunset of the House of Lords and oblivion. The chosen candidate (more truthfully, the candidate imposed by the Transport and General Workers' Union) to replace him was Bob Mellish, a TGWU official.

It was on the hustings then that I learned two political lessons. First, don't threaten what you can't carry out. At one of the perennial Mrs Runge's meetings she had an old friend, a Birmingham industrialist, Sir Harry Selly, to speak for her. He rambled on interminably about the evils of the Labour party until I interrupted and said, "That's enough about Labour; tell us your policy"; hardly original, perceptive or clever, but enough to get under Sir Harry's skin.

"Be quiet, boy," he thundered, "or I will have you thrown out." He paused for a moment, then regretted his tolerance towards me and ordered a rather small, middle-aged steward, "Throw him out." I was standing with a group of dockers, some of them old friends of my late father. One of them, a large man, stepped forward to meet the steward. "Throw him out and you throw me out, too," he suggested. The steward wisely declined the invitation and retreated, much to the disappointment of the audience, almost Labour to a man, who were looking for some excitement.

The second lesson came at the first meeting held by Mellish: never pretend to be what you are not. He was being portrayed by the party as a docker, which he never was. Attempting to ingratiate himself with a crowded hall, he said: "I'm just an ordinary bloke, like you." He was interrupted on this occasion by a docker: "I don't want someone like me in the House of Commons. I want someone more intelligent," he said. Bob was intelligent enough, though. He changed the subject. In time, he became Chief Whip under Harold Wilson and adopted the belligerence of his constituents when speaking to the Cabinet – a case of art imitating nature.

Rotherhithe was still a slum in 1945, despite the targeted house clearance schemes of an energetic local council and the more energetic, though untargeted, efforts of the Luftwaffe, which could carry out its own clearance schemes overnight. The river shore still swarmed with rats. In the down town areas policemen still walked in twos. Today's fashionable Surrey Quays was still Surrey Docks, exclusively populated by the working class..

Suddenly, in the 1950s, the container revolution came and spelt the end of Rotherhithe as a I knew it. The docks died. The casual labour scheme had ended some years before as well as the compulsory overtime that went with it, two appalling practices which compelled a rebellious workforce. But now the militant workers had nothing to be militant about. There was no work. Twice in the late 1940s Dick Barrett had brought his members out on strike and Attlee had declared a State of Emergency; and the local police guarding against any outbreaks of violence played football matches in Southwark Park against the potentially riotous dockers. And then there were none

Barrett, on those strike occasions, was the most vilified man in Britain, not that it bothered him. One day, a *Daily Express* reporter ventured to try to interview him at the dockside. Barrett turned to two of his members: "Throw him in," he instructed, gesturing towards the dock. They moved fast but the reporter moved faster and came close to breaking the 100 yards record as he headed for the dock gates. Now all that had ended. A community as strong as any miners' had disappeared into a forlorn peace; it was to be another 40 years before the miners followed them into history.

As circumstances forced the working class to achieve their ambition of moving out to the suburbs and Kent in the 1950s and 1960s so the middle classes moved in; Anthony Armstrong-Jones, later Lord Snowden, occupied a house in Rotherhithe Street, a few doors away from my youth club, and used it reputedly for what the tabloids delighted in calling a love-nest for himself and Princess Margaret. We were accustomed to the West End travelling East and slumming it and believing they were doing good works, but that was taking the practice to extremes, if it ever did. I never met anyone who ever saw her there. The locals would not have known him from Adam but they would have recognized her in the role of Eve. After all, it wasn't many years since they put the buntings out and held street parties for the coronation of her sister. It is seldom recognized by politicians how patriotic the working class are.

But it all went, comparatively swiftly. The Docklands development schemes changed Rotherhithe unrecognisably. Today, the slums have gone along with the close and closed communities which they bred and the Yuppies have come in. The price of a new one-bedroomed apartment there would have taken the earnings of 1,000 dockers working full-time for a year in my youth. The black bricks of Swan Lane buildings were pressure-hosed back to their original pale yellow colour, the local cooperage has gone and a horse and cart hasn't been seen for decades. The material gains have been immense, the community ones are less obvious.

* * * * *

Working for Associated Press was the first step on a very long ladder, temporarily put back by the sack but immediately re-instated on the same rung by getting a job at the same pay, 25 shillings a week or £1.25 in today's money, in the London Office of *The Glasgow Herald* group of newspapers, a couple of doors away from a shop owned by a sporting hero, the cricketer Jack Hobbs. Between the *Herald's* office and Hobb's shop was the London office of *The Cork Examiner.* One of the senior managers in our office, Cyril Tuke, would hand a new boy a cork and tell him to go next door and get it examined. He was the only one who never tired of the joke.

When I applied for the job I made my request to the most distinguished-looking person I saw, resplendent in a blue uniform. He turned out to be the lift attendant who promptly showed me the meaning of the words "lead-swinger" by falling ill with a bad back, the first resort of the lazy, when I arrived, meaning that my first six weeks in a real newspaper office were spent operating a lift when I hadn't ever been in one three months earlier.

After my stint on the lift, I was switched to selling the company's newspapers and magazines, ranging from the *Herald* to *The Scottish Field,* behind the front counter. My immediate senior was a grammar school boy, Peter, from Wimbledon, with the superiority of manner which is the preserve of the educated idiot. All the money taken during the day was laboriously entered by pencil, sale by sale, on a till roll and the till was handed to the office manager at the end of the day. The amount inside the till never tallied with the sums inscribed on the roll, much to the irritation of the manager. When Peter went on holiday, the responsibility for the till fell upon me. I handled it differently. First, I never noted every penny I got for the papers and just put the money in the till. Then, late in the day, I added up the till myself and then wrote in enough to make sure that the figures agreed. The office manager was amazed at my efficiency in always being accurate. I was promoted to operate the switchboard and to do other odd jobs inside the office - the second rung of the ladder if you like. If Peter had ever deigned to play cards with me I'd have won the clothes off his back.

The jobs were largely drudgery, the management largely kindly. After a couple of months there the second in command, Harry Bundy, gave me a cheque for £70 cash to take to the firm's bankers. I was terrified – I had never seen so much money in my life. I put it in an inside pocket and went back to the office clutching my chest, fearing I would meet a footpad and be robbed on the way. Still, it was nice to be trusted; £70 was more that a year's wages. Unless, of course, he was trying me out.

My interest in politics and journalism became known, largely because I never stopped talking about them and Bundy helped me. I repaid him eventually by persuading him to vote Labour in 1945. He had never done it before and I doubt if he ever did it again, but he was instrumental in getting me transferred to the editorial department, another rung on my ladder, still a messenger but of a more eminent kind. I had to travel to the House of Commons several times during the day and evening to pick up the stories written by the Parliamentary staff of *The Glasgow Herald* and its tabloid junior, *The Bulletin,* whose political correspondent was as talented as any of the better known Fleet Street maestros . I loved it.

I was now the senior boy in the office. But one day, the London editor of the group, James Proudfoot, a Pickwickian figure, about five ft. five, balding and roly-poly, called me into his panelled office. "Can you do shorthand, son?" he asked. "No, sir," I said. "Learn it, get up to 120 words a minute and you can be the telephone copy taker," he said. "You've got three months to do it." That was the biggest rung so far.

I straightaway enrolled in a shorthand and typing class and found myself among a group of giggling girls without any interest in learning anything. I never went again but bought a five shilling teach-yourself Pitman's shorthand book and for the next three months devoted two hours a day, every day, to the tedious memorising of the strokes, curves, grammalogues and shortforms that made up a new language for me. At the end of the three months, Proudfoot called me into his office again. "Can you do 120 words a minute?" he asked. "Yes, sir," I replied. "Then the job is yours," he said. "You can start straightaway." No tests. He took my word for it. I was immensely proud – and relieved – that he did so.

Taking down the reporters' copy by phone, sometimes as many as 60 A4 pages a night, did wonders for my typing speed. My only real difficulty came on my first evening when a *Glasgow Herald* writer (nothing as common as a reporter) phoned two columns from Germany about its growing steel industry and instructed me to take it down in shorthand in order to save money. I was horrified but managed to transcribe most of it. If he noticed the odd cut or amendment he no doubt put it down to a stroppy sub-editor in Glasgow.

Later we were to work together on the sub-editors' desk. His name was Alistair Hetherington and he was the most humourless man I ever met. In the course of time he graduated, naturally, to be editor of *The Guardian*. His job title changed but he never acquired a sense of humour and nor did his paper, except in a bitchy kind of way. I clashed with him more than once when I was Harold Wilson's Press Secretary which led to the paper pompously demanding my resignation, totally misunderstanding the situation which led to its conclusion. No wonder it was known as *The Grauniad*. I got my own back on it much later.

I enjoyed my journalistic work and training with the *Glasgow Herald* group , incredibly stuffy, literally and figuratively, though it could be. For example, even on the hottest days I was not allowed to remove my coat or tie at the subs' desk in London in case a member of the public should appear, which they rarely did. The editor, Sir William Robieson, was Chancellor of Glasgow University, an awesome and distant figure. He was responsible for sending me to Glasgow to work for one rain-full summer. I saw him on the last day of my secondment. "Ah, Haines," he said. "When did you arrive?"

I had, in fact, arrived on a fine sunny day six weeks' earlier. When I left, the sun was shining again. Every other day when it wasn't drizzling, it poured. Emigration of soft Scots taking the high road to England won't stop until they can do something about the weather. I was alone, living in a temperance hotel (I said the paper was stuffy; they weren't going to have a youngster from London falling for the evils of drink). I lived only for when I was at work.

I started on the sub-editors' desk of the *Evening Times,* a highly successful evening paper read by most Glaswegians. It had a practice of lengthy headlines in lower case print. Some of them were notorious. The best I heard was "'Help, help' shrieks unconscious landlady from window." In a novice's attempt to save the paper of the embarrassment of a double entendre, I approached the formidable sports editor, Jimmy McCormack, early one morning with a proof of the previous night's speedway in Edinburgh. "I think this should be changed," I said. He looked at it: "Jack Young on top in exciting night." He glared at me: "You've a dirty mind, young man," he said. "Go away." The headline wasn't changed.

I went from the evening paper to *The Bulletin,* a middle-class tabloid with an appeal to middle-aged spinsters, but a paper for which its journalists, including me, had great affection. It was very tightly written and imaginatively sub-edited but its readers were slowly disappearing. Its ability to say in one word what its more austere companion, the *Glasgow Herald* said in six was great training. It was, however, influenced by its female readers and its female journalists who mirrored them exactly and who would not have been able to understand why their male colleagues laughed at a headline for the Daily Menu, which read: "Baby Peas in Butter."

My time in Glasgow ended with a stint on the *Herald*, which was dominated by a fiercely Presbyterian chief sub-editor, Andy Anderson. His practice was to pencil the font size on a piece of copy (which determined its length) and throw it to the sub-editor of his choice. A youthful Peregrine Worsthorne, a Roman Catholic, who was to rise to the eminence of a Fleet Street editor, was also trained there. I missed the incident but was told by others, gleefully, that Anderson had agency copy about a speech by the Pope and threw it to Worsthorne with the instruction: "Get on with that, you papist bastard." The dry Scottish humour, I supposed.

Later, after I had returned to London, my "dirty mind" got another run out when *The Bulletin's* chief lady writer (I couldn't describe her otherwise), all long tweed skirts, no chin and the minimum of make-up, came down to cast her eye over the London Fashion Fortnight.

I was given her first day's copy to prepare for transmission to Glasgow. I took one look at her opening sentence and took it into the office of the London editor, Comyn Webster. "We can't let this go," I said. He smiled and said, "I agree." I turned to leave. "Where are you going?" he asked. "I thought you would tell her," I replied. "Not likely," he said. "You do it." At that stage in my career I couldn't possibly have done so – suppose she asked me to spell out my objection? - so it was sent, as written, and appeared, as written, with no one in Glasgow with the temerity to take her on, either. Her report began: "Short skirts for the day and long sheaths for the evening..."

I received great help from the Scots I worked with in London and so did the other English messenger boys who followed me. No racism there. One, Gordon Greig, became a very close friend and eventually political editor of the *Daily Mail*, and another, Gordon Leak, who succeeded Gordon Greig, was to become political editor of the *News of the World*. As I became political editor of the *Daily Mirror* it was a notable hat-trick for the small London office of a Scottish group of newspapers. None of us went to university but in his day Greig was without peer among tabloid reporters, many of whom were graduates.

As I grew up, I became acutely aware of the divide in the British nation. It was not then race and racism of the kind which divides most countries today but class and classism. Emphatically, it did not affect me in my work but it did exist there as it did outside. Today, the class war lingers on mainly in the minds of those left-wing intellectuals who see something romantic in it or something to be exploited, among those right-wingers who yearn for the days of a real-life Downton Abbey and in snobs. Romantic it was never was. *The Ragged Trousered Philanthropist* was about hardship not heroism. So was Max Cohen's *I was One of the Unemployed,* or the gritty realism of A.J. Cronin's fiction, an author seldom read today. It was vicious, harsh, crushing for those on the wrong side of wealth. It raged on in the minds of those who suffered from it and was only partly relieved by those members of the upper classes, or the elite, who sought to alleviate some of it by good works. But to alleviate is to perpetuate. The choice was often between that and violence, which erupted over the years in disastrous strikes.

I greatly benefited for the years I spent as a member of two youth clubs sponsored by Cambridge colleges, Queens' and Clare. Both were run by wonderful public-spirited women, but neither their homes nor their upbringing were among the youngsters they served. The first club was named after Queens' college, the second was named Gomm House, after the one-time Lord of the Manor in Rotherhithe, Field Marshal William Gomme. The nearest pub to it was named after him, too. The road that ran through Southwark Park was Gomm Road. (The "e" wa usually dropped)

My wife's parents were tenants of the Gomm Estates. She lived in Abbeyfield Road, where one of the men I most admired came to start what became known as the Abbeyfield Society to help house the elderly. His name was Richard Carr-Gomme, a Guard's officer of the military family who resigned his commission to start the project, with his own money. The first house he bought he scrubbed and cleaned himself. He became a good friend. He meant and did well but he was still on the wrong side of the divide with the people he so much wanted to help. It was sad but inevitable that he was eventually forced out of the Society by the professionals who took over as the project mushroomed into a national movement.

He and the others – including a member of the MCC – undoubtedly did a great deal for those of us who were members of the clubs. So did some Oxford colleges, too. But it only healed some of the wounds of the class war. By themselves they couldn't end it. Their presence only emphasised its existence.

The battles of that war during my childhood, youth and young manhood were one-sided, fought between the working classes, largely unskilled, and the upper classes, who employed them. Between blue collar and white-collar workers. Between slum dwellers and the owners of slum estates. Between those well off enough to have a servant or a nanny or an au pair, the modern Pooter class if you like, and the servant class. Between the ill and the well, where the environment was the determinant of health, between the haves and the have-nots or the never-haves. Between the educated (university graduates and the grammar school pupils) and the uneducated with only a basic learning. Even between the working class and the under-class because no one likes to be at the very bottom. It was fought for many generations and there was usually only one winner, the one on the next rung up. It was always there, since the first aristocrats and knights acquired and strutted the land. But they didn't always get their own way.

Part of the history of my family was that my grandfather took part in the great Dockers' Tanner strike of 1889, after the dockers had formed a union and demanded to be paid 6d (2 and ½ pence in today's decimal currency) an hour. Eventually, with their families on the point of starvation, they had an astounding victory. Anyone who wants to understand the later rise of the Labour party will find its roots in that strike and the victorious match girls' strike just before it. It didn't begin in the mines. Though it is conveniently forgotten now, the National Union of Mineworkers opposed the creation of the Labour party and supported the Liberals.

My father took part in the general strike of 1926, two years before I was born. That was a humiliating defeat. It was, perhaps, the last great success of the bosses until Arthur Scargill led the miners to defeat and eventual extinction in 1984.

The snobbery which the class war bred, a vice to which there was little answer, was instinctive, almost unconscious but often deliberately designed to hurt by those who practised it.

Fortunately, as I said, there was little discrimination, class or racial, in my work. But sometimes aspiring young Scottish stars were sent down from Glasgow for experience in the London office. They came brought with them an ineffable air of superiority (for example, Hetherington) which infuriated me and my colleagues. One such, Stewart Yorston, never sought to make friends among us, only enemies. He was more successful in that than in his journalism. One day he demanded to know what my salary was. I suspected I knew why and what his reaction would be so I told him. "£700 a year," I said. He exploded: "Why do you get more than me?" he demanded. "I went to university and I have a degree." "I get more than you," I said, "because I am better than you." Kick 'em back. My mother would have approved. Yorston left journalism altogether and became a chemist.

The only other incident of that kind came some years later when I was political correspondent of *The Bulletin* and Gordon Greig was my deputy. Harry (later Sir Henry) Boyne had been in the same post for the *Glasgow Herald* before moving on to *The Daily Telegraph* and being replaced, as was the paper's wont, by a university graduate, Ian Waller. Ian was good on the theory of politics but a hopeless news-gatherer at the time. If I ever had a good story, I would pass it on to him. One night I told him of the government's intention to build a new strip steel mill at Ravenscraig, a major story for Scotland and a project for which it had been agitating for some years.

At 10pm Ian's editor, James Holburn (ex-*Times)* phoned him to ask if he was sure the story was right. "Yes," said Ian smoothly, "I've checked it twice with my source," which meant that he had twice come to me to ask if I was certain about it. "Well," said Holburn, it's not in *The Scotsman,* but I see it is in *The Bulletin.*

"Why is that? "We share stories," said Ian bravely. "It has got to stop," said Holburn. "Let them find their own stories." It was part of his insufferable arrogance that he could not see any other explanation.

When the brilliant Harry Bunton, *The Bulletin's* political correspondent died tragically young from lung cancer, his deputy, George Lochhead, who always wanted to swim among bigger fish, replaced him and I was made his deputy, becoming the paper's parliamentary correspondent with my own seat in the Press Gallery, the youngest reporter there. I had my dream job at last. The late nights in the London office, the disruption of any social life they led to, the tedious hours learning shorthand had paid off. Or I thought they had. When I poised my pen over my note book on my first day in the Commons to note the first Scottish question to be asked, it was asked and answered before I had written a line. I had to start learning again.

Fortunately for me, I had become engaged to a Rotherhithe girl, Irene Lambert, before I took up the job at the Commons. Throughout the next nearly-40 years of my journalism, she never once complained about not going out with friends, or to dinners, or to the theatre, or missing the bright life because of my work. I once totalled up the periods I had to spend away from home as a journalist and as a Press secretary and it came to four years. Not many wives would have put up with it. Like me, Gordon Greig had a pretty young wife but she wanted a social life he couldn't give her. Their marriage ended in acrimony.

I had listened to the great speeches of Winston Churchill during the war and had thrilled at Clement Attlee's success in deposing him in 1945. Now, they were both sitting below me, most days, and I was seeing it all for real. For a brief while, I was star-struck. Attlee, Herbert Morrison, Will Griffiths, Harold Wilson, Jim Callaghan, Denis Healey, Roy Jenkins, Barbara Castle, Chuter Ede and Aneurin Bevan, the greatest orator I ever heard, among those on the Labour benches, and Winston Churchill, Anthony Eden, Harold Macmillan, Ted Heath, Enoch Powell, Iain Macleod and other to be well-known names on the Government side. Altogether, seven past, present and future Prime Ministers.

I knew the names and constituencies of a large number of their supporters from my days as a copy taker, but now I saw them in the flesh. One of my first impression was how short the men were. I don't think a survey has ever been done about the height of politicians but I'll bet most of them are under the average. John Le Carre, in *The Night Manager* noted how powerful men are short in stature

I worked away reporting their speeches for over four years, but the greatest events, the best-ever speeches, came after my first two years when, in the biggest act of deception in 20th century politics, the Prime Minister, Anthony Eden, decided to invade Egypt and seize the Suez Canal to thwart Colonel Abdul Nasser, who had nationalised it. We are all captives of our past. Eden had fought in the Great War of 1914-18 and was awarded the Military Cross for gallantry. He resigned as Foreign Secretary from the pre-war Neville Chamberlain government in protest at Chamberlain's appeasement of Hitler policy. His greatest supporter for the Suez invasion was Harold Macmillan who had been seriously wounded in the 1914-18 war.

Both served the Government well in the war against Hitler. They saw the rise of Nasser as the reincarnation of the fascist dictators (and so, briefly, did Hugh Gaitskell the Labour leader, until he came to his senses). Nationalisation was a threat to Britain and its trade, they said. Nasser must not be appeased. The West had to take back the Canal. But with what excuse? Most of our allies, especially General Eisenhower, president of the USA – who had hard experience of fighting in North Africa – were opposed to military action.

In a deliberate, calculated (badly calculated) act of deception, Britain and France, which was equally concerned and militant, concocted an elaborate lie to deceive their publics. Their plan was to persuade the Israelis, who had their own genuine battles with the Arab states and needed no persuading, to attack Egypt; when that happened the British and French forces would land in the Suez area "to separate the combatants" and, of course, retake the Canal. There were secret meetings in France between the generals of both nations and at Chequers, the Prime Minister's country home, where the French delegation foolishly signed the visitors' book. Harold Wilson was to show me it, nearly 20 years later, with two pages missing, torn out to preserve the secrecy of the meeting.

It was the last battle of imperial Britain. Britain was forced to give in by threatened US sanctions against us and a run on the pound. The Chancellor of the Exchequer, Harold Macmillan, the early and leading backer of Eden, told the Prime Minister it was all over, earning him the soubriquet of "First In and First Out." The retreat from Empire gathered pace after that. For me, it re-awakened my passion for party politics. I was among a small group in the Press Gallery, mainly *Daily Herald* and *News Chronicle* journalists, who argued against the war. Not only the newspapers but so many of their employees supported Eden. Journalists can be led by the nose, too.

The upshot was that Eden resigned because of ill-health which was evident at the start of the campaign and was given an Earldom. His Foreign Secretary, Selwyn Lloyd, the other of the two main conspirators so brutally and memorably savaged by Aneurin Bevan during the Suez debates ("Why attack the monkey when the organ grinder is present?") was awarded the highest honour in the gift of the Commons and made its Speaker. Contrast their treatment with the vilification of Tony Blair after the Irak war, which in the scale of lying scandals from one to 10 was at the bottom of the scale while Suez was at the top.

It was Suez that re-aroused all my old political allegiances. When I decided to move out of London in 1960 and into a new house in Tonbridge, Kent, my wife and I immediately joined the local Labour party and eventually we both served on the local council, me for nine years. Apart from a period when Ken Livingstone was re-admitted to the party and I resigned in disgust, I've remained a member ever since.

In 1959 George Lochhead moved to the *Daily Express* and I took his place as the paper's political correspondent and became a member of the mysterious group called the Lobby, which had their own language, their own secrets and their own habit of disappearing from the Press Gallery at 4 o'clock every afternoon to go to their meetings. Sometimes, a notice would appear on the Press Gallery notice board saying "Blue Mantle" or "Red Mantle" and state a time and off they would go. Blue of course was the Tories, red was Labour and the Liberals in those days had no status whatsoever. They were as secretive as any Masonic lodge. Their privileged entry to the Lobby Room, way up a spiral staircase in the upper reaches of Parliament enabled them to talk mysteriously to their offices about "my sources in Downing Street" and impress them mightily. More importantly, their membership gave them access to the Members' Lobby where only MPs could go. And, of course, it gave these journalists privileged access, twice a day, to the Press Secretary's room in 10 Downing Street where he would give convoluted answers to convoluted questions and anything he said was deniable because he hadn't said it.

They really were impossibly stuffy and full of their own importance. They were the elite of an elite. They knew their place, and it was to be deferential. Each new member of the Lobby was handed a small book of his rights (few) and responsibilities (many). A member must never take notes in the Lobby. He (there was only one "she" in those days, the veteran Nora Beloff of *The Observer*) must never interrupt an MP if that MP was speaking to someone else. Of course, if an MP were to interrupt your conversation that was a different matter and you would have to put up with it. Also, you must never "see" anything. If someone kicked the Prime Minister in the pants you didn't "see" it and could only report it in a circumlocutory fashion. Equally, you couldn't hear, therefore not report, anything, not even a blazing row or fisticuffs. It was confirmation of second class citizenship, which was willingly accepted. After all, that was a better class than the mere scribblers in the Press Gallery. Also, shorthand wasn't necessary although those who, like me, had graduated from the Gallery, could do it. It was a cynical definition of the difference between Lobby Correspondents and Press Gallery reporters: that the former couldn't do shorthand and the latter could.

In the early 1970s, a notorious murder trial of a serial killer was taking place at the Old Baliey when an attempt was made to introduce members of the House of Lords to Lobby journalists and a small group of Lobby men were invited to dinner by some senior peers. After introductions, they all sat down. There was an awkward silence and then one of the peers turned to the splendidly named The Hon E. Spencer Shew, secretary of the Lobby, and asked, brightly, "This fella Neilsen" (naming the killer) "D'you know him?"

I will always remember my first day, slightly nervous and dressed in a dark suit, being taken aside by an elder of the Lobby or Lodge and told, in kindly fashion, that I should not repeat my sin of that first day and never again wear Hush Puppies. I assumed that has all changed today. And when in the confines of the Lobby room you were able to question a Minister you had to be careful what you said. On one occasion I and a group of other Scottish journalists were given the Scottish Secretary, John Maclay, a gentle, timid man, a hard time (off the record, of course) when the chairman of the Lobby, Harry Boyne, stopped the meeting. He told us that he would not have Mr Maclay "harassed."

I continued to enjoy my work more and more, though, but I ran into trouble when the 1959 general election occurred. I was writing each day's political leads for *The Bulletin* from the Glasgow office. One such lead infuriated the Scottish Tories for its alleged Labour bias. Most importantly, so far as the editor, Comyn Webster, promoted from London, and I were concerned, it infuriated Sir Hugh Fraser, the draper who owned the group and very much a Tory. He instructed the managing director to tell Webster it must never happen again. Webster bravely resisted: "The question," he told the managing director, "is whether Hugh Fraser edits this paper or whether I do." "No, replied the MD, "the question is whether Hugh Fraser edits this paper through you or through somebody else." It was a not uncommon example of the freedom of the press as seen by proprietors

We racked our brains to see how we could both comply with and defy Fraser and then I discovered on the agency tapes a speech made by Field Marshal Lord Montgomery, whose abilities on the field of battle were diminished by his blunders in civilian life, and we led the paper on it. "Monty Says Labour Voters Are Bonkers" shouted our headline, sufficient to galvanise any Scottish Labour voter to go to the polling station and yet meet Fraser's requirements.

Unfortunately, a month before my wife and I moved into our new home in Tonbridge, *The Bulletin* closed down. It had lost 25,000 of its circulation during the Suez campaign, which it opposed, and it never recovered them. For a year or more I had been its political correspondent (called "editor" these days) after Lochhead had moved to the *Daily Express*. My salary rose to £1,050 a year, I was drawing £1.10s (£1.50p) in weekly expenses and went on holiday to Spain for the first time. With my wife working we could afford a mortgage (£14.25 a month) on our newly built detached property which cost all of £3,550, including legal charges. Yuppies.

As soon as news of my paper's closure became public I was offered jobs by different newspapers. I needed one quickly, with my new mortgage looming and I accepted the first to approach me, the *Scottish Daily Mail,* based in Edinburgh (wrong city), offering a salary of £1,750 a year, a huge increase - only to be offered even more a few hours later by the *Daily Record*. But, as I had promised the first, I stayed with it. It was to give me the first taste of what working for a national newspaper, even though it was its Scottish arm, was like.

First of all, it was much more demanding. Its editor, Donald Todhunter, was an outcast from the London paper, having lost one of the power battles that intermittently raged there. He ran it like a London newspaper. If wanted, I would work on Sundays, which I'd never done with *The Bulletin*. Second, they were delighted to have their own political correspondent working from the Commons, which they had never had before. Third, praise was calculated, not heartfelt and it was rare. At the level of the News Desk they knew little about the political scene. I did, however, think I would be smothered in congratulations when, together with my friend, Gordon Campbell of the *Scottish Daily Express,* I broke the story of the decision to build a new Cunard liner, the QE2, at John Brown's shipyard on the Clyde.

The office went crazy about the news, the biggest industrial story to break in Scotland for years. But office politics took over.

Next morning, the editor demanded to know why I hadn't given the story to the London office - the then editor, the famous Bill Hardcastle, having long believed it was going to happen and furious with the Scottish editor that he hadn't been told about it. Fortunately, on my way to phone my copy the night before, the paper's political editor, Tommy Thompson, has asked me what I was writing. I told him. "Good story for Scotland," he said. Technically, that should have freed me from criticism.

But somebody had to be blamed: Hardcastle blamed Todhunter, Todhunter blamed me; I blamed Thompson; Thompson, reasonably (though with hindsight) blamed Edinburgh for not passing the story back to London and, as I was bottom of the political pile the eventual somebody was the poor bloody infantry - me. Pity no one remembered that I had got the story in the first place, but national newspapers are like that.

Still, things were varied and different in my personal life. My new home forced me to become a gardener; I laboured while my wife designed. I advanced in local politics and narrowly won a seat on the local council for Labour. That was in 1963. (The following year we won a majority for Labour for the first and, I fear, the last time). My mother was proud of me, but died soon after in the autumn of 1963. I gave up smoking in the spring when an elderly Liberal party press officer (the worst job in Parliament then) died of lung cancer. I had always felt sorry for him but his death had a marked effect upon me and I gave up smoking Then I was laid low for a month with pneumonia. I reckon my lungs couldn't cope with the fresh air.

But it was also the period of *That Was The Week That Was*, an exciting new development in broadcast political commentary if you like satire, and I wrote several sketches for it. The biggest impact was one about Henry Brooke, who had just deported a black woman against all the evidence and appeals in her favour. Its format was changed by David Frost and Christopher Booker but I did all the ground work; altogether, the BBC paid me £600 for that one sketch. It helped with the mortgage. And it had an amusing consequence many years later.

I was sitting in the Prime Minister's study in 10 Downing Street when Tony Benn, who had briefly been a BBC producer and was therefore regarded as the party's expert on broadcasting, came in and embarked on one of his customary outbursts against the Corporation. It led to a general denigration of the BBC during which he referred to the programme about Brooke. It was, he said, the most disgraceful ever broadcast. Harold Wilson agreed. Which only went to show that politicians will defend each other as a class no matter to which party they belong. I kept quiet. If I had admitted my role it would only have confirmed the suspicions Benn already had about me. But the sketch was perfectly justified.

But back in Parliament I was growing increasingly unhappy with my day job and when the new political editor of the *Mail*, Walter Terry, a good friend, told me in the summer of 1964, with a general election looming, that he had received instructions that "from now on we support the Tory party 100 percent" I resigned. In the past I had refused a job on the *Daily Herald,* the paper started by the trade unions and which was totally loyal to the Labour party. That was the bit I couldn't accept. It was too restrictive for a journalist, whatever his political views, even though I was a member of the Labour party. I had to be free to criticize.

At the time, I didn't have another job to go to, but a new newspaper, *The Sun,* was the Phoenix about to arise from the ashes of the *Daily Herald* and its editorial director, Sydney Jacobson, offered me £50 a week to join them. I hesitated for a week until I saw what the new paper looked like. I liked it, told him I would join and he immediately raised the salary to £55 a week. At last I was on a national paper, not a satellite of one, nor one based in Scotland.

In truth, *The Sun* was still too much like the *Daily Herald,* but it was freer in its thinking. What's more, its political correspondent was Harold Hutchinson, a seasoned journalist without peer in experience and background or the ability to type and think at great speed. He was the son of a trade union leader and regaled me of stories at his home when he was a child, where political and union leaders would gather to plot and plan At one such, they were accompanied by the Duchess of Warwick, the notorious "Darling Daisy," indiscreet mistress of Edward VII and a supporter of the young Labour party. By the time of Harold's childhood she had grown old; as the men gathered, she took hold of Harold and led him into the garden. "They are boring," she said, "you don't want to listen to them" and kept him entertained with stories of her own. I was fascinated to hear of someone who had links to a different age.

Throughout my four years and more at *The Sun*, I learned more about political writing from Harold Huchinson than from anyone else. He always took the long view, especially when he had seen it all before. He was not interested in personal glory. When he had first grown famous in Fleet Street, Lord Beaverbrook, the moneybags of the industry, called Harold and asked him to join the *Daily Express* as its senior feature writer at what was then a fabulous salary. "What do you want me to write about?" asked Harold. "I want you to interview Marshal Tito," replied Beaverbrook. "And if he says No?" queried Harold. The Beaver hadn't thought that far. Harold didn't join.

Harold was more than a cynic; he was a sceptic of that "Why is that bastard lying to me?" school. If he smelled a rat he wasn't happy until he found it. One remarkable night, March 14, 1968, he and I were strolling the corridors and members' lobby of the Commons, usually a fruitful time for finding stories as MPs and ministers returned from a refreshing dinner and we were struck by an astonishing fact: there was no one to be seen, except for the occasional backbencher scurrying off to the library or scurrying from it. There wasn't a minister anywhere. Harold muttered that there was something up and we couldn't detect it. At 10.45pm I left for my last train and Harold drove home to Wimbledon.

The difference between us was that Harold was still unhappy. He undressed to go to bed and promptly dressed again, drove back to the Commons and walked straight into an extraordinary row, past midnight, in which the deputy Prime Minister, George Brown, an appalling and well-lubricated bully, had demanded that Harold Wilson should come to the Commons and hold a Cabinet meeting there to discuss a decision to close the banks the following morning. That had been taken by Wilson, the Chancellor of the Exchequer, Roy Jenkins, and Peter Shore, Minister for Economic Affairs, and the Cabinet as a whole had not been consulted. Wilson's reply to

Brown was tart: "I'm the only one who calls Cabinet meetings and who decides where they are going to be held." Brown was fomenting insurrection to any minister who would listen, but there were not many apart from the Commonwealth Secretary, George Thomson, a long-standing acolyte.

Brown may have been more sober in the light of day but he was no more sensible and he delivered his resignation letter to No.10 that morning. One of the legends of Wilson's reign was that one day, as he was working in the Cabinet room, a young private secretary stood nervously beside him until Wilson looked up. "What do you want?" he asked patiently. "I've a letter here, sir, from Mr Brown saying he is resigning." "Put it with the others," said Wilson and continued working.

This time, he didn't put it with the others but accepted it and appointed a new Foreign Secretary straightaway and abolished the post of Commonwealth Secretary, merging it with the Foreign Office, and an almighty crisis was defused within hours of it starting. And Harold Hutchinson had scooped Fleet Street because the smell of a rat wouldn't go away. Or the dog that didn't bark or roam the corridors of the Commons. That was partly experience but it was also a journalistic instinct that cannot be taught. As for George Brown, I'm tempted to think that he had never heard of the Ides of March and its significance for political assassination, otherwise he wouldn't have chosen to assassinate himself on March 15. Even if he did know, he was more brutish than Brutus. He might have been able to out-drink Wilson but never to outwit him.

The man at the *Sun* with the title of Political Editor was Ted Castle, convivial husband of Barbara and an Edwardian in appearance. He phoned me as soon as I joined, telling me I would be given the by-line of "Joseph Haines." I told him I preferred "Joe" to "Joseph." He said Joe sounded like a bookmaker; instead they would make it "J.T.W. Haines," and that's how it remained. At least it was unusual in the popular press.

I had some success at *The Sun*. I rapidly got to know a large number of Labour MPs, which I couldn't do on a Scottish Tory paper. Two of them, James Wellbeloved and a man who was to become a dear friend and colleague, Albert Murray, would faithfully take notes of Parliamentary Labour Party meetings and tell me what happened. Another friend, Rowley Summerscales of the Tory *Telegraph,* would have equal access to 1922 meetings of Conservative backbenchers. We had an understanding: I told him what the PLP was up to, he told me about the 1922. It's how the Lobby of political journalists works – a mutual insurance society. The idea that specialist journalists fight like Formula One drivers is absurd. Their first rule is: Never be scooped.

Then I met the fabled Hugh Cudlipp at last. He wanted to see "the man with the initials" and a dinner was arranged at *The Sun* with editor, Dick Dinsdale, and Sydney Jacobson present along with various executives. I sat next to Cudlipp and in front of three bottles of Chateau Latour. A heavy night was in prospect. At first, our conversation was genial. He was an expansive and amusing host. Then he led me into a trap. If he thought I would rise to provocation, he was right.

He began to praise Ian Smith, the rebel and racist white prime minister of Southern Rhodesia who had defied the British Government and was refusing to accept any form of black rule. Smith was the best man, the blacks in Africa couldn't govern, democracy wouldn't work there, etc.etc. The Chateau Latour flowed, I got angry and finally told him that he was the most immoral man I had ever met. Sydney Jacobson, sitting opposite, was almost quaking with anxiety as the conversation developed. I thought I had gone too far and slumped back in sullen silence. Cudlipp ended the argument by saying I didn't know what I was talking about and ought to go to Rhodesia and find out, and he started on another bottle.

To my astonishment, when I went into the office the next morning, my flight to Rhodesia was being booked and hotels arranged. Such was the power of Hugh Cudlipp's whim. I was only saved from what would have been an unpleasant assignment when the Diplomatic reporter, Michael Leapman, protested that if anyone should go to Rhodesia , he should, and he had been banned. Cudlipp must have decided it was too much bother to fulfil a fanciful idea on his part and the trip was abandoned.

I had an interesting experience of "lobby" rules in 1966, one of which said off-the-record conversations should not be reported without the express consent of the politician concerned. I was on friendly terms with the Tory Chief Whip, the perennially cheerful Willie Whitelaw (the man of whom Mrs Thatcher was to say, "every Prime Minister should have a Willie"). Strolling through the inner lobby of the Commons shortly after Harold Wilson had called a general election, I met Whitelaw coming from his Whips' office, bags packed and going off to his constituency for the campaign.

"What's going to happen?" I asked him. "Dear boy," he chuckled, "we are going to be slaughtered." I didn't mention it to the office. It was a private, friendly, off-the-record conversation. If I had written it, it would have been a sensation. Prim I may have been, but it never occurred to me to do so. Rightly or wrongly, it would have been written today, he would have had to deny it or resign and I would have been praised and blamed in equal measure for my scoop or my treachery.

They were exciting times to be reporting politics. I was assigned to following the Prime Minister, Harold Wilson, on his general election campaign. In those days we had to find our own way to his meetings. No buses and few aircraft on which the party leader could ingratiate himself with the press. One night he was speaking at Slough on a deserted industrial estate. The meeting was running late. It was 11 o'clock. Almost all the journalists left before Wilson finished, including me. We only left the faithful reporter of record from *The Times* behind us. Our first editions had already gone to press. We had a train to get to Norwich early next morning. But before I had travelled 100 yards I had a guilty feeling, a Harold Hutchinson moment, about leaving the story and went back. Lucky for me.

Immediately, I ran into Alf Richman, a reporter from the *Sun* who had been seconded to Wilson to be his bag carrier during the election. He told me Wilson had just been hit in the eye by a boy throwing a stink bomb and it had apparently cracked an eyeball. "How is he?" I asked. "He says, 'that boy should be bowling for England,'" replied Richman. It was typical Wilson. Quick on his feet, guaranteed to win over his audience and a headline. He told the police he did not want them to take any action. He got the applause. He didn't need retribution. And I scooped all the popular papers in Fleet Street when our second edition came out. Only *The Times* had it among the broadsheets. The others in the Wilson caravan joined the train the next morning, already mortified after talking to their offices

Wilson sparkled on that tour. At Green's Playhouse in Glasgow he was being fiercely heckled by an SNP supporter in the audience (in those days, anyone could attend political meetings and Wilson thrived on hecklers). At last, with feigned impatience, Wilson turned on him: "If you would only shut your mouth and open your ears you might learn something," he snapped. At Isleworth, he was constantly interrupted by an attractive girl dressed in black leather, an Empire Loyalist as it turned out. After one particularly hostile shout, he said with forbearance, like a kindly uncle: "You know, if you were as intelligent as you are pretty you wouldn't have said that." She gasped and never uttered another word.

Night after night, one town after another, until I woke one morning and didn't know where I was. I got out of bed and went to the window and saw the headquarters of the Norwich Union opposite. I was in Norwich. Soon afterwards I got a call from the office. Harold Hutchison had to absent himself from the campaign. He had hepatitis. His deputy, Trevor Williams, who as an unemployed Welsh miner in the 1930s had walked from the valleys to London in search of work, had found the stress too much and was unable to carry on. I had to go back to London and run the political operation, which I did until the night of polling day. Then I sat down at my typewriter and wrote and changed and upgraded my opinions throughout the night as the results came in until I decided we could go with a Labour landslide.

After all, Wilson had a majority of 101 and Ted Heath, in his first election as Tory leader, had been thrashed. Heath was on the phone to Jacobson that morning complaining bitterly about my use of the word "landslide." I thought he should have had worse things to worry about. We never did get on.

Work was a pleasure then until one shocking morning when I arrived at the Commons to be told that Trevor Williams had had a heart attack and had died on the way to hospital. In truth, he died at the Commons but if it could be helped, no one ever "died" there. It was, apparently, a complicated business involving the coroner and deaths in a Royal Palace. A casualty either died after the ambulance had passed beyond the gates or in hospital. Not on the premises.

Harold Hutchinson gave me the rope and encouragement I needed. I went to the US and the United Nations Security Council in 1967 but all the action was back at home in London with the seamen's strike and a looming economic crisis. The same occurred when I went to the Soviet Union and my report from Moscow began: "Something always happen when Harold Wilson goes abroad, but it happens in London," but Jacobson, who always kept an eye on political news, thought that too frivolous an introduction to a story about a crisis. It was on one of these visits abroad that I decided it was wrong for journalists to accompany the Prime minister in his plane.

Wilson was incurably curious about newspapers and journalists. As we were trying on his plane home to cobble a story together out of almost nothing, he came to where Ian Aitken of *The Guardian* and I were writing, looked over our shoulders and asked: "What are you two up to?" That's the wrong sort of relationship between a politician and a reporter, certainly too far from H.L. Mencken's definition that it should be that between a dog and a lamp post.

Ted Castle was not really a journalist in that he couldn't write a column if needed, but he was jolly and supportive, with the experience of being a former parliamentary candidate and the vast asset of being Barbara's husband. He told me one day that he had decided to withdraw his request to Ian Mikardo to speak the eulogy at his funeral because Mikardo had attacked Barbara but didn't know who to get. "Don't worry, Ted," I said. "I'll do it." He was pleased and thanked me. Then he said, "What will you say?" I said: "I'll say you were always difficult to get ahold of when you were alive, now it's bloody impossible."

Ted had fallen out with Mikardo, the portly, beetle-browed frankly ugly, hard-left winger who Churchill had described as "not as pretty as he looks" after that criticism of Barbara. They were an affectionate team. He told me his role was to listen to her at home in the early hours making a speech she hadn't been called upon to make in the House. When she was a back-bencher, that was often.

Mikardo was a nasty piece of work. One every Labour leader could do without. He was chairman of the Tribune group of Labour MPs, named after the left-wing weekly of that name. The group had its own whip (Mikardo's secretary and later an MP herself, Jo Richardson) and its own policies and had flourished most menacingly when Aneurin Bevan was alive, but it was still powerful. One week, Mikardo was preparing another new policy designed to antagonize the Labour leadership. Neil Carmichael, a close friend who I knew well before he ever became an MP, and a member of the group, gave me a copy of it several days before it was due to be published. In the genre of trouble-making it was a good story.

Regrettably, it led to a falling out with Summerscales. I told him I had the story and that he could have it once the first editions had gone to print. He feared criticism from his office if he missed it and went to Mikardo and told him I had a document (he didn't know what) that I was intending to run that night. His purpose was to get Mikardo to give him a copy, too. Mikardo was not that generous. Instead, he phoned Jacobson and told him I was intending to break an embargo on the document and attacked me for being unprofessional. It was a straight lie and Jacobson accepted it as such. He knew Mikardo. But he still suppressed the story. The influence of the old *Daily Herald* still lingered. I was also told of an ingenious corruption scheme being carried out in Glasgow City Council, a Labour fortress. That was also suppressed. Later a couple of prominent councillors were jailed for the offence

I then had a falling out with the paper's hierarchy. One evening I was having a drink in her room with another old friend, Judith Hart, Minister of Social Security, and watching *Panorama* on BBC. They were running a story that the government were going to pay immigrants to return to their home country. It wasn't new; it had been included in legislation many months earlier and Judith was infuriated with it being raked up and presented as a new exclusive. When I got back to my room there was a demand from the office that I write the story.

I told them it wasn't new. I was then instructed that Ernie Burrington, the night editor, insisted I should write it. I refused. Nevertheless, the paper led on it the next day, written by another reporter. As soon as I got to the Commons that morning, Ted Castle phoned, sorrowfully pompous. "I must tell you, Joe," he said "that I am disappointed in you, the editor is disappointed in you and Mr Burrington is disappointed in you for missing that story."

I retorted that I was disappointed with the editor, disappointed with him and disappointed with Mr Burrington and that unless I got an apology from the editor, himself and Mr Burrington by two pm I was resigning. I put the phone down and went for an early lunch. When I got back at 2pm Ted Castle telephoned a handsome apology on behalf of the editor and himself. Ted had called Judith Hart and she had confirmed my stand. It sometimes pays to raise the stakes.

I never heard a word from Burrington, but he was to play a central part in the Robert Maxwell saga at *The Daily Mirror* more than 20 years later. The old resentments were still there on both sides, with possibly catastrophic consequences.

I went on comfortably in my job after that. It was a good paper to work for, with some outstanding journalists on it Then, early in 1968, I was approached by the Prime Minister's political assistant, Gerald Kaufman, asking me to become deputy to Wilson's Press Secretary, Trevor Lloyd-Hughes. Hoping to tempt me, he said impressively: "It pays £3,000 a year." I said I didn't want the job and that I already earned more than that, anyway. If Lloyd-Hughes knew about the approach, which was doubtful, I suspect he heaved a sigh of relief. I had clashed with him many times at the anonymous Lobby briefings and I'm sure he didn't want me. He had had a bad year before and after devaluation and had lost the confidence of the Lobby. On one occasion, criticizing us, he had pointed to the clock on the wall in the Lobby room which had not gone for years as an example of our inefficiency. I said, "At least it's right twice a day which is more than you are." That didn't make for us becoming happy companions.

I heard no more about joining the Downing Street staff until December of that year when my phone rang at my desk in the Press Gallery and a voice said, "This is the Downing Street switchboard. The Prime Minister would like to see you in his room at the House of Commons." That was an invitation no journalist could refuse and I went downstairs to see him.

The Boy Wonder

The Prime Minister's room at the House of Commons is off the corridor which runs behind the Speaker's chair; it is large enough for a Cabinet meeting but rarely used as such. When I entered, he was by himself, a small figure sitting hunched in a large gentlemen's-club-like chair reading his papers, all of which emphasised the burdens of the great office he held. It was just as a film director might have wanted it, and very impressive, despite an instinctive suspicion I had that it was all put on for my benefit. He politely waved to me to sit down and went straight to the point: "I hear you don't want to work for me," he said, putting me on the defensive. I was doomed from that moment and my fight was brief.

"It's not that I don't want to join you," I said, "but I don't want to be deputy to anyone." It would have been vulgar to mention that the salary on offer (£3,000 a year) was lousy for such a job. (It was interesting to see in 2016 the post was advertised at £117,000). "I don't want you to be deputy," said Wilson, playing his ace straightaway. "Take a few months to learn the job and then I want you to replace Trevor Lloyd-Hughes," which would have been a nasty surprise to Lloyd-Hughes if he had had any inkling of it. Not for the last time in life – I was to repeat my mistake with Robert Maxwell 15 years later – I had walked into a trap of my own making. I was quite happy with my job at the *Sun* and was reluctant to change it. Still, Press Secretary to the Prime Minister was too tempting to refuse for that reason alone. After asking him to square it with Sydney Jacobson, editorial director of my paper (and others), and on the strict understanding it would be for two years and no more, I agreed to become his deputy press secretary until I found my feet. I then went back to the Press Gallery and finished the story I was writing when he phoned.

* * * * * *

My suspicion that our interview was stage-managed was, not, I think, well founded but it sprang from Wilson's reputation: a brilliant smart Aleck, a wily politician, regarded by Tories with the same dislike and in the same terms as they regarded their own Iain McLeod, as too clever by half and too soon, not so much economical with the truth as a spendthrift with it, accompanied by a sardonic and wounding wit. At the astonishingly early age (for those days) of 46, he had won the party's leadership in 1963 over the doubters in the Parliamentary Labour party and the opposition of almost the entire Labour shadow cabinet. Only one of them voted for him, Fred Lee, known derisively as "flea" by Labour right-wingers. He had friends in the PLP but they were never wholly reliable. Dick Crossman, for example, was a close but untrustworthy ally – he wasn't known as Double Crossman without reason - and Barbara Castle a fond but often trying colleague. The sudden, premature and unexpected death of Hugh Gaitskell, who had admired his skill in the House of Commons but neither liked nor trusted him and who had roundly defeated him in a leadership contest in 1961, gave him the chance for which he had prepared almost throughout his life.

His academic career was brilliant, a council and grammar school-boy who gained first class honours in PPE at Jesus College, Oxford, and was a lecturer in economics at New College at the age of 21. He was a dedicated swot. The idea of joining a frivolous gang like the Bullingdon Club would never have occurred to him in a thousand years. He became an assistant to Sir William Beveridge, the pioneer of Britain's welfare system, on leaving the university and was chosen to speak at the British Association at the age of 23. The day of his speech, however, was not felicitous – September 3, 1939, when the attention of the world was occupied with weightier matters.

When Clement Attlee won the general election of 1945, Wilson was among the tide of victors who carried him to power, winning a seat at Ormskirk he was expected to lose. Not for the first or last time, the new dawn had arrived, but this one was the most promising. He became a junior minister immediately, a Cabinet Minister as Secretary for Overseas Trade at 31 – the youngest in an ageing government - and, later, as President of the Board of Trade, made his first significant public impact when he promised a "bonfire of controls" to an over-regulated country.

The first real crisis of his political career came in 1951 when he resigned from Attlee's Cabinet along with Aneurin Bevan and John Freeman, a junior Minister. A usual with Wilson's moves, moods, tactics or manoeuvrings – call them what you will - the circumstances were complex. Bevan resigned quite simply because he opposed the decision of Hugh Gaitskell, the Chancellor, to impose charges on prescriptions on the NHS to contain an alarming rise in costs. Wilson also opposed these charges, not on the principle of preserving a free National Health Service but because he thought they were unnecessary and could be avoided if a huge and unrealistic increase in the defence budget, because of the Korean war, was scaled down. In fact, he was proved right on that when the subsequent Churchill Government reduced defence spending to the levels he advocated, but he was denounced by the party's right-wing as "Nye's little poodle," an appellation he resented.

In fact, he was never that close to Bevan. He was of the Left in those days but not a Bevan follower, never a member of the Tribune group, which coalesced around Bevan and he was swiftly an object of Bevan's anger when he later accepted a post in the Shadow Cabinet. Again, the situation was complex. Bevan resigned from the Shadow Cabinet after he had made a previously unheard-of interruption of Prime Minister's Questions to contradict the views of his leader, Attlee, on German rearmament. Attlee's strictures about his behaviour left him no option but to go. Under the then system of an election for 12 Shadow Cabinet places, Wilson, who had come 13th in the vote, would automatically be offered co-option to it.

Ian Mikardo, the staunchest of Bevanites, pompously declared the issue was a battle between the principled and the pragmatic, thus grabbing for himself a description that few who knew him would ever have granted. But Wilson was always prone to pragmatism and thought principles without power were for the vain. After all, both he and Bevan had stood for election to the

Shadow Cabinet, so there was no difference in principle in being a member of it. He accepted.

He told me more than once that his socialism owed more to the Methodists than to Marx, which in those days was heresy to the hard Left. When I asked him if he had ever read *Das Kapital* he shook his head and said: "Never. Too many footnotes. I never got beyond the first page." In fact, he never flirted with Communism at all – as distinct from flirting with its leaders - a fact which the Left of the Labour party, as well as the leaders of the Soviet Union were slow, to realise. That was due in part to the frequent trips he made to the Soviet Union, when few Western politicians were welcome, as an employee of Montague Meyer, whose timber business depended upon East-West trade.

The war between Hugh Gaitskell and Aneurin Bevan held centre-stage in the Labour party throughout the 1950s. At its peak, Bevan made his renowned jibe about a "desiccated calculating machine." "He mentioned no names but it was universally accepted as an insult to Gaitskell. Only Wilson disagreed. He was convinced, he told me, that Bevan had him in mind and not Gaitskell. Given that Wilson was unemotional in public, rather like Sir Stafford Cripps, the Attlee Chancellor he so much admired, and Gaitskell was highly passionate, Wilson had a case.

In 1953 he wrote a book, *The War on World Poverty*, which led to the creation of the charity, War on Want. It helped establish his international credentials as a knowledgeable and caring left-winger. The fact that it was published by Gollancz gave it a stamp of approval which was highly valued by anyone on the left. He also wrote a damning report of the Labour Party, comparing its operations to that of a "penny farthing" bicycle. It was the more wounding because of its accuracy, though if anything he under-stated the situation. He became the party's chairman in 1961. He got to know the party inside out. He won over the party members long before he won over the MPs. I never ceased to be amazed at his knowledge of regional delegates to Labour party conferences who he would greet as old friends and ask about their wives (or husbands) whose names he remembered. Like all his predecessors as Prime Minister in the 20th century, he took the long, hard road to the top. And yet he generated mistrust among those who also hoped to travel the same road.

Wilson worked hard as Shadow Chancellor and he was a great success politically. His speeches were sharp, witty and well-informed and "the gnomes of Zurich" was a phrase he made famous even if he didn't coin it. It was in Opposition that he made what I have always regarded as his best House of Commons speech and the episode which brought out the worst and best of his qualities. The late Reginald Maudling, whose own record should have aroused more distrust over the years than it did, accused Wilson of keeping his ear so close to the ground that it was little wonder that it was full of dirt and it seemed to be apposite on this occasion. It was ironic that when Maudling left the Government because of what Edward Heath's biographer called his "unwise associations" with dubious people, he travelled to No. 10 in the car of Eric Miller, who was more than dubious. He was crooked. Much later, when he was a close friend of Lady Falkender and a regular donor to Wilson's political office, he blew out his brains as the Fraud Squad closed in on him. Hangers-on in politics are like football managers: they switch smoothly from one failure to another, ever hopeful, but ultimately disappointed..

The event which seemed to doom Wilson to political extinction and instead opened the door to his future leadership attempts was the Bank Rate Leak Tribunal which was set up by Harold Macmillan after a startling series of staged Commons events in 1957-58. There is no doubt that its purpose was to destroy Wilson politically and from the start it looked as if he were on a loser. Bank Rate had suddenly been raised by the lightweight Chancellor of the Exchequer, Peter Thorneycroft, from two per cent to seven per cent. The suspicion that the decision had been leaked in advance for the benefit of unnamed speculators was first raised in the Commons by Sir Leslie Plummer, the MP for Deptford, and closely associated with Wilson (and an object of interest to MI 5). There is no doubt the two arranged it. It was a fix. Wilson took it up. When he named Sir Oliver Poole, a wealthy Tory banker, as recipient of the leak the situation became more serious, though still treated with scorn by the Tories and with some misgivings on the Labour benches. The press, including me, remained sceptical. I remember sitting next to Bernard Levin, the renowned columnist of *The Spectator,* in the Press Gallery and scribbling a joke headline: "Plummer seeks leak, finds Poole," which he used in his magazine that week. I thought Wilson was chasing a hare as false as any which ever circled a greyhound track. And in reality, he was.

The inquiry, as intended, cleared Poole and Thorneycroft but left enough loopholes for Wilson forensically to demolish it. But when he rose in the House to make his speech in the two-day debate on the report it was to the jeers of the Tory benches and only scattered support from the Labour MPs behind him. But it was one of those rare occasions when a debate was changed by the speech of one man. It was widely described as "brilliant" and "superb." Even Tory newspapers who had joined in the hunt for his blood praised it. Rather than fight on the narrow front of the tribunal's report, Wilson widened his attack to take in the whole of the City of London's money-making culture. It was said that the City would never forgive him, but the City exists to make money not to take revenge.

More important than its reaction was that of the PLP. For the first time, he was seen as a possible successor to Hugh Gaitskell should anything happen to the leader. But he stayed outside the close circle around Gaitskell. His challenge for the leadership when it came in 1961 was another example of the straightforward being complicated by mixed motives. He argued, privately, that Gaitskell should remain leader, at least in the short term, but the unilateralist Left were determined he should be challenged and Anthony Greenwood, son of Arthur and an elegant, smooth-talking politician of little ability, decided to stand. Wilson thought he wasn't up to the job he himself coveted and would only strengthen Gaitskell's position. He also, more importantly, thought that would make Greenwood the standard bearer of the Left if ever the post became vacant. That would have been intolerable to his long-term ambition. He stood and was well beaten, but not ignominiously so.

He sided, but not wholly, with those who opposed the independent nuclear deterrent, arguing it was neither independent and, consequently, nor a deterrent, an argument he was later to abandon. He didn't publicly disagree with Gaitskell's famous conference speech denouncing the Common Market though he was later as Prime Minister to make strenuous, even desperate, attempts to join it. He appeared to sit on too many fences at this period of his life, fulfilling James Maxton's maxim "That if you can't ride two horses at once you shouldn't be in the bloody circus." But it was also part of the basic insecurity which affected him all his political life, in office, in opposition and and even in retirement. To change the metaphor, he couldn't put all his eggs in one basket. He trusted none of his colleagues in the PLP 100 per cent and they, in turn, did not trust him.

The shocking death of Gaitskell in 1963 changed his political fortunes. The three candidates to succeed the late leader were Wilson, the deputy leader, George Brown - the choice of the Labour establishment, largely because of their detestation of Wilson – and Jim Callaghan, who was wisely laying down a marker for the future, even though he was older than Wilson. Wilson, who was now supported politically and strategically by a formidable secretary, Marcia Williams, who joined him in 1956, won after a second vote over George Brown. Looking back today, whatever one's final conclusions about Wilson, the election of Brown would have been dire for the party and a calamity for the country, whatever it might have done for the brewing industry.

Every politician who aspires to top the greasy pole has a good speech in him to make on the right occasion. Churchill, whom Wilson greatly admired, had many. Gaitskell and Aneurin Bevan, the most remarkable orator of my time, had several, Macmillan, who was often too theatrical, had one world-changing speech, about the "winds of change" sweeping through Africa, and Wilson had at least two outstanding ones – during the Bank Rate debate and at his first Labour conference as leader, in Scarborough 1963 – and several of high quality.

But Opposition was one thing, Government another. Though Wilson had a record of Cabinet membership and despite the fact that his nimble-footed campaign during the 1964 general election left impartial observers gasping with admiration and the Tories leaden footed and clumsy, he still only just scraped home and didn't need the fingers of two hands to count his majority. The inevitable crises, expected and unexpected, stated soon afterwards. Wilson, mimicking John F. Kennedy, had promised 100 days of action, which hardly happened as intended and on the last of which Sir Winston Churchill, a Tory for whom Wilson never had a bad word, died and Wilson spent it writing his parliamentary tribute to him.

Some of the events during that first Labour Government since 1951 were almost routine, speculation against sterling; a mandatory visit to Washington where President Lyndon Johnson first asked him to send troops to Vietnam; the loss of a by-election contested by Patrick Gordon Walker, who had been defeated at the General Election by a racist Tory, Peter Griffiths, at Smethwick, and a narrow victory in another by-election for Frank Cousins, the unilateralist leader of the Transport and General Workers' Union, who Wilson brought into the Government where he was an uncomfortable colleague and all-round failure. In Rhodesia, the white government of Ian Smith made a unilateral declaration of independence, a situation which, despite dramatic, even melodramatic, attempts to resolve it over the years, Wilson was never able to overcome.

The PLP were always demanding Wilson condemn the US war in Vietnam. The Left were then, as today, always more enamoured of protest at a problem than a solution to it, and Wilson was contemptuous of it. He told President Johnson that Britain had more troops in Malaya fighting communism than the US had (at that time) in Vietnam and refused even to send a token force. The Left were never satisfied. Their appetite for protest was insatiable. Thy wanted him to condemn the United States. Wilson did send his parliamentary private secretary, Harold Davies, a voluble Welshman who represented Leek in Staffordshire, on a secret "peace" mission to Vietnam in the feeble hope that he might help bring the Vietnamese to the conference table. But whatever slight hope there was of success - and I believe there was none at all – was scuppered when John Harris, a devout Gaitskellite, Roy Jenkins's closest ally and confidant, and special adviser at the Foreign Office – leaked it to the *Daily Mail* and *The Sun*.

Davies was an interesting choice to be Wilson's p.p.s. and one which aroused seldom dormant suspicions about the Prime Minister's true political ideology. In 1961, only four years previously, he was on a list of 16 Labour MPs handed to MI 5 who the then Labour leadership believed to be covert communists and whom they would be willing to expel if the secret service confirmed their betrayal. The list was drawn up by Gaitskell, George Brown, and Patrick Gordon Walker. None of the other Shadow Cabinet Ministers, including Wilson, were told. MI 5 refused to be involved, saying it was a question of party politics. More interestingly, they didn't believe that any secret of which Brown had knowledge would be secret for long because of his heavy drinking (and the fact that he was a regular informant of Chapman Pincher of the *Daily Express*, a constant irritant to the secret service because he knew too much about them). Of even greater, and more secret, interest and unknown to Gaitskell was the fact that soon after his election to Parliament in 1945, MI 5 opened a file on Harold Wilson. It was so sensitive that it was kept under the name of "Norman John Worthington." MI 5 maintained that they had no suspicions about Wilson but did have them about some of his associates, including a civil servant.

Rumours and allegations about Wilson's association with and sympathy for the Soviet Union were to dog his career before and after he became Prime Minister. I firmly believe there wasn't any substance to them whatsoever but there is no doubt that some of those people he mixed with, negotiated with or appointed – for example, Jack Jones, the formidable and much-honoured trade union leader - were sympathetic to, or paid agents, of the Soviets and, what's more, he knew it and so did MI 5 from the very beginning, hence the "Worthington" file. It did not help those who would swear by his innocence. Wilson was aware of Jones's past when he appointed him to sit on the National Economic Development Council. Jones, unknown to him, was forbidden to see confidential papers, but he should never have been appointed in the first place, despite the insistent demands of other trade union leaders, most of whom would not have known of his Soviet connection. His deputy, Alex Kitson, however, is likely to have known. He was a suspect himself.

Wilson's frequent trips behind the Iron Curtain in the 1950s, representing Montague Meyer, his "friendship" (the word is too loosely used in politics) with Soviet leaders such as Kosygin and Gromyko, and his lack of transparency about his concerns and his political attitudes did not help his greater cause. His refusal to sign a motion condemning the Soviet Union for its invasion of Hungary in 1956 was shameful and noted by MI 5 as well as by the Kremlin. It was a time when great events should have risen above personal ambition, either as an emissary of a private firm or a future Shadow Foreign Secretary. This ambivalence was also a sign of his insecurity. It may have been no coincidence that the Kremlin decided to start an "agent development file" on him in that same year, codenamed OLDING. But it was also commonplace for the Soviet Union to be given the benefit of the doubt by the Left in Britain at a time when a serious, rational politician should not have seen a doubt. Kruschev, for example, was a political thug and mass murderer different from Stalin only in degree. Aneurin Bevan in the 1950s praised the Soviets in extravagant language by which he would have been embarrassed had he lived and there were many others in the Labour party who agreed with him. It wasn't necessary to be paid in Russian gold to do their work for them. The "useful idiots" would do it for nothing. But, somehow, the stigma of being a Soviet sympathiser attached itself to Wilson particularly.

When he became Prime Minister, MI 5 would have told him of those MPs, recent or still sitting, who were suspected of being risky on security grounds and some of them were on Gaitskell's 1961 list, including the Silverman brothers, Sydney and Julius, Leo Abse, John Mendelson, Tom Driberg, Stephen Swingler, Davies, Sir Leslie Plummer, Arthur Lewis, Judith Hart and Emrys Hughes Gaitskell listed 25 in all, either as secret CP members or as suspects.

Of those, Driberg was a member of the Labour party's National Executive Committee for many years and a notoriously promiscuous homosexual (before and after the act was decriminalised), the ground on which Wilson refused to give him a peerage in his first two governments, though in his last government he conceded it at the persistent request of Michael Foot; Swingler was made a minister by Wilson, but, according to Christopher Andrew's History of MI 5, Clement Attlee, Labour's first post-war Prime Minister, told the general secretary of the Labour party, Morgan Phillips, in 1947 that he was certain Swingler was a communist; Sir Leslie Plummer was Wilson's partner in promoting the Bank Rate Leak "scandal" in 1961 and his wife Baroness (Beattie) Plummer, I was told when I worked for Wilson, certainly was a Soviet agent. There was a period when she was a frequent visitor to No. 10 and Mrs Williams, but those visits had virtually stopped by the time I joined the staff there.

Arthur Lewis, on the other hand, was one of the most stupid men ever elected to the Commons, too stupid to be a communist but stupid enough to be a security risk if had he ever known anything sensitive. He used to send me abusive unsigned letters about Bob Mellish making allegations of corruption with bookmakers in Bermondsey. His near-illiteracy was such that he didn't need to conceal his name, but after one such letter I replied beginning with the words, "Dear Arthur, Thank you for your anonymous letter...".and I never heard from him again.

Judith Hart was an old friend of mine. Her husband was undoubtedly a communist and never hid the fact. I don't believe she was, but she was sympathetic. In 1974 Wilson offered her a post in the Government and then withdrew it after MI 5 told him they had intercepted telephone calls between her and Bert Ramelson, industrial organiser of the British Communist party in King Street, London. (Wilson announced in his first Government that calls made by MPs would not be tapped by the security services; that prohibition did not extend to calls made by suspects *to* MPs) and he showed me the intercept. It was a conversation about the situation in Chile after the murder of its Marxist president, Salvator Allende. But she protested to Wilson she had been asked by Labour's NEC to find out about the state of affairs in Chile. Wilson should have remembered: he was a member; Ramelson was the best-informed person in Britain she could ask. Wilson reversed his decision and she was reinstated. There was a persistent story much later about Judith Hart being confused by MI 5 with a Mrs Tudor Hart, but that wasn't the case.

Right to the end of his premiership Wilson persisted in his unwise associations with people who had come under the surveillance of the security services. One of the most sinister of these was Rudi Sternberg, an East European businessman. When it became clear during the drawing up of Wilson's final and infamous Honours List that he was intending to make Sternberg a peer, a senior Foreign Office official protested to me: "But he's a Russian spy!" I went to Wilson and told him what had been said. He replied: "He's a double agent." I couldn't contradict him and Sternberg's name went ahead. When I made further investigations later I was told absolutely that Sternberg was never a British agent and that Wilson was not telling the truth. Why did he do it? The short answer was money, which was key to some of his honours and to his insecurity, and I deal with that below, but it is also true that some of the dubious characters he relied upon showed him a loyalty, for whatever reason, that the bigger beasts among his Parliamentary colleagues did not.

The Prime Minister's principal private secretary, Ken Stowe, reported to Wilson when his resignation Honours List was being drawn up that the Department of Trade did not favour an honour to Sir Sigmund Sternberg on the grounds that he was an "unsavoury" character. Sir Sigmund, who I knew for some years, always seemed to me to be an honourable man; he never gave money to Wilson's office, only to the Labour party and was a passionate supporter of Israel, as was Wilson. I believe the Department of Trade confused the two Sternbergs (unrelated). Interestingly, Brian Brivati, biographer of Gaitskell and of (Lord) Arnold Goodman, Wilson's solicitor, asserts that Wilson suspected that Sternberg was involved with the Soviets and that Sternberg's house was being watched by the security services at the time of his death, which directly contradicts what Wilson had told me.

It was not possible in the days of the Soviet Union to be in left-wing politics without being forced to associate with people who, frankly, were treacherous, but it was possible to keep a distance. Wilson certainly kept a distance from many in the parliamentary party whom he knew to be suspect, but there were others to whom he was too close. And this was the man and the organisation that I agreed to join. Little did I know the world I was entering, but fortunately I was not clairvoyant.

*****

Lord Goodman was Wilson's solicitor, the fixer of fixer, the "cab for hire" as he described himself, and a firefighter frequently called in to settle political problems for Wilson (for example, Rhodesia) and the personal problems of Mrs Williams.

He was the chairman of a secretive committee – described euphemistically as a "trust" - whose purpose was to provide funds for running Wilson s office. Other members included Sammy Fisher, chairman of the London Mayors' Association, Jarvis Astaire, a boxing promoter who was included in the first draft of the infamous Resignation Honours List of 1976 and later deleted, Donald Gosling, and Arieh Handler, London manager of the International Credit Bank of Geneva which was forced to close in October, 1974 after a row about a deposit account he opened in Wilson's name unknown to Wilson.

Lady Falkender was also a member of the committee. There was one aspect of Wilson's affairs from which I was completely excluded during my seven years with him, and that was the financing of his office. That was controlled, in effect in not in name, by Lady Falkender when she was Marcia Williams. If ever the committee were due to meet during the years of Opposition, Wilson would send me home early before the members were due to arrive. In Government, other money-raising meetings, with different members and more informal and secretive, were held but I heard about them. They were purely (!) and simply to raise funds. At least one took place at Chequers, where each wealthy man present – there were never any women, apart from Lady Falkender - was bluntly asked to contribute £1,600, a sum which the ill-fated Eric Miller said was inadequate and should be increased.

Money was the essential bane but lifeblood of the office's existence. There is no doubt today that the methods of raising and receiving it would be regarded as illegal, but the same could be said of the bankrolling of Ted Heath and Winston Churchill. Other Prime Ministers may have accepted the route of the Honours List – Lloyd George notoriously so - to bring in the cash, but morally they were no different. It's the way the British system works: if the state doesn't officially provide the funds for a political leader and Prime Minister to do his job adequately then he or she finds other, dubious, ways of doing it. When Wilson first left office in 1970 he was £14,000 in debt with a ridiculously overstaffed office to pay for. Though that was dramatically reduced in number it was still costly and the contribution of Labour's headquarters at Transport House - £6,000 a year – was ludicrous. At one point, Transport House told Wilson that while they would pay for his visits to other constituencies and regions they would not pay for his wife, Mary, to accompany him. Wilson ended that dispute by telling them that in that case he wouldn't visit anywhere as his wife was more popular than he was.

Lord Goodman didn't admire Mrs Williams – he told me once that "but for that woman, Harold Wilson would have been a great Prime Minister" – but he had a gargantuan appetite for work (and, on occasions, for food. I vividly remember a pub lunch we had in a bar off the Strand. He ate for England that day). He presided over the private affairs of public figures like an amply-suited Buddha. In the 1974-76 Government he was frequently called in to aid Mrs Williams, or Lady Falkender as she became in 1975. On one occasion, she demanded that Wilson summon Goodman because she was about to be sent to prison for owing the Inland Revenue £20,000 in tax. (I remember wondering how a secretary supposedly on the same salary as me could possibly owe £20,000 in tax). Whatever her debts to the Revenue, her fears were the product of hysterical fantasy. As always, he comforted and counselled her and nothing dire happened.

* * * * * * * *

Wilson's record during his first two governments was of gallant failure, with occasional and, in the case of the Open University, lasting successes. He fought for the University of the Air as it was originally called against the scepticism of opponents and Cabinet colleagues alike, yet it brought pleasure and education to hundreds of thousands of people who might never otherwise have aspired to a university degree., and it wasn't done by dumbing down. In his later Governments, Roy Jenkins, as Chancellor, wanted to end it and Mrs Thatcher, as Prime Minister felt the same, though she subsequently changed her mind.

But wage growth was only controlled by compulsory wage restrictions. The seamen's strike of 1966, more political than it was industrial, damaged the economy severely. In Rhodesia Ian Smith was only interested in wasting time and clinging to white rule and the pressure on the pound which never ceased after the seamen had returned to work eventually led, in 1967 to the most crippling blow he ever suffered – devaluation. He had set his heart and mind against it, but like other Prime Ministers before and after him he found he could not buck the markets. Publicly, he seemed a broken man. George Brown, whose machinations against Wilson in his attempt to succeed Wilson were as malevolent as Gordon Brown's against Tony Blair more than 20 years later, but unsuccessful, had overstepped himself in attempting a coup against Wilson in the early hours of March 15 – the fateful Ides of March – and resigned, not for the first time, from the Government only to find to his dismay that on this occasion Wilson accepted it.

Crises flew in thick and fast. Cecil King, chairman of the International Publishing Corporation, which owned the *Daily Mirror* and my newspaper, the *Sun,* demanded Wilson must go and hatched a bizarre plot whereby an emergency government, led by Lord Mountbatten, should take over. Some of the hereditary madness of the Harmsworth family seems to have afflicted him. The ultimate result was that IPC sacked King. But Labour whips drew up a list of 77 Labour MPs who refused to sign a motion condemning King and it included, interestingly, apart from the usual suspects, Robert Maxwell.

Finally, rebels in the Cabinet, led by Denis Healey, attempted to get lifted an arms embargo on the South African apartheid Government. That was a step too far for Wilson. He refused to concede and his resistance succeeded (Healey later admitted to me that he had been wrong). But as the old song has it, "it was one durned thing after another."

And this, I reflected in December, 1968, was the government - divided, bitter, conspiratorial, jealous and rebellious, and 23 points behind in the opinion polls - I had just agreed to join.

* * * * * * * * * * *

On January 1, 1969, I found myself in charge of a small, tidy office occupied by four ladies in or approaching middle-age. They did their best politely to make me comfortable which made me uncomfortably aware I was an outsider. Government documents showered down upon me, principally telegrams from our embassies abroad, notes of departments about forthcoming announcements and decisions made by Cabinet committees before Christmas which had only just filtered down to the Press Office. No one took a decision on anything without referring it to me, but most of every morning each day was taken up by my staff ringing round government departments to ask questions of their press officers which might be asked of the Press Secretary when he held his first Lobby meeting of the day at 11 o'clock.

I knew that system was wrong from the moment I saw it: why should No. 10 employ press officers to do the Lobby reporters' job for them? Why shouldn't the reporters phone the departments themselves instead of wandering into No. 10 after morning coffee and ask one man to reply on matters, say, of health, defence, pensions, employment, the economy or any other issue on which he usually had only second-hand knowledge? Of course, there was a reason.

It was a common jibe in the civil service that if you had a man or woman who was honest but not very bright, you put him/her into the press office and didn't tell them anything in case they told the newspapers. And so a department at the heart of government was deployed each morning trying to wheedle answers out of departments scattered all over Whitehall who were reluctant to release what little information they had. There was a meeting of

Chief Press Officers each week, due to be presided over by me, which would look forward to the coming week and try to give some coherence to the government's publicity strategy, if it had one. To adapt Oliver Cromwell, it sat there too long for the good that it did. I only attended it once.

There were two dominant figures, apart from Wilson, in No.10 when I joined: Michael Halls, his principal private secretary who Wilson had known back in his days at the Board of Trade, and Marcia Williams, Wilson's private secretary, aide and confidant since 1956. The one to be scared of, even if you were a civil servant – especially if you were a civil servant - was Mrs Williams, a tall, attractive blonde with a toothy smile, an acute intelligence, a charm which could captivate a stranger and a glare which could reduce an enemy to a shivering wreck.

There were also two major figures of importance outside of No. 10 but both genuine intimates of the Prime Minister, Lord Goodman and Joe Stone, his personal doctor and a man totally devoted to Wilson. It took me a while to get to know them but they loom large in the pages of this book dealing with the personal rather than the political life of Wilson. They both hated the influence of Marcia Williams. Goodman would soothe her in her moments of panic, be calm and reassuring but never bent to her will. Stone acted as her doctor as well as Wilson's (and would give advice to all the personal staff if they wanted it). He never said a harsh word to Marcia. His bedside manner with her was impeccable but his hatred was implacable.

Halls was a weakness and deliberately so. Wilson's first principal private secretary had been Derek Mitchell, one of the outstanding young civil servants of his generation. He had left before I joined but his reputation survived his departure and I was impressed when I met him afterwards. Unfortunately , as was inevitable with any strong-minded and intelligent civil servant, he was said to have fallen foul of Marcia. If she and a civil servant were incompatible the civil servant had to go, and go he did. Halls, who was widely judged by his contemporaries to be second rate, served to please the Prime Minister, often beyond the call of duty. In an unguarded moment he complained to me that he had to spend too much of his time sorting out the domestic problems of Mrs Williams. Frankly, he didn't have to, but he did not have the resolve to say No to the Prime Minister when he was asked to involve himself in her difficulties, though if he had done so his days at No. 10 and on this earth might not have been numbered. Those difficulties included the birth of a child fathered by Walter Terry, political editor of the *Daily Mail,* with another on the way. Halls's wife blamed the stresses of No. 10 on his premature death and successfully sued the Civil Service Department for a large sum of money in compensation. But to me he was the White Rabbit of Whitehall, always scurrying to do the Prime Minister's wishes, intrusive and inquisitive and insecure.

One change I made as soon as I found it was happening. Frequently calls for Trevor Lloyd-Hughes were routed through my telephones. I watched a civil servant taking a call telling the caller to hold on and then put it through to his office. But she didn't put the phone down. She covered the mouthpiece and listened. I asked what she was doing. She said that Lloyd-Hughes might say something that we all ought to know. I immediately forbade her doing it again. I was being loyal but I was also thinking of the time in the near future when I would be taking those calls. It would be my job to decide what the rest of the staff ought to know, not hers. I was to find out later that what she was doing was common practice in the civil service. If anyone joining for the first time nowadays wants to make private telephone calls, it would be better to use a mobile phone.

Once I was Press Secretary, I handed over the chair of the weekly strategy meeting, successively, to three permanent civil servants who *were* good at their job and could tell me if anything of the slightest interest ever happened there. The first, George Holt, was a former parliamentary correspondent of the *News Chronicle.* He was wise, patient, polite, impartial and able to do any job given to him with great efficiency; he would have been well able to fill Trevor Lloyd-Hughes's shoes if that was what Wilson wanted. But it wasn't. He wanted a different style of shoes entirely. The second was Charles Birdsall, a Ministry of Labour veteran who seemed at times to run that department. He was a walking encyclopaedia of

Civil Service lore, always telling me why I couldn't do something I wanted to do, but a lovable man, nevertheless. The third was my final deputy, Janet Hewlett-Davies, a young blonde I'd known since 1963 when she was the chief reporter of my local newspaper, the Tonbridge *Courier*. She was very good, had had a previous spell at No. 10 under Ted Heath, was saucy with the Prime Minister but not flirtatious and never once grumbled about the work-load I placed upon her. I only saw her lose her temper once and that was after I interrogated her at a Civil Service Board to make the appointment of my deputy.

The rest of the Board had treated her lightly and she was sailing through. There was an assumption by the others (rightly) that whatever she said she would get the job, but their presumption annoyed me, so I asked her: "Do you agree the Government is very unpopular at the moment?" "Yes," she replied cautiously. "Whose fault is that," I went on, "the Prime Minister's or his Press Secretary's?" Her answer was a gulping platitude. When I got back to No. 10 and my room, she came bursting in, stood in front of my desk, and said: "You bastard! " "What are you bothered about?" I asked her. "You got the job." She almost collapsed with relief.

The greatest advantage of working at No. 10 was its atmosphere, relaxed, calm, confident and unhurried. The elegance of its furnishings, carpeting and paintings made one think almost anything was possible there. In fact, it was the product of a 17th century jerry-builder (named Downing, of course who even had an Cambridge College named after him), which seemed appropriate in view of its later history of the policies that were born there, but countless rebuildings had turned it into a place of beauty and it was a delight to work there. My last visit was in December, 2015, when I made a speech to about 120 civil servants from around Whitehall. One permanent secretary said I had made her week, which was usually boring and routine. I sympathized. I couldn't help thinking how things had changed in Government and that if I worked in No.10 today I would find all its magic had gone. The previous speech I had made was also at Downing Street, when Tony Blair was Prime Minister and it was to an audience of his staff. I was asked only one pertinent question, by one of Blair's economic advisers: "What do you think we should do about Gordon Brown," he said. "Sack him," I replied. I've often wondered how political history might have changed had my advice been followed. But that's the fate of advisers, to be seen to be right in hindsight, to be heard but not acted upon.

The Cameron Downing Street had changed enormously since my time there. A friend described today's front hall and corridor and rooms off it as like a railway station and he was right. From elegance to Euston, in less than a generation. There is an aura about historic buildings; change the appearance and that aura is lost.

The deep red carpeting had been replaced by someone whose taste must have been nurtured in studying the interiors of superior bed and breakfast accommodation on Blackpool's South Shore. The beautifully proportioned rooms upstairs had been carved up out of recognition, and lined with fake distressed wooden cabinets, which would have been bad enough if the distressed wood were genuine. A huge table which looked like middle slice of a diseased elm tree had pride of place in one room when it should have been the centre-piece of a rural bonfire on November 5. A senior civil servant whispered to me: "Don't blame us – It was Mrs Blair's choice." But I blame him and his immediate civil service predecessors, and Gordon Brown and David Cameron, for leaving it there. Downing Street has been vandalised and it would take a Jacob Rees-Mogg to restore it, which might be too high a price to pay.

When I took my first lobby meeting soon after my arrival it was flatteringly described to me as a breath of fresh air as I tried to avoid the traditional circumlocution of the answers to elaborate questions archly asked. But Lloyd-Hughes kept a tight grip on the Lobby meetings after my first by always attending them himself while I sat there listening dutifully to answers I would once have scoffed at when on the other side of the fence.

In the run-up to my taking over, Wilson had offered Lloyd-Hughes the post of the Government's Chief Communications Adviser or something similar grand-sounding. The title was of little importance. So was the job. He was being promoted out of

No. 10. He disappeared into the entrails of Whitehall, but not before telling me he suspected he was being manoeuvred out and if that were true he wouldn't go. For his sake, I was glad he never found it was true because the outcome would have been the sack. Apart from two clashes with him, I saw nothing of him after that. The first dispute was not long in coming, though.

I had asked one departmental press officer when the report of a major commission of inquiry was being published. He told me. I asked when it would be issued to the press. "At the same time," he said. "It won't, " I said. "It will be issued under embargo the day before." "No," he replied. "The contents have been leaked to John Grant of the *Daily Express* and we are paying them back." I disabused him, perhaps too forcibly, and told him to do as I said. He was no doubt totally unaware that John Grant would be a Labour minister the next time there was a Labour Government. In any case, if he objected to the leak he should take it out on the leaker.

Misunderstanding my position, he complained to Lloyd-Hughes, having now taken up his post as titular head of the Government's information services. Soon afterwards, I was walking with the Prime Minister along the corridor that joins the front hall of No.10 to the lobby in front of the Cabinet room when Lloyd-Hughes appeared and stopped us "Ah, Harold," he said (first mistake; when others were present he should have addressed him as "Prime Minister"), "I'm glad Joe's here, I've had a serious complaint about him." Harold bristled, slightly but noticeably. "What is it?" he asked. "Joe has been rude to a civil servant," replied Lloyd-Hughes digging his pit a little deeper. "Good," replied Wilson. "Anything else?" At last, after several weeks, Lloyd-Hughes had got the message. Later in the year 1969, the first American astronauts to land on the moon came to a dinner held in their honour by Wilson at No.10, a grand occasion. Lloyd-Hughes wrote to Wilson saying that the date chosen was the day when a major Government report was due to be published. Wilson passed it to me. I scribbled something like, "We are sometimes at the mercy of great events," and we never heard any more of it - or him.

When Wilson lost the general election in June, 1970, Lloyd-Hughes wrote to the new Prime Minister, Edward Heath, asking that he be kept on in the job he was doing. Heath said No. Some years later, Lloyd-Hughes wrote to *The Times* laying the blame for the loss of that election upon me and my style as Press Secretary. I wrote a tart reply saying that up until then I had thought we had lost it because of compulsory wage restraint, inflation, arguments with the trade unions over *In Place of Strife*, strikes and apparent support for the US in Vietnam.

It was unlikely that Heath would ever have engaged anyone once closely associated with Wilson. Heath regarded Wilson with the contempt which a bully has for an opponent on whom he could never land a blow. Wilson told Philip Ziegler that he couldn't forgive what Heath had done to me. Ziegler asked me what that was. I hadn't the faintest idea what he was talking about unless it was Heath's complaint to Sydney Jacobson. Wilson for his part was suspicious about where Heath got the money from to run his political office. It smacked a little of the pot calling the kettle black. The answer appeared to be the same kind of source as Wilson: wealthy donors in search of a title or the recipients of one already, but a group who acted with more subtlety. Wilson was told, and it seemed plausible to me, that a group of men in the City of London invested large sums of their own money into a fund whose profits went to Heath and helped maintain his yacht, *Morning Cloud*, while retaining their capital. Wilson had the traditional (in those days) doubts about a man in his forties and fifties who never married. When Heath's Government proposed changes in family laws, Wilson sardonic comment was that "those who don't play the game shouldn't make the rules."

When I went to No. 10 I noticed that if I ever said anything amusing to the Prime Minister, Michael Halls always waited to see if Wilson laughed before he did. One day Wilson called me up to his study where Halls was present. He said he had a problem and two solutions, neither of which was quite right, and told me what they were. "Why don't you do both?" I said. They both stared at me, then the Prime Minister said, "Joe, you're a genius" and Halls after a brief delay said, "Brilliant, brilliant." "I'm not just a pretty face," I replied. They both stared at me again. It was obvious that neither of them had ever heard that retort before. Heaven knows what doubts that aroused about my sexuality.

It was difficult to overcome the passive resistance of the civil servants to outsiders. The Prime Minister's personal red box, which was left open in the private office for senior staff to read had vital or secret papers placed in it at the last moment before going to the Prime Minister for him to read, which often meant that I missed them. I had to rely on Wilson to tell me what had happened at Cabinet meetings because the civil servants were unforthcoming. I suspect their attitude derived from the Lloyd-Hughes regime, made worse by the fact that I was obviously a political appointment and, perhaps, by the fact that I was seen as an ally of Mrs Williams's, which I undoubtedly was at first.

I had known her for a long time, but only slightly, but there was no way in which Lloyd-Hughes could have been sacked and I appointed if Mrs Williams had not given her blessing, or even inspired the changes. She made me welcome. She kept me informed on most matters, or so I thought. If Wilson wanted to talk politics or party politics in his study she made sure I was invited, even though I was a civil servant . She was a sometime visitor to the Press Gallery when I worked there, usually at the invitation of Walter Terry who was a long-time friend of mine and worked in the same room as me for some years. I thought nothing of it though one evening Mavis Terry, Walter's wife, asked me what I thought of Marcia. When I praised her, Mavis changed the subject. My wife's constant refrain was that I couldn't see what was in front of my nose,

Marcia had a powerful influence on Wilson, obviously, but it didn't seem to me at the time to be a malign one. Never did I have an opinion which I so totally reversed. In the meantime, I enjoyed watching her sweep into the private secretaries' room, throw down a piece of paper in front of Mark Forrester, the junior secretary responsible for keeping the Prime Minister's diary, and demand: "What is the meaning of this?" "This" would be an appointment which the unfortunate private secretary hadn't first consulted her about. "Take it out!" she instructed and swept out again. As a theatrical performance it was up with Edith Evans's Lady Bracknell any day.

I was drawn more and more in to the political circle around Wilson, which suited me fine; I never intended to ape the perfect civil servant. Early on, I asked him, "Why did you call me Press Secretary?" and he replied: "Because it disguised what you really do." I quickly justified what I really did when a close friend, an MP, gave the news of a more serious than usual plot against Wilson's leadership, with names, including that of the ring-leader, Ivor Richards, a devotee of Denis Healey. It was the first inkling I had of how conspiracy thoughts dominated Wilson and Marcia When I told Wilson, he told Marcia and the action was immediate. Marcia said that Wilson's parliamentary private secretary, Eric Varley, the link between Downing Street and the House of Commons, should be brought back from holiday immediately to quash any signs of trouble in the House. Wilson decided to make a speech showing his awareness of what was afoot. "I know what is going on," he proclaimed. "I'm going on." End of purported conspiracy. But I was becoming aware that no-one was trusted.

One story I told him did not have the consequence I intended but was another sign of insecurity. I went over to the Strangers' café and bar in the Commons soon after arriving in Downing Street for a bite to eat and a quick drink and met Richard Marsh, MP for Greenwich, Minister of Transport and a long-time acquaintance. Richard blithely told me about the last Cabinet he attended, clearly not knowing that I had joined the No.10 staff and thinking I was still a writing journalist. Naively, I told the story while chatting in Wilson's study because I thought it was amusing. Wilson didn't. In the summer he sacked Marsh, swearing to me that he had done so because he was always bringing him problems whereas he wanted his ministers to bring him solutions; and it was true that Marsh would turn up at No.10 late at night to consult Wilson, but I was never convinced that was the reason. I think it was my big mouth.

Worse, shortly before the party conference that year, Wilson showed me a list of the Cabinet changes he was to announce the week-end after it was over. Marsh's dismissal was the most prominent – and I was due to have lunch with him on the coming Thursday. I didn't make an excuse and we had lunch. He was always an engaging companion and he was effusive about the Prime Minister. "If he were to sack me tomorrow," he said, "I would have no complaints." Not tomorrow, as it turned out, but on Sunday. He complained then and for evermore.

Wilson was remarkably cheerful during 1969. He had suffered the humiliation of devaluation in 1967 and it had hurt; in 1968 he had to cope with the foolish abortive coup by his deputy, George Brown, and the warm glow of voter approval he had enjoyed in 1966 had long disappeared. But there was one sign of stress and it constantly reappeared – he would grow a sty under his eye. They looked bad and felt worse. Eventually, a special antibiotic designed for him cured them and he began to think of when to hold the next general election.

George Brown, deputy leader of the Labour party still though no longer a member of the Government, would pop in to No.10 occasionally as though he owned the place, but he was an irritant to the professional civil servants who nevertheless had to treat him with respect. He would walk into the private secretaries' room asking questions they could not properly answer, look at papers when he had no right to do so and on one occasion at least in my presence, demand to know when Wilson was going to award him "my peerage." I avoided him; he was a drunken oaf who had bullied his way to the top backed by the Transport and General Workers union and that mysterious element within the Labour party which were not themselves brought up in Peabody Buildings and would venerate anyone who was, their "bit of rough." It eased their consciences about being so upper middle class. It helped that he had a loud voice and belonged to a powerful trade union and they excused the fact that he effed and blinded in front of young women which I found intolerable, stared down the cleavages of women he met at diplomatic parties and was publicly rude to his long-suffering wife. The classic definition of a long-time drunkard also applied to him: One sniff of a barmaid's apron and he'd fall on his back.

It was astonishing to me that in the election for the Labour leadership after the death of Hugh Gaitskell he won more votes from MPs than Jim Callaghan and more votes from the Shadow Cabinet than either Callaghan or Wilson or both combined, though Wilson only got one.

In the summer of 1969 Brown embarrassed everyone attending the dinner in honour of Buzz Aldrin and Neil Armstrong, the first men to land on the moon, and Michael Collins, who orbited above them. After the customary speeches and toasts, Brown rose unsteadily to his feet and proclaimed we should all toast "the real Michael Collins," the Irish Republican murdered by his fellow-IRA members for making a peace deal with the British. It was insulting to Collins the astronaut and no one responded to Brown's toast. Shortly afterwards he left and I followed him and his wife, Sophie, down the stairs to the front door to ensure nothing further went astray. They were oblivious of me walking behind them as she rebuked him for his behaviour. "Shut Up," he shouted and disappeared from No.10.

I never saw him there again, though I was involved in another of his bizarre incidents some months later. He saw me lunching at the Connaught Hotel with the chief press officer of British Steel, deduced, wrongly, from that that Wilson and Monty Finniston, the BS boss, must be upstairs holding secret discussions and phoned the *Sunday Express* to give them the exclusive non-story. The drink had finally addled his brain.

It was an indication, however, of how Wilson had been weakened by *In Place of Strife,* especially among the trade union group of MPs, that he considered bringing Brown back into his government that summer, though without a specific department; nothing came of it because when he spoke to Brown he was met by the same obtuseness which dotted the former Foreign Secretary's career. Brown insisted that as he was deputy leader of the party he should be made deputy Prime Minister. Wilson told him that was impossible. The arrogance that caused his resignation hadn't abated and the reputation of the Government, the party and Wilson himself was saved further embarrassment.

Wilson was always cheerful in private. I never saw him despondent as, say, I was often to see Robert Maxwell. He was a delightful raconteur in the privacy of his study. He often brought a different vision to a problem. Present him with a four-sided problem and he would provide you with five answers. His ruminations on politics when he was relaxed and with a glass of whisky in his hand would have made any lecturer on politics green with envy and he knew the Labour party from A(ttlee) to Z(illiacus).

He thought of little else because he loved politics so much. He told me that in 1953 he feared that Churchill would suddenly call a general election on the back of the Queen's coronation when patriotism, which Churchill always thought favoured the Tories - mistakenly in my view – was at fever pitch. "I was too young to think like that," I said. "Were you?" he replied. "I've thought like that from the moment I was born."

He still managed to read, and ranged from Kant to Agatha Christie, but his preferred choice was political biography. He surprised me when I asked him his favourite and he chose the life of Arthur Balfour. When I asked him why he said it was because it was the only book of its kind that understood what being a Prime Minister was like. Most biographies were sequential, dealing with one issue after another, but Michael Young's realized a Prime Minister was a juggler, having to keep a number of balls in the air at the same time, fearing to drop one of them. If that wasn't understood, he said, then the biographer didn't understand his subject.

Occasionally he would drop in one of his famous "Wilson's Laws of Politics," which I suspected he made up as he went along. The most famous, of course, was "A week is a long time in politics," which was generally, and wrongly, taken to be a cynicism. It did not mean "Don't bother, the public will forget about it in a week," but that if an issue was still at the forefront of the public mind it was serious and had to be dealt with, however distracting it might be. It was like throwing an extra ball into the juggler's equipment. A more profound law, which did have a touch of cynicism but was instructive to any politician, was "Never go into a room without knowing where the exit is." Without that to guide him, he would never have survived 1969's battle over Barbara Castle's legislative proposals in *In Place of Strife.*

That attempt to curb the excesses of the unions was Wilson's as much as hers. The seamen's strike of 1967 was a direct cause of devaluation and Wilson never forgot it. Like most Labour leaders he had been friendly and supportive of the unions but that was a strike too much. It caused devastating harm to the economy. What's more, the secret bugging of the strike leaders' meetings demonstrated to him that the strike was political, aiming to make the Government subservient to the unions. Wilson had seen dossiers on the leaders of the strike and on others in the movement whose sympathies seem to lie more with Moscow than Westminster. If the unions had not shown their habitual myopia, Wilson's proposals for a strike ballot before stopping work and ending unofficial strikes would have been accepted without a struggle. They were to get laws much worse from their point of view under later Conservative governments.

As it was, union reform was the last and biggest battle of the 1966-70 Government. A balanced history will show that Wilson emerged from it with enormous credit, but contemporary newspapers will show they thought that he was an appalling failure. The fact was that Wilson and Castle were willing to go the brink and beyond (even entering the room with no exit) rather than let things go on as they were. It is all described graphically in Barbara Castle volume of diaries 1964-70. In an attempt to halt the spate of strikes Wilson had the intransigence of the over-mighty unions with 12million members to contend with as well as the cowardice of his Cabinet who lost their nerves in the closing stages of the negotiations with the Trades Union Congress and were waving white flags whenever Wilson spoke to them. But there were two moments in talks that lasted for nearly six months when Wilson showed he was not bluffing and his listeners realized it and those moments demonstrated his strength rather than weakness.

One was at a meeting at Chequers on Sunday, June 1, 1969, when Hugh Scanlon, half of the powerful Scanlon-Jack Jones axis (and Wilson was aware at the time of Jones's role as a part-time

Soviet agent – it was always the last shot in his locker), said to Wilson that he would never accept the principle of penal powers that a Tory Government could use. "if you say that, Hughie," said Wilson "then you are claiming to be the Government. I will never consent to preside over a government that is not allowed to govern. There are two types of Prime Minister I have made up my mind never to be: one is a Ramsay MacDonald and the second is a Dubcek. I am not going to surrender to your tanks, Hughie." At that moment, the unions realized he was serious and began the process of relaxing their inflexibility.

As the negotiations were reaching a climax, the Cabinet began to rat, one by one. Jim Callaghan was a known opponent, but some of the others were a shock, especially Peter Shore, who was one of the authors of the reform proposals more than six months earlier. Dick Marsh was always a carping critic and was sealing his fate, little did he know it. Roy Jenkins, who from the beginning had wanted "a short, sharp Bill", was obscure, saying the party could accept Wilson's resignation but not Castle's, Tony Crosland ("always weak" according to Castle) and others. Of the senior members only Denis Healey stood by Wilson, accompanied by junior and lesser-known people like Cledwyn Hughes, the Welsh Secretary, and Jack Diamond, Chief Secretary to the Treasury. Wilson decided to make the cowards suffer.

On the final make-or- break date, June 18, the anniversary of the Battle of Waterloo, the TUC met Wilson and Castle for the last time. The Cabinet, apprehensive and fearful, never courageous, sat waiting for hours in the Cabinet room, shut off from the outside world (no mobile phones in those days) and strictly forbidden to leave it. Civil servants were instructed to tell them nothing and to accompany them if they went to the toilet. Wilson and Castle had secured the basic agreement of the unions to do what the politicians wanted by signing a "binding" agreement provided there was no legislation. This was later called a "solemn and binding" agreement, immortalized by Bernard Levin as "Mr Solomon Binding." Wilson had no choice but to accept it: his left wing, his right wing and his centre had all crumbled. But he wasn't done.

Wilson would go from one room to the other, offering the Cabinet little hope of an agreement. He said to me: "I'm going to make those buggers pay." They were left to sweat until Wilson had settled every dot and comma of the agreement and Wilson went into the Cabinet room and announced that a deal had been reached. What Barbara Castle was to call "a ragged cheer" went up, but it was hardly from the ranks of Tuscany; - more the ranks of Munich, 1938. They were relieved that at the last moment their jobs had been saved, for a short while at least. Wilson was contemptuous of them. He had saved the government at the expense of his own reputation.

Relations between him and Callaghan were at their worst and between Wilson and Jenkins disastrous. Over the coming years, he and Callaghan became close together, but there was no way he and Jenkins could ever have more than a barely tolerable relationship. "Old Beaujolais," as Wilson called him, had burned his last boat, especially after his initial enthusiasm for legal action to curb the unions. It wasn't Jenkins's affected voice or his superior manner that irritated Wilson most, but his practice of finishing work by about 7pm. As a politicoholic, Wilson could never understand it.

The effect of the settlement on the poll ratings was bad, but as I thought the polls were fundamentally flawed – because they asked a hypothetical question in a hypothetical situation, because their margin of error was too great and usually unstated and because their methodology was inadequate – I was not bothered. After all, when I joined Wilson Labour were 23 points behind in the polls and anything less than terminal was bearable.

There was one party political incident which took place just before the summer break where Wilson put his foot down and won. A pro-European dinner at the Guildhall, aimed at raising £750,000, was due to be addressed by the three party leaders – Wilson, Ted Heath and Jeremy Thorpe, the Liberal leader. A few days beforehand, Wilson discovered that the firm organizing the fund-raising would get 10 per cent of the monies donated, meaning that if he raised £10,000 by his speech £1,000 of it would go to the organisers and he pulled out, supported by Thorpe. He got his way and the organisers, Arrow Enterprises, received only a flat fee. Wilson generously did not mention in his history of the 1964-70 Government that the PR firm was run by Jeffrey Archer, whose reputation was questionable or, in the sweeping term used by Wilson, "crooked" but it was Archer's involvement that revolted Wilson.

At the beginning of September, 1969, Wilson went to Portsmouth to speak at the Trades Union Congress, where he warned the delegates against any backsliding over the agreement reached in June. They didn't like it. The press said the reception was chilling. Wilson said he had no intention of mincing words to get a good reception. It was ominous for the future after the general election which was due by April, 1971, at the latest.

I went to the party conference at Brighton at the end of that month, the first Press Secretary to do so. It seemed to me absurd that I should be in charge of the Prime Minister's publicity for 51 weeks of the year but not on the week which in political terms was the most important, when I was expected to hand it over to Transport House, the party headquarters, riven by factions, including dedicated opponents of Wilson, and watch from the sidelines. Michael Halls was nervous that a civil servant would be attending a party conference but I pointed out that the Prime Minister's civil service private secretary would be there and so I went. Tom McCaffrey, Jim Callaghan's Press Secretary after Wilson retired, did the same but Bernard Ingham, who did the job for Mrs Thatcher, reverted to the old pre-Wilson regime. A foolish mistake.

Wilson made a statistical speech but he cheered up the delegates. Two million new homes – an average of 400,000 a year – under the Labour Govenment, for example, an achievement which, if it had been repeated in the governments of Blair, Brown, Cameron and May would have transformed the social scene in Britain. On the whole, his Government had a good record, but it was fragile. From Wilson's point of view the conference could have been irredeemably wrecked and his reputation permanently damaged by a demand from Marcia Williams that he leave Brighton and return to London to see her, saying she was ill. But he did consider it. It was the first real indication I had of the corrosive effect she had on the Government. He could not possibly do as she demanded and keep it quiet. His sudden absence from the conference would have devastated it. I couldn't see it from her point of view, unaware as I was that she had just given birth to her second child by Walter Terry. I argued vehemently against the projected visit and he eventually agreed it made political sense not to go. It would have been madness.

After his autumn reshuffle which merged some departments and removed one or two ministers who had passed their Use By date, he began to think seriously about exactly when he would call a general election. As I wrote in *Glimmers of Twilight,* there was no right more jealously guarded by Wilson than his right to ask for the dissolution of Parliament and he had no intention of allowing his Cabinet colleagues to share in it until after he had taken the decision.

In fact only one Cabinet Minister was consulted before the decision was made – Peter Shore. He was among the small group – Williams, Kaufman and I were the others – who met in Wilson's study on April 13, 1970 (for a superstitious man Wilson was careless in his choice of dates), to make the final decision. He explained his reasoning for going in June, nine months before it was strictly necessary. First, decimal currency would begin legally in February, 1971; to wait until after then would have the advantage of going on a new electoral register but it would sacrifice all flexibility, going to "the bitter end" and at a time when the new currency would be hugely unpopular. To go in October, 1970, was possible but he had had information from a Tory MP (Captain Henry Kerby, a regular snout as it turned out) that the Conservatives were planning a large and expensive advertising campaign in August/September (£2million) which we could not possibly match. Shore and Kaufman, both with safe seats to go to, agreed with him, enthusiastically; I agreed reluctantly and Williams agreed "provided we do not lose," a proviso that made her opinion right whatever happened but useless.

June 11 was the date chosen and I began the softening up by suggesting to Rowley Summerscales of *The Daily Telegraph* that an early election was worth speculating on provided he didn't tell anyone it came from me. (Leaking it to the *Mirror* would have been a hint stronger than Wilson wanted to give). From then on, speculation continued. On May 12, Wilson asked his Cabinet whether they would like an early election. The polls were getting better and they jumped at it with one, fatal as it turned out, change: the Leader of the Commons, Fred Peart, pleaded for the date to be delayed for a week until June 18 (once again, Wilson's historical sense deserted him: it was not only the Waterloo anniversary again but now also the anniversary of the "capitulation" over *In Place of Strife*). Wilson agreed, saying to me that he had to give something to keep up the pretence that the Cabinet were making the decision. What he didn't realise was that bad balance of payments figures were due on the Monday before the new polling day. The days before that the opinion polls showed him romping home to another victory and on the Monday they went into sharp reverse.

It had never truly looked good. When Wilson asked Roy Jenkins to take sixpence (two and a half pence) off income tax in his April Budget, the Chancellor loftily refused: he was not going to risk his reputation for financial prudence to win an election. It was another example of what Wilson despised in Jenkins: his prim refusal to get his hands dirty in a dirty profession. The Budget is, above all, a political occasion, especially in an election year. At the start of the campaign, Mrs Williams urged (i.e., instructeded) that Wilson should fight a presidential campaign on the grounds that he was far more popular than the Labour party. Instead of making speeches everywhere, which had won him the two previous campaigns, she wanted him, dressed in a smart new suit of a style which didn't suit, to tour the country waving his hands to the admiring throng. I simplify, but that was basically it. What was wrong with it is that was not the Wilson the voters knew.

I didn't understand why he agreed to it though I was to discover it was what he usually did. It showed a fundamental misunderstanding of the voters, especially those of the Labour party, the core of whom were a right-of-centre working class whose allegiance was tribal. Rather like the old story of Newcastle United, that if you put black and white striped shirts on 11 monkeys you would still get a crowd of 50,000 at St. James's

Park, that core would vote for any candidate who had the label "Labour" attached to them. But that vote alone was not enough. In any case, they might not have voted if the monkeys wore monkey suits.

The Wilson the country had voted for over the past six years was like a Labour Stanley Baldwin, rugged, open-faced, pipe smoking, ex-grammar school boy in a rumpled suit with a northern accent who offered some hope of getting the country out of whatever mess it was in. It also ignored the fact that there was – and still is - a considerable body of voters who are not Labour voters but are anti-Tory, but have to be won. It is a question of class and culture and habit and remains the bedrock of the British electoral system though it has shown some fissures in recent general elections. Mrs Theresa May should have taken heed of the lesson, too, before she embarked on her failed presidential election campaign in 2017, but perhaps no one in her entourage read political history.

Anyway, he quickly returned to a normal mode after an early mocking press. But it wasn't a good campaign. I played little part, not that that had anything to do with its lack of success. Gerald Kaufman, wrote some speeches, but was more concerned with his own election and Wilson wrote others. I did a radio broadcast for him on housing, something I knew about, and some newspaper articles. But the drive and inspiration which led him to success in 1964 and 1966 were missing. It was still basically a campaign run by him and Marcia, but he was tired by six years of being Prime Minister and she was irritable and erratic and a mother of two children born within ten months. Nevertheless, on the Friday before polling day things were looking hopeful and I asked him to release me from the two years I had promised him so that I could go back to Fleet Street. He refused and held me to my promise - and I stayed another five-and-a-half years.

Wilson came back to Downing Street on June 19, where the dining room was wrecked by half-eaten sandwiches and stale beer partly consumed by a disconsolate staff, with a sheaf of notes in his hand. He had spent the journey by car through the night from his constituency outside Liverpool writing an outline of the book he was intending to write on his 1964-70 Government. "It will be a handbook for our canvassers for the next election," he said. As an example of optimism in the face of adversity, it couldn't be bettered, including the bit about it being a "handbook" seeing it weighed over three lbs and ran to 836 pages - even after I edited 50,000 words out of it (surreptitiously, after Marcia had announced that I was to have no part in the writing of it as punishment for attending a secretary's leaving party to which she had not been invited).

He and his wife, Mary, first had to find somewhere to live; they had long since sold their house in Hampstead. Desmond Brayley, an industrialist who up until that time I had never heard but unfortunately I was to hear too much of later, offered him a penthouse above La Caprice restaurant and gave him a supply of the largest cigars I have ever seen. Soon after that he moved temporarily into a house in Vincent Square belonging to Dick Crossman at eighty guineas a week which I thought at the time (1970) extortionate.

He swiftly agreed a book deal with George Weidenfeld, the publisher who was a close friend of Marcia's, and it was published under the Weidenfeld/Michael Joseph imprint. Weidenfeld fawned on Wilson and in the end got the peerage he craved, but he had to work for it. *The Sunday Times* paid about £240,000 for the serialization rights, which I thought was generous, but the book reads better today than it did at the time. There were various add-ons to the price: Marcia's sister was employed to type the manuscript and I was paid a year's salary (£5,000) by the newspaper to write or rewrite it. The two appointments were contradictory. I didn't need anyone to type for me. I don't know what Marcia's share was - £60,000-£70,000 was the general belief – but I know it was substantial and too much. Future historians seeking to determine the influence of his close advisers over that period will find no mention of Marcia Williams (as she then was) or me in the book, but if it were to be a handbook for future canvassers, then we were irrelevant. The book's dedication was to "the hundreds of thousands of members of the Labour party whose efforts and idealism created the Government and who in dark days and brighter ones, sustained it with their unwavering loyalty." Well, up to a point.

There was little personal profit in the book for Wilson. Most of it went on paying the salaries of the absurdly large number of secretaries – nine -we started in opposition by employing but that was rapidly reduced. The shortage of money was significant: if Wilson had no money of his own then it would have to be found elsewhere. The squalid and tainted path towards, effectively, the selling of honours, began there. To make financial matters worse, some officials at Transport House were hostile to him, hence their decision to allow him only £6,000 a year in travel expenses and not to pay for Mary Wilson when she accompanied him on party visits. As usual, he outsmarted them: "In that case," he said, "I won't go. She is more popular than I am." They gave in.

Desmond Brayley (later Lord Brayley, of course) turned up at the Wilson house one day and handed Mrs Wilson a small parcel, containing about £8,000 is £50 notes. "What shall I do with it?" she asked Wilson's driver, Bill Housden. "Shall I put it in the bank?" Housden, more street-wise, hastily urged her not to do so. From then onwards, for nearly a couple of years, Wilson would hand me my salary each month in £50 notes. There is no doubt that Wilson, Heath and Winston Churchill would not have survived today's level of Parliamentary scrutiny of monies received. The problem is still there, however much attempts are made to hide it. There is no moral way of selling honours or favours and no way to run a leader's office without doing so.

From the beginning of Ted Heath's premiership Wilson determined to give him a free run for a while. "He will make mistakes," Wilson said to me, "but no-one will listen when we point them out. I'll wait until the turn of the year before attacking him," which was largely what he did. It was a time for memoirs and reflection.

The 1964-70 Government is still derided by many, but mistakenly or out of political bias. To take his juggler's metaphor, he had an awful lot of balls to keep in the air and eventually there were too many. During that first spell in Government, Europe was always on his mind and he met de Gaulle early on. In a way, both men shared a vision of Europe. Wilson thought Britain in the European Community would naturally lead it; de Gaulle felt the same about his country. When de Gaulle in 1969 proposed a secret deal in which Britain and France would virtually control the Community, the British Foreign Office deliberately, and against Wilson's explicit orders, leaked a secret telegram from the British ambassador to Paris, Sir Christopher Soames, in order to wreck it. The Treasury and the Foreign Office regarded themselves as semi-autonomous states within the state. They would deliberately flout the Prime Minister's wishes, or seek to subvert them, in order to push their own departments' views. I have seen nothing since up to the current day which suggests they have changed.

Wilson tried to get into the Community and was repeatedly rebuffed. But his reasons for joining were wrong. The old idea of the sun never setting on the British empire still evoked a thrill and phrases like "East of Eden" were used almost regretfully. He was torn between the coming reality of Europe and the romance of the Commonwealth. He thought he could have them both.

The seamen's strike of 1967 and the subsequent devaluation of 1968 pained him, the conspiracy of the trade unions to defy him in the first and the ordure heaped upon him personally when his efforts to prevent the second failed, wore him down. He was constantly the subject of plots, real or imagined, to overthrow him, mostly fanciful but one or two serious. But he retained the support of the bulk of the PLP, not least because he defied a revolt in the Cabinet over the sale of arms to South Africa, led by Denis Healey (who many years afterwards admitted to me he was wrong). He successfully frustrated the playing the Test matches against South Africa but in the last resort was prepared to ban them by law. (He said to me that the last thing he was going to allow was a riot at Lords on Polling Day). He lost by-election after by-election, five of them on one day in 1969, but still remained optimistic about winning the next election. The spirit was willing, even if the flesh was weak. But he nearly did it.

The test of any administration is whether it leaves the country in a better position than when it started, and, on the home front, that government did, despite inflation and a worsening economic crisis which was global, not national. Democracies suffer at the hands of weary electorates. After the war the Tories ruled under four different Prime Ministers but Churchill was too old, Eden was ill to the point of derangement, Macmillan was a brilliant politician but weary , in part for personal reasons, out of touch and complacent and Sir Alec Douglas-Home was the last aristocrat in No. 10. They were old in political and physical terms. They governed for 23 years By contrast, the Wilson of 1963/4 was the new kid on the block

Today, it is infinitely harder; 24-hour news leaves no time for reflection. Government policies now no longer make the news but are made by it. Every change of mind is a U-turn to be denounced whatever its merits. Cabinet Ministers are watched for any slip of the tongue which would justify, however ludicrously, a demand for their resignation. The Commons is no longer a comradely place but an abusive pit. Aneurin Bevan said the 1956 Parliament was the "squalid" Parliament, but his wit was usually elegant. How often does a witticism in the Commons linger in the memory today?

Wilson was proud of many things in his first Government, perhaps the Open University most of all. But he was also proud that in one year of it not a single British soldier was killed in action anywhere, probably for the first time in over a century. Now the killings were about to start again in Northern Ireland. In a briefing of the Cabinet before the election of 1970, the commander of the British forces there gave a gloomy assessment to the Cabinet of the sporadic outbreaks of violence there. "This is going to go on for many months," I said to Wilson afterwards. "No, Joe," he replied, "it is going to go on for many years." I don't think either of us thought it would go on for another 27 years. And, suddenly, he found there was nothing he could do about it, so he settled down to write his book.

I have written elsewhere how Marcia Williams tried to stop my having anything to do with the writing of it, and she succeeded. It wouldn't have mattered had she not been such a powerful influence on the Prime Minister Her venom against me for having tea and cakes with a departing secretary was almost indescribable, but it was the start of our own private war which went on for a further six years. If I had all the other ranks on my side, she had the general on hers.

* * * * * *

While Wilson devoted too much time to his memoirs – he boasted to me that he had written one day, by hand, 12,000 words without even getting up from his seat and any professional writer would have told him his work-rate was physically and mentally damaging - the work of Opposition had to start somewhere and the BBC offered us what seemed to be a good start. Relations between the Corporation and Wilson were never peaceful and had worsened in the last year of his Government. He didn't trust the BBC and with good reason. As a journalist, I was suspicious of coincidences. As a politician, he didn't believe in them and there were too many unfortunate coincidences in our relationship with the BBC.

Breaking all convention, Ted Heath when in Opposition had been invited on *Panorama* to comment on the Queen's Speech. When we protested, the BBC said it was a mistake and should never have happened and that therefore to invite Wilson on to discuss the same subject would compound the error. A wiser man – a football referee, for example – would correct a mistaken sending off by deliberately mistakenly sending off an opposing player. The BBC's way is a theoretical rectitude, the second is a sensible way of defusing a situation. There were other occasions, too petty to retell, when Wilson was treated badly, but they culminated in a meeting between Wilson, the BBC's chairman, Lord Hill, and me in which Hill, as a former Tory Minister practised in defending a bad case, deftly argued it and then shot himself in the foot by asking the Prime Minister to invite Charles Curran, the BBC's director-general, to dinner because he was lacking in self-confidence. Wilson could have told him he wasn't a counsellor to nervous BBC employees, or even ask why a man lacking in such a basic management attribute should be employed in such a high-ranking post. Instead, he ignored the request altogether.

But a new life in Opposition couldn't be continued by paying back old scores, or so I thought, and when in November, 1970 we were approached by David Dimbleby, a young reporter wanting to show he was more than his father's son, to take part in a documentary called, apparently, *Her Majesty's Opposition,* as part of a series of *Tuesday Documentaries,* I persuaded him that he and the Shadow Cabinet should take part. In my worse moments, I sometimes feel that my career has been sign-posted by my mistakes, though in this case I could rightly say that I was deceived from the very start. Part of that mistake was to assume that the professionalism and impartiality of Richard Dimbleby had been inherited by his son.

First, the programme was changed from the Tuesday slot ("too dull") to another, not a documentary series, called *24 Hours* without our being told or consulted. Secondly, its name was changed to *Yesterday's Men,* mocking a Labour publicity campaign against the Tories. Needless to say, we were not told of that, either. Thirdly, a right-on young producer, Angela Pope who talked in what I took to be modern jargon, like "get off my back" and "give me an easy ride," pleas which I told her were contradictory, was caught filming in the House of Lords and said she had been given permission by the Serjeant at Arms, a clumsy lie that was quickly disproved and she was ejected from the Commons. The Serjeant at Arms's writ does not run in the Lords. It was only on my plea that the Serjeant reluctantly allowed her back in. Fourthly, the Wilsons had recently bought a house in Buckinghamshire called Grange Farm. The police were firm that in view of the current terrorist threat from the IRA its location should not be identified and I told Pope so. Surprisingly, she resisted, even though I told her there had been a number of threats to Wilson's life, including four in one day. Finally, she gave a promise that she would not film the house, under threat from me that without her agreement we would abandon the programme. She cheated: they didn't *film* the farm, they photographed it, without care for the fact that it was occupied for much of the week by an elderly housekeeper. Television breeds a reckless arrogance among its practitioners whereby only what they do matters and everything else is secondary and unimportant – even the safety of a lonely housekeeper.

Six weeks later, an electrician working for the Wilsons challenged a man who had climbed the fence and was taking photographs of the house. He claimed he had Mrs Wilson's permission. Totally untrue. And if he had permission why did he have to climb the fence?

Finally, the BBC publicity people had promised me that I would have a private view of the programme before it went out. In fact, I got an invitation to the press preview the day before it was to be transmitted. If there were passages I objected to and were deleted the press would have seized upon them.

In its conception and execution it was the shabbiest, most disgraceful film ever produced by the BBC on a political subject, then, before or since. It may have made David Dimbleby's reputation, if that kind of reputation was what he wanted, but it shamed the BBC and tarnished his family name and the attempt to hide it from us could only have been conceived by dishonest minds better suited to pranks in a junior school. The whole programme was accompanied by a pop group, unknown to me, called the Scaffold, singing a specially-written song called Yesterday's Men and hired months before, which demonstrated that deception was always the BBC's intention. They never made a serious attempt to apologise.

It went from bad to worse An interview with Wilson, which was supposed to be the crux of the programme quickly became a row when Dimbleby persisted in turning it into an inquiry about Wilson's money, saying the deal with the *Sunday Times* had made Wilson rich, which it didn't, as I have set out. Wilson felt he had been deceived and ordered the filming to stop and I stood in front of the camera, but the audio continued. John Crawley, Curran's special assistant told me, in a conversation I took down in shorthand, that the whole of that section would be destroyed, Angela Pope promised that section would not be used, Dimbleby promised it would not be leaked and Curran sent Wilson a tape which he said was the only one in existence. He told Wilson: "Heads will roll over this." So far as I know, the only head to roll was that of a comparatively junior figure only peripherally involved, a classic example of punishing someone way down the line. Who leaked it? No one ever confessed, bu the *Daily Telegraph's* correspondent, a man of good reputation, told me he got it directly from Dimbleby.

We tried, of course, to stop the transmission after I had seen the preview but the lies and evasions continued, led by Lord Hill who was too scared to take a phone call from Wilson and told his wife to tell Marcia Williams that he was out when she called on Wilson's behalf. The wriggling went on for months Even when Jean Seaton, the BBC historian, held a seminar on the show the BBC supplied a copy of it that had been edited to remove the offensive bits. I wrote a fuller description of the whole affair, including an appalling and shameless excuse from Huw Wheldon, the biggest name in TV at the time, for one aspect of it and it appears in *Glimmers of Twilight*. I only recall it now in attenuated form because it goes to the root of the political argument that has raged between the political parties and the Corporation for decades. Wilson firmly believed in an anti-Labour – or, more precisely, anti-Wilson – conspiracy at the BBC. The Tories proclaim, from time to time, that there is an anti-Tory bias, an anti-Brexit bias or a pro-European Union bias, but it is much deeper than that.

Television can be a force for evil as well as a force for good. It is a magnet for ambitious young people who want to appear in the public eye, sometimes at all costs. It is like a python, enveloping all those who tend to it, but unlike a snake, the venom is not in its head. Self-appointed by their own egos, they seek to articulate what they believe to be the thoughts and beliefs of the inarticulate. Those who are promoted, or chosen, to run it day by day from the board room or govern it month by month under whatever guise the Government deems right, have got where they are by playing safe, by being part of an establishment, a network of dinner parties, who are besieged by the eager young men and women they employ, who are frequently talented but not establishment. These are the young Turks, thrusting, often unprincipled and anarchic. What is right is what they can get away with, whether in politics, pseudo-biographies or violent drama. Politically, It is not just Labour or Conservative or any other parties they oppose (though they might look kindly on *Private Eye* and the Socialist Workers' Party, which are also anarchic); they oppose everyone, anywhere someone else is in charge. They don't inform, they insist; they don't debate, they confront; they don't educate, they assert. They are not responsible (and many good journalists will argue it is not the place of the press to be responsible) but irresponsible. But they differ from the written press because their influence is so much greater. The quantitative difference makes a qualitative difference to the argument.. They will never be changed because who is to change them? Not politicians. Some of them would miss their own mother's first marriage to get on *Question Time*.

The distraction of the Dimbleby saga was enormous at the time. In the short-term the damage was done to the Labour party, but politics is not a short-term game. After the row had subsided I made a decision which I never changed over the years until Wilson retired: he would never again appear on a programme with David Dimbleby. If, as they did, the BBC, ever insensitive to their crimes, telephoned to ask if Wilson would appear on their television, my first question was to ask who the interviewer would be; if it were Dimbleby, the answer was No.

In the end we had to put it to rest and not be distracted any further. Wilson had three main issues that concerned him through the early years of the Opposition apart from the continuing eye he kept on the worsening economic condition: Northern Ireland, Europe, and keeping the Labour party from tearing itself to bits, all seemingly intractable from time to time.

He made the courageous decision – and, given the violence going on in 1971 it was courageous - to go to Ireland himself and I went with him. It was too soon. They were all still playing for position. Talks with the Rev. Ian Paisley, Gerry Fitt of the SDLP and others got nowhere, except that we learned a few new Irish jokes from Fitt, who delighted in calling his daughters the Miss Fitts, and Dublin was little better. When he suggested to the Dublin Government circumstances in which it might be possible for a united Ireland to join the Commonwealth they all looked as if they wanted to be somewhere else. Armed policemen outside our bedrooms doors seemed to epitomise the problem, as did the sudden appearance of John Hume, the rising star of democratic politics in Northern Ireland who fled to Dublin fearing assassination and turned up in Wilson's hotel room for safety. We met IRA leaders three times, once on the edge of Phoenix Park at midnight and twice at Grange Farm but we got nowhere because they were looking for surrender rather than a compromise. We were 25 years too early and they were still airing the grievances of the 17th century.

He took another decision, too, early on in Opposition: he told me he would have to duck and weave and appear to retreat against the rising tide of opposition in the party to entering the Common Market but that he would not give up on his determination that Britain would become part of the European trading area. He only conceded a referendum to Tony Benn's insistent demands because he was certain he would win it and thus defeat Tony's purpose. I was frequently asked when Brexit suddenly emerged after the 2016 referendum what Wilson would have done. I could only give the famous Irish answer that he wouldn't have started from there, not a second time. There was always a hard-left faction on the National Executive Committee of the party which was determined to wreck the European project come what may, but in those days the leadership had no difficulty in defeating it; nowadays, they are part of it.. For Labour and Tory alike, Europe was then and remains today the most divisive issue in British politics.

Sometimes, the NEC went too far and attempted to commit the party, at its annual conference, to opposition to the market and each time Wilson thwarted them. But, like the opposition within the Conservative party to membership, no set-back ever kept them quiet. They crowed over Roy Jenkins's resignation from the deputy leadership; he went because he didn't believe Wilson's intentions not to give in and become an opponent to Europe because he didn't want to. His dislike of Wilson was greater than Wilson's dislike of him. He preened himself and thought that the leadership of the party would eventually fall into his lap. It was never going to. He revelled in being the King over the water but, in truth, he was the King with no clothes, no visible support apart from a group of hardened acolytes.

Throughout all this time the machinations and tantrums of Marcia Williams plagued our lives, which, as I wrote in *Glimmers of Twilight,* ranged from the bizarre to the ridiculous. She brought in her brother, Tony, as office manager, and he brought an unsavoury character into the office who was further to damage Wilson by stealing his notepaper and forging a damaging letter under Wilson's name . Tony married Joe Kagan's secretary and left us and was replaced by an excellent, organized and efficient man, Ken Peay, wealthy enough to work for nothing. He transformed the working of the office, quickly realized its fundamental fault – Marcia – and told Wilson she had to go. His logic was impeccable but his solution was impossible, and so he departed instead. It was the last chance we had to construct an efficient structure for the office.

Albert Murray, ex-MP for Gravesend, an old friend, seemed ideal for the new and regrettable vacancy and I proposed him for it. Astonishingly, Marcia agreed, convinced Wilson it was her idea, and he got the job. All went swimmingly until, inevitably, she turned on him and abused him, withholding his salary on one occasion when he could ill afford it and leaving him unable to pay his mortgage, and complaining to Wilson about his heavy drinking when, earlier in the day, I watched her insist on his having two gins. The absurd became normal. The wickedness became commonplace. Marjorie Halls, Michael Halls's widow, had complained in Government that the behaviour of Mrs Williams had contributed to her husband's death (the Civil Service Department settled out of court). It was distressing to see Albert Murray under the same kind of stress for the same reason and his eventual death several years later – at a comparatively young age, collapsing at The Den, his beloved Millwall Football Ground – was a blow to all his friends.

In the spring of 1973, the oil crisis which was to lead to a general election less than a year later, began when the Arab oil producers quadrupled their prices and restricted their exports to countries which favoured Israel, including Britain which had its supplies cut by 15 per cent – thus we were paying four times as much for 15 per cent less. Suddenly, coal became fashionable again.

The vulture of inflation was gathering its wings. The National Union of Mineworkers demanded a 35 per cent wage increase; impossible to meet when the Government's pay policy held wage increases to five per cent. The Government wriggled and twisted the policy to get a settlement for the miners nearer to 16 percent but the miners had been there before in fights with coal owners and governments. The familiar steps followed. First an overtime ban, which cut coal production by 40 per cent. Then a State of Emergency – about the fourth in my lifetime because of industrial disputes – was proclaimed and Heath stoutly announced he would not give way, though few believed him. Lighting and heating restrictions were brought in and, disastrously new, television programmes ended at 10 pm. Train drivers banned overtime in sympathy with the miners. Street lighting was halved. A three-day week was introduced from New Year's Day. Probably the only people to benefit were the manufacturers of candles. In Wilson's office a general election seemed inevitable and it swiftly came.

The politically sensible thing for Heath to do was to hold it immediately before a new electoral register came into force; the old one was 15 months out of date, thus excluding hundreds of thousands of new voters and favouring the Conservative cause. But in a crisis one mistake is usually followed by another. He dillied and dallied before making an announcement on February 7 that Polling Day was to be on February 28: on the new register, just what Labour wanted. His chosen theme was "Who Governs Britain?" which was precisely what we didn't want and it was imperative to switch the terms of the debate. Fortunately, there was a robust public response to Heath's slogan: it said, "You were elected to govern Britain, you have a healthy majority so why don't you get on with it?" They suspected a rat, and rightly so. The Government's private forecast for inflation was that it was going to go beyond 20 per cent in the coming months which we didn't discover until we took office.

Wilson, as the most experienced politician around, suspected a decaying rodent, too. He told his small group of advisers – Marcia, me, Murray, and Bernard Donoughue, temporarily seconded from the London School of Economics, that Labour would campaign on the rising cost of living; that Heath was going to the country not to defeat the militant miners but because he had to strengthen his majority against the tide of inflation before the voters were aware it was coming. Not for the last time - witness Theresa May in 2017 – the country did not take kindly to giving people in power even more power. And Wilson was proved right in thinking that they wouldn't be happy with a one-issue election. But it was hard going,, distinctly hindered when Alf Richman, a reporter seconded from the *Sun* to act as bagman and anything else Wilson wanted, slammed a car door shut before Wilson had put his foot safely in it.

The afternoon and evening on the day Heath announced the election was spent discussing the coming election. Wilson was no longer the young and fresh (comparatively) leader who scraped home in the 1964 election and won a landslide victory in 1966. He had suffered too many blows in policies which came unstuck and by-elections which had been lost when in office. He was no longer a one-man band nor a shoo-in for president which he had tried briefly, and disastrously, in 1970. I knew he had declined from the man he once was, but he was still formidable.

This time he used what was to be his favourite football metaphor. No longer centre-forward and goalkeeper combined but a deep-lying centre half, surrounded by expert team-mates who outshone anyone in experience and wisdom, which was, to a large extent, true. The Shadow Cabinet, fissiparous as it had been, had quality players, including Roy Jenkins, Denis Healey, Jim Callaghan, Shirley Williams, Tony Crosland Ted Short and even Tony Benn as well as others. It was a powerful team. If a team game was his tactics, his strategy, he said, was that of the Battle of Marston Moor – soak up the enemy's attack and then launch a devastating counter-attack. He loved these historical comparisons.

He was not well and he knew it but he had a plan for that, too. The tensions and battles between me and Mrs Williams were wearing, tedious and distracting but they were essentially trivial. He asked me – and presumably her, too - to put aside our enmities and work together as a team, especially with Bernard Donoughue joining us unknowing of what had gone before. I was happy to agree. I am convinced a small team, working harmoniously, is the best way to fight an election or do most other jobs, which is why, on returning to office a month later I dismissed nearly half of the bloated Press Office of Heath's regime. What's more, it brought out the best in Marcia. In her better moments, she knew how to run an office. She announced after the Polling Day was given as February 28, we should all go home and get a good night's rest. I didn't. I got home at midnight where my wife was waiting with a message to ring a London number, whatever the time was.

It was Andrew Alexander, former Parliamentary sketch writer for *The Daily Telegraph,* once a Conservative candidate in a by-election, an outspoken right-winger and close confidant of Enoch Powell, who had announced that day he was not standing in the general election because it was a fraud. Politics always has a hate figure, few more so than Powell so far as the Labour party was concerned. He was toxic. Beyond the pale. Untouchable.

Alexander's proposition was simple. Powell was offering to make speeches on Europe which would be anti-Heath and favourable to Wilson and he was suggesting that Wilson should follow them up on the succeeding days with similar speeches – in other words to co-ordinate our campaigns. Powell was hated by the political classes but not by the voters who, on the whole agreed with his anti-immigration stance which had produced his unpopularity at Westminster.

So far as I could see, our object was to win the election, for three weeks everything else was secondary. I told Wilson and our team the next morning about the call. Wilson was excited and willing, Marcia dubious and astonished. Bernard took my view. In the opinion of all of them it was to be a Haines-Alexander operation only. If it leaked, the blame stopped with me. Nothing to do with Harold Wilson. What's more, if Alexander called when we were all together, Marcia would announce: "It's Joe's friend" and everyone but me would leave the room, making them technically innocent. It was part of what Harold meant, I suppose, when he said that the title "Press Secretary" disguised what I really did. Wilson made only one stipulation, that he would make a speech and Powell would follow it up, not the reverse as Powell was proposing.

Years later, Wilson told a newspaper lunch that it was all agreed between him and Powell while they were standing in the stalls of the men's lavatory in the Commons. Powell told Wilson's biographer that there were "several meetings of this kind," a regular co-ordination of bladders which seems unlikely. When, for example? Wilson didn't use the Commons once the election and dissolution was announced. Powell was no longer an MP or a candidate. When did Wilson have the time? Did he and Powell really stand side by side, not knowing or caring whether anyone was listening behind closed doors of the toilets, and agree to put Haines and Alexander in the frame which would have cost Alexander his job, almost certainly, and led to clamour within the Labour party for my head had it leaked out? The more complicated a plot, the more liable it is to fail, especially if the fall guys discover they had been set up. Loyalty has to work both ways, even for party leaders. I suspect their later claims were designed to get the credit for something that worked, neither wishing it to be known they got others to do their dirty work for them. Powell didn't win the election for Labour but he helped Heath lose it. It was another issue, apart from "Who Governs Britain?"

The alliance between Marcia and I did not start auspiciously because she insisted Wilson should write his own speeches. It didn't work. She was reliving the past. He didn't have the time or even the ability to do it all himself. But when Marcia was good she was very good. She swiftly changed her mind after he took five hours to write a speech which was not up to the task. She cruelly told him it was rubbish and that we should revert to my writing the speeches. So I was handed the job, with Bernard Donoughue playing an important role in their concept. Then everything went swimmingly. Wilson and Donoughue went to Transport House, the party's headquarters, every morning at 9 am while I worked on handouts for the evenings speeches (Bernard told me the campaign committee meetings they attended were a waste of time; they had no idea how to fight the election). At the start of the campaign I prepared a master speech of several sections; each day we would choose the day's subject and drop it in to the speech and that would be the handout for the press. On the whole it worked, except for the BBC who wouldn't record what we wanted them to (the hand-out) and made their own choices among those subjects which were repeated night after night. No news like old news but we expected no more.

Wilson's strategy worked superbly. He recovered from the bad cold with which he started the battle and was enjoying himself. While he was away in the evenings I would write the next day's speech which Marcia would take to his home in Lord North Street and place on his pillow. The final copy and the press hand-out were completed the following morning. The ugly side of Marcia's nature was to crop up over Wilson's TV broadcasts. She was increasingly star-struck and, without consulting me, recruited John Mortimer, creator of Horace Rumpole, to write them. It was not his field, any more than mine would have been writing about Rumpole of the Bailey. For all his talent, it was no good. Wilson asked me what I thought of it and I told him so. I asked him to look at it himself but he refused. Mortimer was asked to do it again. It was still no good. Wilson asked me to resume writing them and I did. It was not the last event of its kind to disturb the artificial harmony of the office. Odd incidents apart – like when I threw John Allen, a perpetual cadger and former lover of Marcia, out of the office when he tried to raid the drinks' cabinet – our tight little team worked well, helped, crucially, by the two bodies which wished us least well.

Heath – did he have no one to advise him about anything? – decide to refer the miners' pay claim to the Pay Board. I don't know what he expected but he got more than he wanted. The Pay Board held a briefing for journalists at which it said that the miners, far from being at the top of the pay list, were only sixth. Roger Carroll, of *The Sun,* called me immediately after the briefing. I caught Wilson just before he left for the night's first meeting. He featured the revelation in off the cuff remarks while I wrote a script for the next meeting. Marcia terrified the school caretaker at that meeting – she was very good at that - to ensure Wilson phoned us before he spoke again and then, to cap it all, the BBC's Nine o'clock News presented the story as a great mistake by Heath. The "Who Governs Britain" strategy was finally blown apart. With enemies like that, who wants friends?

The story was up and running and unstoppable by the time Heath heard of it, courtesy of my friend Gordon Greig of the *Daily Mail* at 11.30 that night. I thought subsequently how things might have been different had Heath had a phone in his car as he travelled from one engagement to another. Much later, I was told that he did have a phone in the car - but it wasn't switched on. "For want of a nail a shoe was lost...."

The campaign went more or less smoothly after that, periods of elation, times of depression, skirmishes, minor rows, Marcia protective of her special position, with Bernard and I brushing aside additions which Marcia seemed to make to the team, like Peter Lovell-Davies and Denis Lyons (where did they come from?), with Thomas Balogh, the Hungarian economist, wandering in and out making incomprehensible and unusable suggestions for speeches and getting on everybody's nerves. That apart all went well. By the time we reached Polling Day, on balance, we thought we would win. In the Adelphi Hotel, Liverpool, Bernard, Albert Murray and I phoned around the country to get on-the-ground reports of the voting. The most significant for me was when I phoned the Birmingham regional agent. He was enthusiastic and put his finger on another of Heath's calamitous mistakes in calling the election. Britain was on a three-day week. Most of the Midlands, he said, were not working that Thursday and the council houses were turning out "100 per cent" to vote for us. Harold and I went for a final walk-round the polling booths in his Huyton constituency.. There were more houses with that day's *Mirror* front page proclaiming "For all Your Tomorrows Vote Labour Today" in their windows than party posters. It was the best slogan the paper – or the party – had ever devised.

Harold Wilson and I went out for a last tour of the polling stations and arrived back at the Adelphi just after 9 pm. A group of miserable junior lobby correspondents were gathered in the lobby of the hotel, all wishing they were back in London where the action would be instead of being in Liverpool waiting for the words of a loser when he finally admitted defeat. They ignored us completely. We were the bit players in a drama in which they all thought the end was certain. Our end. We went to Wilson's room for something to eat and a drink and to watch TV until it was time to go to Wilson's count.

Then things started to happen. Labour MPs in the industrial North began to be returned with higher majorities. The Tories weren't getting the gains they expected, they were beginning to lose seats. There was a nervous tap on the bedroom door. I answered it. One of the group of journalists from the lobby below asked if he could have a word with Mr Wilson, the man he had totally ignored little more than an hour earlier. "No," I said as politely as one can say "No." and closed the door. A few minutes later, I heard noises in the corridor outside the room. I went out determined to be a little less polite this time. Instead, I found the corridor was filling up with plain-clothed policemen. The chief constable of Liverpool and his deputy had always been friendly towards Wilson and they had clearly decided that the next Prime Minister was on their territory and they were going to accord him the proper protection. That was the most heartening event of the night.

We went to the count where Wilson scored more than 50,000 votes. We had no doubt we had won, however narrowly. Few others doubted it, either. The Press knew we had won. Michael Charlton of the BBC tried to get a few words with Wilson, beginning his request: "Prime Minister." All those who doubted we could possibly win, including many at Transport House and in the Shadow Cabinet, knew it too and some said they knew it all along. If so, they had concealed their optimism. The only person who refused to know it or believe it, was Ted Heath. By the time we got back to Wilson's house in Lord North Street on Friday morning it was becoming clear we might not move into Downing Street that day, if at all.

Heath was sticking, trying to arrange a coalition with Jeremy Thorpe, the Liberal leader. There were two obstacles to that. John Pardoe, a powerful Liberal MP and a friend of Bernard Donoughue's, told Bernard that the party wouldn't have it. Secondly Wilson said that if, as strongly rumoured, Thorpe's price would be that he would become Home Secretary then two former ministers, Ted Short and George Thomas, would come forward and disclose his homosexual relationship with a man called Norman Scott, who was obsessed by the belief that Thorpe had his National Insurance records which prevented him from getting work.

It was not intended to destroy Thorpe for being a homosexual but from being a politician. The practice of homosexuality had only been decriminalized a few years before and Thorpe, if the stories were true, had committed criminal offences. Little did we know it at the time but that was the least of the crimes to be laid at his door. We assumed at that time that Heath did not know about Thorpe's secret life, but he admitted some years later that he had been informed by Sir Burke Trend, the Cabinet Secretary, of the allegations against Thorpe, which made the attempt at forming a coalition even more extraordinary. Thorpe would have demanded one of the senior Secretaryships of State, probably Home Secretary, as the price of keeping Heath in power. Scott had already told the police of his relationship with Thorpe and Thorpe had told Peter Bessell, a disreputable Liberal MP, in confidence, and Bessell had told George Thomas who had told Wilson. Heath must have been desperate to stay in power even to consider such an absurd proposal for a moment.

But the exposure of Thorpe didn't come on that occasion, however. Thorpe realized he couldn't carry his party with him and the talks broke down. It was, though, the beginning of a saga which was to become public and make the front pages a couple of years later in the biggest political trial of modern times.

Wilson's interest in Thorpe and Norman Scott didn't stop once the coalition talks were aborted. After all, he had only a bare majority in the Commons and could be brought down by unforeseen circumstances at any time. Once his Government was established, he asked Barbara Castle, the Secretary of State for Social Security, for details of the national Insurance problems of Scott. She was uneasy about doing it but Wilson told her, sharply, to "get Jack Straw", then her special adviser, to do it. Many years later Straw admitted that he had sent a written report on Scott to the Prime Minister. When he was a minister in Tony Blair's Cabinet, Straw complained to me that I had caused him a lot of trouble, but he didn't deny the request had taken place and that he had met it.

There is no doubt that if Thorpe was to prove an obstacle to Wilson taking power in March, 1974, Wilson would have destroyed him politically. But nearly two years later, Peter Hain, a Young Liberal activist and who was to become a Labour Cabinet minister, passed a dossier - what later journalists in another situation were to call a "dodgy dossier," - about an attempt by the South African intelligence agency, the Bureau of State Security, or BOSS, to bring down Thorpe. Hain himself thought it was dubious but felt Wilson should see it. The immediate first question was: why should BOSS bother? What we didn't know at the time was that Norman Scott was a friend of an unsavoury South African journalist, Gordon Winter. They slept together and Scott told Winter of his relationship with Thorpe and Winter passed the information on to BOSS. To that extent, whatever else may have been in the dossier, it was accurate.

Conspiracies to Wilson and Marcia had an irresistible temptation, like Delilah and Cleopatra combined. The dossier was passed to her and she believed it was an attempt to bring down Thorpe and Wilson - though what the latter belief was based on it is impossible to say - which meant Wilson believed it. He began to ask me about Winter, of whom I knew nothing and whether I could find anything out about him, which I couldn't, except what I read in *The Sunday Times*. There was talk of Thorpe resigning in early 1976 but that was over his association with a failed bank, the London and County, not Norman Scott. But one day in Downing Street Marcia demanded: "Harold, we have got to save Jeremy." If ever a book is written about things people wish they hadn't said, that deserves a chapter all to itself. Once again it set him on the path to disaster. He decided to "do something" and he did.

On March 9, 1976, nine days after the proposed original date for announcing his resignation and seven days before the actual announcement, Wilson told an unbelieving House of Commons what that something was. For the only time I can remember, he failed to tell Bernard Donoughue and me what he had in mind, which showed he felt guilty about it: "I have no doubt at all that there is a strong South African participation in recent activities relating to the leader of the Liberal party," he said, going on to add that there were dark forces at work, "private agents of various kinds and various qualities," meaning Winter. John Preston, author of *A Very English Scandal,* the definitive report of Thorpe's plot to murder Norman Scott, thought this a sign of Wilson's approaching dementia. I think not. It was a sign of his decades-long paranoia, fed by a secretary who shared his suspicions of each and everyone.

After the serialization of *A Very English Scandal* in the summer of 2018, Jack Straw spoke more openly about his role in 1974. He said he had been asked to go through the files to help Thorpe find out if there had been a political plot to prosecute Scott for fraud. He said of the files: "there were all sorts of pockets marked 'secret'." He added: "We opened these pockets and there were statements made many years before going into all sorts of details about the contact between Scott and Thorpe which went well beyond their use of social security numbers. They included graphic details... and when and where they had sexual encounters." Straw added that Wilson was "predisposed to believe Thorpe but asked us to look through the files."

Whatever Straw was told by Barbara Castle, the truth was that Wilson wanted the knowledge contained in the files to hold against Thorpe in case the proposal for a coalition with Heath was raised again. And, without question , Mrs Castle did not want to instruct Straw to do anything and only did so because Wilson insisted. The dossier handed to Wilson by Hain changed Wilson's intention to one of saving Thorpe after Lady Falkender's intervention.

So we had reached this bizarre situation: In March, 1974, when he feared that Ted Heath would enter a coalition with Jeremy Thorpe, Wilson was ready to expose Thorpe and his association with Norman Scott, though he had no idea that Thorpe had been planning the murder of Scott as long ago as 1968. Now, in March, 1976, he was standing up in the Commons and accusing the South African government of planning to do what he had planned to do two years earlier, linking it, with no evidence at all, to a plot to bring him down, too, even though he was intending secretly to resign voluntarily in a week's time in a revised timetable, anyway. Meanwhile, in the previous year, the attempt to murder Scott has been attempted and bungled by a hitman, Andrew Newton, hired by Thorpe, whose gun jammed when he pulled the trigger.

Wilson was suddenly defending a man who had already committed a crime, conspiracy to murder, which would have been a capital crime carrying a life sentence had he been found guilty, and risking his own reputation by a piece of utter nonsense born of paranoia. It was at one with his claim in the autumn of 1974 when he claimed that legions of journalists were scouring the country trying to find evidence to destroy him. I had struck it out of a speech to that effect with which he began the general election campaign of that year but he put it back. Maybe that was why he didn't tell me about the statement he intended to make to the Commons about Thorpe.

In the midst of Thorpe's insane intentions, in 1975, I had experienced an attempt by the Prime Minister's doctor, Joe Stone, to enlist my support for the murder of Lady Falkender, which, had I agreed, would have been a genuine conspiracy and, ironically, one they had never suspected. We thus had the intended victim of one proposed crime defending the perpetrator of another. Two parallel plots to kill at the very seat of power. It smacked more of ancient Rome than modern Britain. I return to Joe Stone later in this narrative.

* * * * * * * * *

Almost the first message of congratulations on the February election result result came from Goronwy Roberts, MP for Caernavon, who had lost his seat to a Welsh Nationalist. "I stand ready to serve you in another place," he declared loyally. "Another place" is the Westminster way of describing the House of Lords, often a reward for electoral failure

But all that was in the near future. That Friday afternoon and early evening we waited at Lord North Street for word of Heath going to the Palace to present his resignation to the Queen. All we got was a phone call from Heath's brilliantly adroit principal private secretary, Robert Armstrong, saying he was going out to dinner. In other words, nothing was going to happen. Marcia was all for issuing a strong statement. Bernard and I were for saying nothing. Wilson agreed with us. He went off to Grange Farm saying to me not to tell the press anything, but to be friendly. In one of his favourite phrases, "all aid short of help." When the photographers descended on Grange Farm they got what they wanted: Wilson playing with his dog, Paddy.

We reconvened in Lord North Street on Sunday evening but had to wait until Monday afternoon before Heath finally accepted the inevitable and went to the Palace to resign, then to leave Downing Street never to return. His long twilight in politics had begun. Meanwhile, the old and tiring infighting between members of the Shadow Cabinet seeking jobs in the new government began, with Roy Jenkins behaving like a petulant prima donna laying down conditions and being tiresome. He never realized, as I believed all along, that he wasn't ever going to be Prime Minister whatever the circumstances because the party outside Westminster wouldn't have him. It was as simple as that.

His unpopularity was illustrated for me at a party conference when he was deputy leader. I had gone along with Wilson to one of the many regional parties which are a feature of the leader's schedule at conference. As soon as Wilson entered the door he was surrounded by people who knew him and, more importantly, whom he knew. He shook hands, called them by their first names and demonstrated where his strength lay in the party. Then Jenkins turned up, an elegant fish in muddy waters. Wilson introduced him to all the leading figures at the party because he knew none of them and none of them knew him. It was embarrassing. Jenkins should have learned the lesson that there is no easy way to the top and that the best of generals needs the troops to follow him, but I doubt that he ever did.

We all went to Buckingham Palace on the Monday afternoon, the advisers – Marcia, me, Albert, Bernard, and, for some reason, Gerald Kaufman who hadn't been seen during the campaign but determined to hang on to the tailboard of success. Harold and Mary Wilson went in their official car. We stayed outside while Harold and Mary went in. When they came out, Marcia insisted I get into their car, leaving no room for Robert Armstrong. Civil servants of his class are not to be beaten however: when we got to Downing Street, Armstrong was waiting to greet us, having sped back in the spare car and entered through the back door. The same civil servants who had lined up to clap Heath as he left the building lined up again to applaud us in. No one made any jokes about Heath being "clapped out." It had happened to us in 1970.

Wilson introduced his advisers to the civil servant private secretaries and made it clear how important we were: we had the right to see everything and to be consulted. Bernard and I were to see all Cabinet and other documents. Any official speech written (usually by Robin Butler, senior after Armstrong) had to be submitted to me for vetting, approval and amendment before going to the Prime Minister. The first I got from Butler had the Prime Minister travelling between Scylla and Charybdis; I told him that was not an allusion a Labour Prime Minister would make. He was troubled by the fact that he had written speeches for Heath supporting the Government's prices and incomes policy and now he feared he would have to write the opposite. He needn't have worried. I intended to write them. We became good friends; he was a determined character, shown when he beat me 22-20 in a table tennis match in the Cabinet Office when I had been leading 20-15. The result cost Albert Murray a fiver.

My first job was to go to the Press Office and tell the former Foreign Office man in charge, Robin Haydon, that he was no longer needed. He asked if he could come in the next morning and say goodbye to the staff. I said that was all right provided he was in and out before I came in at 9.30. He never came. The next morning I told four more press officers they were redundant, making five in all. Armstrong asked me, for the sake of civil service morale, not to lose any more. I understood his point, but I had to emphasise that I was in charge and got rid of another. I had already recruited Janet Hewlett-Davies from the Home Office because she was reliable, intelligent and knew Wilson and me very well. I brought in Jean Denham from the Labour party press office for the same reasons and also to jmprove the deplorable relationship between the Wilson office and Transport House. We were up and running.

All went well at the beginning. It reminded me of the cartoon of two men sitting at a bar and one saying to the other, "We were happy at first, but as we left the church, she said..." We were a happy band of brothers and a sister until the sister reverted to her tantrums. No.10 has, or had, a small dining room and it was agreed we happy few would lunch together and discuss our politics and where the Government was going. That didn't last long. Wilson's favourite starter for lunch was whitebait. I found them uninteresting and would have preferred potted shrimps. Marcia found them repulsive and said they were all staring at her from her plate. At one of the earliest of these lunches she walked out, Wilson followed her to placate her and that was the end of the lunches. I fear what she didn't like was that we were all treated as equals.

If this were a history of the Labour Government, then I would spend less time writing about Marcia Williams. She should have been a ridiculous figure, consoled by a "there, there", a pat on the knee before that constituted sexual assault, and relegated to the back of the mind. But it is about Wilson, the influences that swayed him, bothered and sometimes bewildered him. It is not about the work he did or the policies he enunciated, but about the conditions in which he had to do that work and advance those policies. Not about the matters that inspired him to action, but about the obstacles which often depressed and dismayed him.

It is about the Prime Minister as a politician and as a man, his strengths and his foibles, and his future place in history

He had already told us, in Lord North Street as we waited for Heath to accept the inevitable, that he intended to spend no more than two years in Downing Street. Perhaps symbolically, but with Mary Wilson's urgings, he had decided he would not live there in the inadequate top floor flat but stay in Lord North Street. After the first flush of victory, there were signs, insignificant at first, that he was ready to go, but his was a role that had to be played; there was another election to be fought. He had told us before we entered Downing Street when that would be - on October 10 that year. What we did from then on was directed towards winning that.

By the end of the first week in office, Bernard Donoughue was already thinking of resigning, not least because of the Marcia tantrums. He was still learning how to ride them. She blew hot and cold with him. She liked attractive men but disliked those who did not respond to her. She demanded he phone her at all hours of the day or night and would then scold him. She attacked me and Albert as well as Wilson. She wanted to end the lunches we started with the senior civil servants, but as we were paying for the food and the services of the cook she was reduced to complaining that official premises should not be used for such a purpose. These were constant irritants, time- and thought-consuming.

For my part in the build-up to Octobe 10, I wanted to keep Wilson away from set-piece television appearances as much as I could. I wanted viewers, if faced with a programme featuring him, to say, "Keep it on!" not "Oh, it's him again, turn it off." Rarity can have a value in politics, too. It was my job to choose when he appeared and that was when it suited us, not when it suited the TV producers. We were no longer the supplicants and his appearances were strictly limited in the run up to October. I did, however, take pleasure, when the BBC asked him to appear in a special programme of *Panorama* with David Dimbleby, in refusing them and offering the spot to ITV who jumped at it..

Wilson decided to ask each Cabinet Minister to publish White Papers on their future plans and policies, all designed to prompt the voters to support Labour when the next election came.

All sensibly did so except Tony Benn and his perpetually scowling acolyte, Eric Heffer, who produced a wild and woolly White Paper on industry which would have sent the electors and business deserting in droves. Wilson said he would throw it into the waste-paper basket and do it himself. We simply needed a few months now without diversions. We didn't get them

There is a book to be written about the Paranoia of Power. I encountered it twice, with Wilson and Robert Maxwell, and some of it is detailed in this book. Wilson's particular paranoias were about the Press and the belief that someone, somewhere was determined to do him down, and showed most in his paranoia about defending Marcia against all comers and all the evidence..

From the general election onwards we suffered from the growing and distasteful saga about the Field family (Marcia was born Marcia Matilda Field) and their investment in some slag heaps at Ince-in-Makerfield in Lancashire. If the heaps were cleared and the necessary permissions granted they supposedly would be a valuable, profit-making development. If it weren't for the fact that Tony Field, the driver of the investment, and his sisters, Peggy and Marcia, all worked for the leader of the Labour party it would be a matter of local interest only. But Wilson had spent most of his political life denouncing speculators and this was clearly speculation. Interest centred particularly on Marcia's involvement and at times she was hysterical about the press attention. Over a period of three weeks, Bernard, Albert Murray and I were despatched by Wilson to her elegant home in Wyndham Mews, one of two she occupied, to calm and pacify her and keep her company. Our jobs were inevitably neglected. It was no way to run a railway, let alone a government. The behaviour of journalists camped outside her house was disgraceful, though. The curtains had to be drawn because reporters were peering in through the windows. They knocked on the door themselves and they paid children to knock on the door as well. It was harassment of an intimidating kind, with two young children inside. We even sympathized with her.

The scandal, as the press saw it, was all made worse by Tony Field's business acquaintances, particularly by a man called

Ronald Milhench who had visited Tony in Wilson's office in Opposition when he was manager. Milhench stole Wilson's notepaper and crudely forged Wilson's signature implicating Wilson in the slag heap deal and then tried to sell the letter to the *Daily Mail* for £25,000. It was tawdry, messy and criminal and for those of us who were dragged in never having heard of the slag heaps in Ince-in-Makerfield before, totally exhausting. The Lobby meetings I had to take when I was there were naturally consumed by the affair and reached the depths when an old friend and former colleague, Ian Waller of *The Sunday Telegraph*, who had lunched too fluidly, drunkenly made absurd insinuations against Marcia and I walked out. These allegations of impropriety coming from the man who had secretly approached me to obtain a peerage for Captain Henry Kerby, MP, in return for the sale of Tory party secrets (and been turned down) was too much. I couldn't help remembering that when he was lobby correspondent for the *Glasgow Herald* and too ill to do his work I wrote his stories for him in his style and his paper never knew about it. There is little gratitude in politics or in journalism, either.

Stories have a natural life and a natural death and this one would have died had Wilson not decided to make a statement about it in the Commons. His draft was impossible in its original wording and Bernard and I protested strongly against it, saying "...in its present form [it] invites disaster. You would inevitably involve yourself in the transactions which were not your concern." He greatly modified it but refused to take out a phrase we particularly objected to but of which I think he was secretly proud, that the land deal involved "reclamation, not speculation" and which received the derisive laughter in the Commons which we had predicted for it.

Things went from what my mother used to call "worse to worser." Wilson had launched himself on a campaign which was to imperil the plans he had made to win the October general election. His next disastrous step was to announce to us that he had decided to make Marcia a baroness. Back in January, 1972, he had told me how Marcia had sent for Mary Wilson to call on her at Wyndham Mews where she declared that she had been to bed with Harold six times in 1956 "and it wasn't satisfactory." That cruelty was in retaliation for Wilson taking his wife out to lunch that day, the 12th, her birthday, without telling Marcia first. Mary was upset, Wilson was outraged, Marcia was banned from the office for six weeks (a punishment which, as I told Wilson at the time, was ameliorated by the fact that she rarely came into the office), but from one Wilson extracted one gleam of hope: "She has dropped her atom bomb. She can't hurt me any more," the significance of which grew the longer one examined it. And, now, inexplicably, he was risking the future of his Government to get back at the press, a self-inflicted wound if ever there was one and, what's more, a wound made by her demand to achieve a public respectability after the slag heaps affair. He tried to mollify us by saying that she would retire from his office now she had a peerage and join the board of Cavenham Foods, the principal arm of James Goldsmith's business, an assertion she later denied. In any case, we didn't believe it and it didn't happen.

I have written some years ago of our attempts to get the peerage cancelled, of the Queen's willingness to allow Wilson to change his mind, a fact of which we had certain knowledge, and of how I told Wilson of my inability to defend her any more now that she ceased to be a private person and was to become a member of the Upper House of legislature. All to no avail. As of the date of writing (winter, 2018/19), more than 44 years after her "ennoblement" she has yet to make her maiden speech and seems unlikely to ever do so. She is now, as she was at the time of her peerage, an outstanding argument for drastic Lords reform and an everlasting stain on Wilson's record. The fact that she insisted that he write her letter of acceptance of the honour, rejected the first draft by scrawling "rubbish" over it and told him to do it again added humiliation which no man, let alone Wilson, deserved.

For a Government with such a short life (March-October, 1974), we certainly had trouble pile on us. Sleaze allegations against Ted Short based on a forged letter (of course) and Bob Mellish, concocted by that fat and obnoxious ignoramus of an MP, Arthur Lewis who hated Mellish. Plus, of course, wage demands, strikes and the collapse of British Leyland and, closer to home, rumblings in the Lords about Lord Brayley, an army friend of the notorious spy-hunter George Wigg. Brayley had been very generous to Wilson after the 1970 defeat and was rewarded with a peerage and a job as junior defence minister. He was a kind and affable man but on an intellectual level with Lewis. How he ever became a colonel remains a mystery to this day. Wilson agreed with a deputation from the Lords to sack him, but not yet, but the *Daily Mail* published a story about his misuse of his company's money before he became a Minister. I raced up to Wilson's study as soon as I saw the story and said Brayley had to go immediately – and he did. As, it seems, with every government before and since, personal scandals of one kind or another were a constant distraction from what they were supposed to be doing.

Personal issues involving Marcia continued to distract both Bernard and I throughout that summer. The attacks on Bernard grew in intensity and we heard, in the usual civil service friendly way, that Bernard's unit was to be removed from Downing Street and placed in the Cabinet Office, which was like being removed from a cathedral and put to work in the graveyard. There was no organizational, political or managerial reason for it. Its purpose was not to increase efficiency or add to the expert advice available to the Government. Its sole purpose was to carry on a personal vendetta by someone whose constant refrain was "Mirror, mirror on the wall, who's the fairest of them all...?"

Furniture was already being taken out of the Policy Unit's offices ready to be put in place in the Cabinet Office for the move when Bernard came to my office to tell me about it. He recalls the occasion vividly and how I said to him, "I know how to stop that" and asked the switchboard operator to put me through to the Prime Minister, who was at Bradford University in his capacity as Chancellor. She told me he was on the platform and I asked her to ask him to come off. He did and I told him what was happening. "Why did you get me off the platform to tell me that?" he demanded. "Because if you don't stop it I won't be here when you get back," I replied. He stopped it and a bewildered Cabinet Secretary, Sir John Hunt, asked Bernard: "What's going on? One day I'm told to make arrangements for the move and the next day I'm told the cancel it." Bernard might have replied, "That's politics," but I suspect he merely laughed.

Marcia then made me a target again. My wife and I decided to take a two-week holiday in Ardentinny, in a former farmworker's cottage in a remote hamlet in Argyllshire owned by Kay Carmichael, without a phone and eight miles from any newsagent's shop. Just before we left, Robert Armstrong warned me that he had been present when Marcia told Wilson that he must sack me and replace me with Peter Lovell-Davies, a current favourite of hers, an ambitious man with a lean and hungry look (which is more than I can say for his partner, Denis Lyons, who was not lean and looked as if he had not experienced hunger for a very long time) and little obvious talent except for sycophancy. To this day I don't know where the two of them came from but they were both involved in the publicity business.

One of Marcia's weaknesses is that she would interfere in matters she didn't understand. One essential requirement of a plot is not to disclose it in front of witnesses who are not irrevocably wedded to your side, which is what she had done. Also to understand that every plot has a counter-plot. It took one phone call to obstruct her.

I called Gordon Greig of the *Daily Mail*, told him what was happening and we agreed that he would run the story of my proposed sacking in the Nigel Dempster column in his paper after I had been away for a week, which meant no one would blame me for it. It was one of those stories which, though true, became untrue immediately it was published. As soon as I got back, Wilson sent for me to say there was absolutely no truth in the Dempster story. "What story is that?" I asked innocently. He explained, adding, of course, that Marcia had never suggested replacing me, one of the three or four direct lies I ever heard him tell, and that was that. But Lovell-Davies and Lyons (who, not least because of their physical shapes, were known in the office as Laurel and Hardy) were to crop up more hilariously when the October election was finally announced.

But before then, as though he were determined to lose the election and as another off-shoot of the slag heap affair, Wilson decided to embark on his all-out assault on the press. It was as if he and Marcia were unable to realise that some, at least, of the criticism of the slag heap affair was justified; that making her a peeress was making a mockery of the honours system and public life, that shady characters willingly connected to a government demeaned that government and insulted those hundreds of thousands of party workers and supporters who had worked to put it back in Downing Street. It went on and on: it was always the fault of the critics, not the perpetrators.

Peter Lovell-Davies then told Marcia that he had heard that there was to be a newspaper exposure of Wilson's tax affairs on the eve of Polling Day, which had not yet been announced. The usual suspect was the *Daily Mail.* Harold asked me about it; it was a fear made worse by the fact that his tax papers had gone missing. My simple explanation that he had thrown them away when clearing his desk – his method of tidying up was to pick up a pile of papers and if the top papers looked to be disposable or of no further interest, to dump them in the waste-paper basket – was not accepted. I asked Bob Carvel, of the *Evening Standard,* one of the best-informed and knowledgeable lobby correspondents if he had heard anything ; he said there were rumours that the person with a damaging Wilson story was a Tory journalist on the *Mirror.* Terry Lancaster said it wasn't true, but when I reported it to Wilson he and Marcia saw it as a confirmation of the Lovell-Davies story, except by now they had convinced themselves it was to be in the *Daily Mail,* come what may. It was a rumour chasing its own tail, but time-consuming and, as ever, distracting.

Wilson decided to write the speech attacking the press himself. He passed it to me for editing and polishing. I edited it almost to extinction and deleted his pet phrase about a "cohort" of journalists scouring the country trying to uncover scandals about his Government (meaning, principally, about him and Marcia). "You've taken too much out, Joe," he said and put most of it back. So we started the election campaign with an attack on the press. It was too awful.

Inside No.10 we had an embarrassing private meeting to plan the campaign. Terry Lancaster asked about the speeches: "Joe will do those?" he inquired. Harold muttered that they would be done "under the direction of Marcia," who had never written a speech in her life, couldn't make one and whose main contribution to anything Wilson wrote was to scrawl "RUBBISH" across it in capital letters and at an angle. It became clear that "under the direction of Marcia" meant that Lovell-Davies and Lyons were to do them. It was getting more hilarious by the minute as Lovell-Davies and Lyons were instructed to write the first speech of the campaign. That was enough for me, except when Wilson asked me, in a whisper and outside her hearing, to "have a look at it."

I gave the pair three hours to work on the speech and then I called in on them to ask how it was going. They produced a single sheet of A4 paper as their work. When I started writing Wilson's speeches I would go to the back of the hall and listen, not only to him but to the audience's reaction. I learned a lot. They had no such experience. Lovell-Davies and Lyons had never heard a speech by him in their lives. They asked me what I thought of their labours. First, I told them it was no good, not least because it would not take him five minutes to deliver and he needed a speech 45 minutes long and, secondly, it didn't say anything. Anyway, in a comradely spirit I wished them well. If they were going to do the speeches, I said, I was taking a three-week holiday at home. Their panic showed in the sweat on their faces. Lyons said he had a business to run. If Lovell-Davies said anything I've long forgotten it and I left them to sweat it out.

I went to Wilson who asked me how it was going with the speech. I told him it was no good and offered to show him a copy. "No, no," he said. "You do them." And so I did, but it was another afternoon wasted in pursuit of a jealous woman's vendetta. And it went on throughout the campaign, right up to the eve of polling, when she refused, for some imagined slight, to allow Albert Murray to go to Wilson's count. So, in solidarity with Albert, Bernard and I refused to go, too. Not a day had gone by without a new problem with her but we overcame them, albeit with more time wasted. The election was won, but the result was disappointing. Labour won 18 seats and the Tories lost 20 and our overall majority was only three. Given the way we had fought the campaign from the top it was as much as we could have expected and probably more than we deserved.

The one campaign that didn't stop was hers. Wilson was weary of it but couldn't rein her in, despite all his promises to us. I said to Bernard after the count: "From now on its all downhill," and so it was. We were no sooner back in Downing Street than we heard that Marcia was on the move again. This time it was to fire Bernard, remove him from the Government altogether. Once again, we had to spend, or waste, time to forestall another threat to our efficient working.

A victory party was arranged to celebrate, with staff from Transport House invited and our own staff and some other peripheral helpers. Bernard and I walked up the stairs to the room where it was being held, shook hands with the Prime Minister and his wife waiting formally to greet the guests with Marcia hovering to see who they were . We had a quick drink and then left, before Wilson had a chance to make his speech. As we turned round and walked out and down the stairs again, I have a vivid memory of looking up from the bottom and seeing the terrified face of Marcia looking down at us, as though she had just realized the effect of what she was planning.

Wilson, in Government and in personal relationships, in good health and bad, never wanted to fight on two fronts. The struggle to get rid of the Policy Unit went on for a week but on Wilson's side it was to get out of the mess which she had got him into and which would have threatened his newly-elected government. I never told Wilson I would leave if Bernard was dismissed but I didn't need to. I had also said to Bill Housden, Wilson's talkative driver, that if I went I would not go quietly. To tell Bill something was a sure way of letting Marcia know without actually speaking to her. Eventually Wilson sued for peace, showered praise upon Bernard, as did Marcia at a subsequent lunch of false bonhomie, and both denied rumours that they had ever thought of dispersing the Unit. It was all contemptible, a fine man, in obviously deteriorating health, entangled in a web which was choking the political life out of him. He offered to make Bernard head of his "Kitchen Cabinet", empty words for an empty job which would have left Bernard trapped with him in her coils. But nothing came of it and we went on as before, ever wary, ever cautious and only left with one ambition , to get Wilson out looking the decent man he was rather than part with him dishonoured and disgraced.

Bernard Donoughue set out in detail the full horrors of the day-to-day disputes in his *Downing Street Diary* covering the Wilson years and I did much the same in my books, *Politics of Power* and *Glimmers of Twilight* and it would be tedious to repeat them all here. Dozens of people, ranging from Bill Housden to Joe Stone, Wilson's personal doctor witnessed the rages, the vendettas, the spitefulness which peppered those last Wilson years, but we – apart from Wilson, of course – had a better view than any. Government, however, went on.

The economic crisis had never gone away, wages were rising to beat inflation and thus causing inflation to rise even more. In the classic phrase of the hopeless, "something had to be done" and Wilson decided to make a definitive speech to the National Union of Mineworkers conference in Scarborough in July, 1975. He was to write afterwards: "Never in 30 years in Parliament had I prepared a speech with such care – dictating, writing, amending, inserting, discarding and drafting again." It was all so sad. Ever since the previous election, when she had been foiled in her attempt to get Lovell-Davies and Lyons to write Wilson's speeches, she had been trying to prevent me from doing so. It didn't work because neither she nor they were capable of doing them. As I remarked wryly a long time afterwards when Wilson wrote of the hard work he had put into that particular speech, what couldn't be done at the time was done retrospectively

Wilson wrote the personal touches which only he could do, recalling past miners' leaders he had known and his relationship with them. He had thoughts which I translated into paragraphs, he tinkered here and there, as was his practice with every speech and, as with every speech, it was his because he stood up and delivered it, and very successfully, too. But he didn't "write" it. I did. He knew it, Marcia knew it and Geoffrey Goodman, then running the Counter-Inflation Unit, knew it.   Indeed, the peroration, the final paragraph, of that speech was Goodman's suggestion. And the truth will be buried somewhere in the archives of the Government if the drafts of the speech were kept because Wilson wrote across the first draft of the speech I submitted to him, "This is your best ever." Not for the first time and not for the last he was to claim credit for something he hadn't done. He did it, not out of vanity, because he was generous enough in his praise to me in private, but because he dared not admit publicly that he had defied Marcia's wishes.

(In one successful foray against me, she once had me banned from the preparation of a speech to the Labour party conference. He dictated it, she organized the typing and collation of it: the result was chaos. He didn't realise until he rose to his feet that the most important part of the speech was missing from his typescript, a fool's mate kind of secretarial error. He sent a message to me via Shirley Williams who was on the platform near to him and she told me. I dashed back to the hotel room where they had been working; various drafts of the vital section, unnumbered and unidentified, lay scattered on the floor. I picked up one and dashed back to the conference hall. Shirley Williams gave it to him on the platform and he slid it into his speech. Trouble was that when it came to speeches Marcia couldn't organize the proverbial in the proverbial. I was never excluded again and it was her last appearance at conference speech-making discussions).

His appeal in the Scarborough speech to the British workers to give a year for Britain fell on the deaf ears of the Treasury and wasn't heeded. They were determined more was necessary and persuaded Wilson that it was time to revert to the tried and untrustworthy method of compulsory wage restraint. I had a vigorous disagreement about it with him in in the lobby outside the Cabinet room (what the tabloids would have called "a stand-up row") on June 30, 1975 and he ended it with a weary, "The trouble is, Joe, that when old problems recur I reach for the old solutions, I have nothing to offer any more." There was a further row later in the day with Bernard taking part as we were preparing for a formal dinner with the Belgian Prime Minister, M. Tindemans. Wilson still refused to budge on a statutory wage policy and accused us of being neurotic on the subject It was on that occasion that I understood that the mental deterioration Bernard and I had feared was taking place.

There is a history to be writing of the conniving ways of the Treasury. No change of government ever seems to reduce their power. They are arrogant, independent and ineffably superior in attitude, the perpetual paladins, those who believe they were born to rule. As a result, they never give up, even though they are sometimes compelled, by events or a strong Prime Minister, to give in. They can be devious or simply obstructive. In this instance they were both.

They knew, because they always knew, that I and Bernard Donoughue were the most vocal and determined of their critics over a statutory wages policy for three principal reasons: it went against the party's manifesto, it would be nigh-impossible to get it through the Commons, and it wouldn't work, anyway. Therefore the promise that I was to receive at 7 pm a copy of the statement they were preparing for the Prime Minister to make at a special meeting of the Cabinet the following morning was never likely to be fulfilled. Nor was it. Instead, a single copy arrived just before midnight for the Prime Minister, ready for him to read when the party for Tindeman's finally broke up and before he went to sleep. Fortunately, the Prime Minister's new principal private secretary, Kenneth Stowe, was on our side and he ensured that the copy came to us first. Soon after midnight, Bernard and I composed our objections to the statement, attached it to the top of the Treasury draft so that our case would be seen first and went home. It was impertinent. It could have been that we would both only return the next day to collect our things and say goodbye to our staff. With some prime ministers that would certainly have been the case.

But there was still a lot of the old Wilson left. When I arrived home at 1.50 am there was a message from my wife: to ring the Prime Minister immediately I got in. I did and he was brief. "You are right," he said. He had cancelled the early start to the next morning's Cabinet, arranged so that members could read the Treasury draft to be circulated by Denis Healey, the Chancellor. The cancellation was received too late by some. Shirley Williams arrived on time at 9.30 and there was nothing for her to read. Both Bernard and I have writing extensively about the intrigues, the arguments, and the exhausting meetings of those days and it is not my purpose in this book to recount them, but they are the seed corn for a future historian. I'll only remark that at a time of genuine major crisis, Lady Falkender had no contribution whatsoever to make, either destructive or constructive. She was at the party of celebrities upstairs.

The importance of Lord Goodman and Joe Stone began to show in the summer months of 1975. Goodman was frequently asked to issue write for libel, one or two of which he did but nothing ever came of them because of his constructive negligence. I ended a writ by Marcia against the *Evening Standard* by pointing out that she would have to give evidence and that the paper's QC could ask her "anything." "What sort of thing? she demanded. "About the children, for example," I replied. She flew into a purple-faced rage, tapped her handbag and said that if they did she would destroy him – "him" being Wilson. I heard nothing of the writ again.

But the big event involving Goodman came after, in a state of hysteria, she had told me that the Inland Revenue intended to send her to prison for failing to pay £20,000 in tax. That is not the way the Inland Revenue behave but Goodman was sent for. He calmed her, as he usually did, and promised to look into it. Independently, Wilson asked Harold Lever, the richest man if the Cabinet, if he would pay £20,000 to meet Marcia's capital gains tax on the sale of the Wigan slag heaps. Lever politely refused. "Why not?" Wilson demanded, "it is only a drop in the ocean to you." Lever replied that on principle he didn't pay other people's tax bills. Like so many other stories, I never learned the conclusion, but someone clearly paid it. Lord Goodman was fulfilling the role he described as "a cab for hire" but he never disguised to me his dislike for her.

As for Joe Stone, he had been seriously worried about his charge's health since a visit to Paris to see Giscard d'Estaing, the French president. As Wilson came out of his meeting he asked me to get Dr Stone immediately. He said he had had a heart flutter.

Joe prescribed immediate and complete rest. When we returned to London Wilson went straightaway to Chequers and I announced he was suffering from influenza. Soon after the prime minister's return, Dr Stone came to my office with an astonishing suggestion: that we should discuss ways of removing the burden of Marcia from Wilson. When I said I saw no way of doing that, he replied that he could "dispose" of her in such a way that her death would seem like natural causes. He would sign the death certificate and that would not be a problem. I said I couldn't go down that road and he dropped the subject.

But soon afterwards, when the three of us – Bernard, Joe Stone and myself -were walking across the main square in Bonn, he raise the subject again and again Bernard and I refused to contemplate or discuss it. Even if we had agreed, it meant that three people were in the secret, which for a secret was two too many. Supposing one of us had had a fit of remorse and went to the police? The grim process of digging up the grave and carrying out an autopsy would follow, unless, of course she were cremated. Then who would believe the whistleblower? Apart from the fact that it was an evil deed, how could any one of us live with it? And would it have relieved Wilson of the burden of Marcia alive? Of would he have sunk into a deep depression? And why did Joe Stone need our agreement?

We now began to move, secretly but remorselessly, towards Wilson's retirement. He had never deviated from his intention to retire within two years of re-taking office in 1974. Those summer weeks in 1975 intensified that intention. He was drinking too much, not because he was addicted to it but because it helped him get through difficult events, such as Prime Minister's Question Time which had become an increasing burden. He mooted the intention of announcing his resignation at that year's Labour party conference and Lady Falkender retained enough political sense to veto it; memories of the chaotic Tory conference in 1963 as rival candidates paraded and manoeuvred to win the throne of the stricken Harold Macmillan were too fresh. Instead, he suggested to me that he might go at Christmas. I said his MPs would love him for that - having to forgo their Christmas break in order to elect a new leader at the peak of winter. At the Labour conference, he finally made up his mind. One night he handed me a sheaf of papers from Cabinet ministers on which decisions needed to be taken and said, "Joe, you deal with them." He had never done anything like that in all my time with him. He never delegated that kind of work to anyone. It was an irrefutable sign that his mind was made up and he would not change it.

Then he said he wanted me to draw up a timetable for his resignation, to be announced on the afternoon of the last Wednesday in February, 1976, because the National Executive Committee of the Labour party would be meeting in the morning and "I'm not going to allow those buggers to have anything to say about it." He never lost his sense of humour. He further instructed me to give him the original proposal once it was ready and not to copy it (Too much to ask of a journalist; I made a copy and it is still in my files somewhere). I was to discuss it with no one except Kenneth Stowe, his principal private secretary; it was necessary for him to be involved on the official governmental side.

My paper therefore started the process on February 28 and after allowing the maximum time for the necessary elections to choose a successor had him going to the Palace to tender his resignation to the Queen on April 5. The starting date slipped, not because of any decision by him but because of a sudden financial crisis, which his resignation would have made worse. but he kept to the end date. He pretended to be indecisive up until the last moment, partly, perhaps mainly, because Marcia still steadfastly opposed his going at any time and still thought he could be persuaded; according to Bill Housden, she complained bitterly to him that her family had worked their fingers to the bone for him. Another version might have it that as he gave jobs to her, her brother and sister and enabled her to enjoy a peerage, two houses in London's West End, up to five servants, two children at private schools and a further house in the country, life might not have been to hard. Those fingers may have been worked to the bone but they were covered in rich gravy.

Whether he showed her my document, I don't know. He persisted in saying that only three of us were in the secret. By my count, due to his inability to keep a straight face when discussing his future, there were 22 of us who knew he was resigning. After all, Mary Wilson was the first to know. I naturally told Bernard and Albert Murray, Wilson himself dropped such heavy hints to Jim Callaghan, one of them on a train to Brighton, that there was no way in which such an acute mind could miss them, and also to Harold Lever. My deputy, Janet, knew. She was totally to be trusted to keep a secret. And Marcia, without giving a date or knowing it for certain, told anyone she thought might dissuade Wilson from going. Lord Goodman, his solicitor knew. Joe Stone, his doctor, knew and probably breathed a huge sigh of relief, and so did Bill Housden. In the same way that a gentleman's valet always knows his master's inner secrets, so does a minister's driver.

But once the decision was taken, Wilson relaxed and was more Prime Ministerial again with the winning post in sight. But there were still problems with which he felt he was unable to cope. Joan Lestor, a friend of mine before she entered Parliament, resigned from her post as a junior education minister on a matter of principle and such resignations always worried Wilson and on this occasion he wanted to make a smooth exit. He asked me how he could replace her. I told him to appoint another left-wing woman. "I don't know any," he said. "Do you?" I suggested Margaret Beckett, whom I had known since she was a highly efficient secretary at Labour h.q. He asked if I would ask her without committing him to anything. If she said "No" I would be the one free-enterprising and he wouldn't be snubbed. I saw Margaret in Downing Street over a coffee and after persuasion she agreed. Joan Lestor never spoke to me again.

One problem arose with the *Daily Mirror*. Marge Proops, the Grande Dame of Fleet Street, had arranged to interview Wilson for his 60th birthday on March 11. That was fine when the arrangement was made - he would have resigned by then. But the financial crisis upset the timetable and postponed the announcement. When Marge came, his intended resignation was still a secret. When she asked at the end of the interview the inevitable question about his future, he said he would stay as long as necessary, or words to that effect. A few days after the interview appeared, I made the official announcement of his departure. Terry Lancaster was hurt and Marge particularly so. It was made worse by Terry asking me shortly before the interview: "He didn't mean it, did he, when he said he would go after two years?" "You heard him, Terry," I said, which was as far as I could go. The trouble with Harold was that even his friends didn't always believe what he said.

That was only a small cloud on the horizon. Another, lasting, storm was brewing: the Prime Minister's Resignation Honours List. It is often a blot on a prime minister's record. This was the biggest personal blot of all. Primarily, this list is to honour those who have rendered faithful service to the prime minister during his years of office, plus a deserving few who don't fit into that category, like substantial donors to the party. A classic example for inclusion in such a list was the prime minister's personal driver over the years, Bill Housden. But the principal, headline awards were outrageous for that time in politics although subsequent prime ministers have further debased the system, either during their time in office or on leaving it. To put it bluntly, honours are bought today and have been for a very long time and to say otherwise is to make words say what they don't mean. Buying is not necessarily with money, but by using influence, by opening doorways to a celebrity lifestyle beyond No.10 and by maintaining friendship with the prime minister of the day and his closest advisers. The 1976 Honours List met all these unsavoury criteria in spades.

I was shown the initial, tentative list by Ken Stowe. One name that jumped out was that of David Frost, the entertainer, to be recommended for a peerage. Nowadays, particularly when people like Jimmy Savile have been honoured by a prime minister (Mrs Thatcher) against the advice of civil servants, it may not seem so shocking. But I had known Frost for a good many years before Lady Falkender did. He was fun, compulsively sycophantic but a better interviewer than anyone else on the British TV scene and without a breath of scandal to his name. But that's all he was. A creation of TV. I never heard him express an opinion on any topic of political or social concern. The idea of making him a legislator was absurd (then), as absurd as the similar transformation of Marcia Williams/Lady Falkender, who had her political opinions but was never to voice them publicly.

The trouble was that she had already arranged with Frost (unbeknown to me, whose job it was to deal with such matters) that when Wilson resigned he would do a major interview with him for Yorkshire TV. It still wasn't worth a peerage. What's more, I objected then, and do now, to journalists, particularly political journalists who are still active, receiving honours from the government of the day. Too many have done so, especially chairmen of the Lobby. I always admired Francis Boyd of the *Guardian* who refused a knighthood because he was still working. As happens, word that I was responsible for blocking Frost's peerage seeped out. Another friend lost.

But Frost was by no means the worst of it. As the potential list trickled out to us it became more appalling. Wilson did ask me to inquire about honouring Jarvis Astaire, the boxing promoter and a contributor to office funds. I did, via the *Mirror's* crime correspondent. The word came back that he should not be included, subsequently, I learned that the Home Office had also voiced their objections. I was, at the same time, warned from a different source that Joe Kagan, the manufacturer of the raincoat that Wilson wore, boringly, for many years and a certain provider of financial assistance to Wilson's office and to Marcia, was being investigated for tax fraud. Wilson accepted what I said about Astaire – after all, he had asked me to make inquiries - but said it wasn't true about Kagan. He had similarly dismissed my fears when I reported to him, from a very high source, that Rudi Sternberg, a physically sinister-looking person like Kagan, was a Soviet spy. "He's a double agent," he said. Sternberg was also a contributor, too, and ended up as Lord Plurenden. Kagan became Lord Kagan and not too long after had a prison number attached to his name when the investigation I had told Wilson about and which he denied proved to be true.

The saddest moment of all came when Wilson said bitterly to Bernard, after the scale and enormity of the list had begun to leak: "Why are the press attacking me? I hardly know half of them."

[the list's proposed beneficiaries].That's why it was called the lavender list, after the colour of her notepaper. Too many of them were better known to Marcia than to him.

Albert Murray was properly included. He had worked tirelessly for Wilson under great stress and strain for years, was a former minister and MP and his attachment to the Wilson office, which was unpopular in some constituencies, undoubtedly prevented him from regaining a seat in the Commons. But I had to make a direct request to Wilson after I had been told by Housden that he was not to be included.

But Lew Grade and his brother, Bernard Delfont? Showbiz, to which Marcia was incurably addicted. Not Wilson's type to be included in his very personal Resignation Honours List. John Vaizey, an ex-Labour Tory academic who had helped Marcia find private schools for her two children but most notable politically for being an opponent of Wilson? George Weidenfeld, publisher of Wilson's (and Marcia's) books and regular social escort to Marcia? James Goldsmith, knighted despite the fact that Wilson said to me: "Why should I give him anything?" but who, according to Wilson, was about to offer Lady Falkender a post as director of his main company, Cavenham Foods, and was said to have offered her later a directorship of a subsidiary company. Goldsmith was furious, I was told, at not getting a peerage, only a knighthood, but, in fairness to Wilson, he was never included for a peerage in any list or part-list that I saw. But for Lady Falkender, most of these people would not have been included in the List, anyway, and Wilson's reputation would have been immeasurably the better for it.

On the return flight from a visit to Luxemburg on what may be thought an appropriate day, April 1 – we had been at one of the incessant European Common Market meetings – Wilson asked me if I would become a peer to be included in his list. I refused. I said I wanted to abolish the House of Lords, not strengthen it, but the truth was that there was no way I was going to be associated with this shabby betrayal of what I thought we all stood for. I thought he breathed a sigh of relief when I said, "no." That, at least, averted another row with Marcia. He then offered me a knighthood. Again I refused. I said my wife didn't want to be called a "Lady" and that a knighthood was a permanent invitation to cocktail parties, which we both disliked. The truth, however, was the same for both of us. Anyone in that list who had been closely associated with Wilson would have looked a dirty knight indeed. Anyway, I wanted to become a journalist again.

About the same time, Bernard Donoughue refused to be included in the list. When the storm was breaking, Wilson was showing Bernard the inscriptions in the books stored in the cabinet room. Suddenly, he said to Bernard: "What do you want, a peerage, I suppose?" Bernard replied, "Like Joe, nothing..." Wilson never mentioned it to him again. An additional proof that it was Marcia's list in the main? Neither Bernard nor I were in the tentative list although we would have been automatic candidates because of our seniority.

It was a typically Marcia tactic that when the names seeped out into the press Wilson asked for an official inquiry into the leakage and Sir Douglas Allen, head of the Home Civil Service, was asked to conduct it. That was only to pile more criticism on that already current. There is no doubt that Sir Douglas, later Lord Croham realized that the scandal was not about the leaking of the list but about its contents. Though it was not disclosed until Lady Falkender sought to auction the Lavender list and associated papers at Sotheby's in the summer of 2018 – having for 40 years said it was no more than names which Harold Wilson had given her written on notepaper issued by 10 Downing Street – Allen himself, in his role of head of the political honours scrutiny committee,- had sent a memorandum to Wilson saying that the effect of the list "could only be detrimental to the prestige of the honours system." Exactly: that's what the complaints were all about.

But quoting Lord Croham and also Kenneth Stowe, who wrote to the Prime Minister saying that the Department of Trade's report on the intended honour to Sigmund Sternberg was "unfavourable," was enough to block the sale temporarily when the Cabinet Office questioned her right to sell what might be government papers. Lady Falkender's son blamed the security services for the objection, demonstrating he shared some of his mother's conspiracy beliefs.

Gabriel Heaton, of Sotheby's said the Honours List was a political scandal that had turned on a group of documents.."even the existence of which was denied for many years. It is an interesting insight into that moment, which does feel a long time ago, but so many of those issues are still with us today."

The next few weeks after the resignation were spent trying to add further names to the list to improve its respectability, but the respectable had already read enough. Dick Crossman's widow was phoned in Italy (by Weidenfeld, of all people; what had it to do with him?) to see if she would accept a peerage. Again, the answer was "no." Meanwhile, previous recipients of Wilson honours fell by the wayside, Eric Miller by his own hand as the Fraud Squad closed in on him and Lord Brayley , who died before he appeared at the Old Bailey on charges relating to his company's funds. Lessons hadn't been learned. Kagan's imprisonment was still to come.

Lady Falkender says that the derision which greeted the Honours list when it was eventually published was "anti-semitic." Totally untrue. Bernard Donoughue, Albert Murray and I all had many Jewish friends and were all strong supporters of Israel; indeed, the Israeli Government later that year invited me to a three-week tour of their country. What was anti-semitic was the ennoblement of Jewish people whose conduct was dubious if not downright unlawful. They were criminals; being Jewish had nothing to do with it, but by honouring them they allowed anti-semites to rant against Jewish influence. There were fine members of the Jewish community in Britain who could have adorned the House of Lords but weren't given the chance. And when honest Jewish MPs were honoured it wasn't always for the best of reasons. Leslie Lever, the MP who had strenuously worked to get Gerald Kaufman to be his successor in the Gorton constituency, got his barony for that alone. I was present when Kaufman demanded immediately after the 1970 election that Lever should get "his" peerage there and then and Wilson said "All bets are off".

The press and public vilification of the Lavender list largely dissipated the goodwill which had been bestowed on Wilson when his resignation was announced. He left office with unaccustomed praise from the press, a rarity in his lifetime. Of course, the conspiracy rumours began and still persist, even to this day: That he was deeply involved in a financial/moral/sexual scandal; that he got out while the going was good; that somewhere there was a British Watergate. The truth was that his mental health was failing, that he had recognized it more than two years earlier, that the date of his going had been chosen, broadly, by him the previous October and by me, precisely, at the beginning of November and that nothing happened in the meantime to change his mind, not even a barrage of demands from Lady Falkender that he should do so.

A few weeks before he left one of the private secretaries, Nick Stewart, exasperated, like all the others at her behaviour, asked me whether I intended to write a book about her and my time in No.10. She was undoubtedly unpopular among the civil servants who crossed her, which was all of them. In turn, one of the private secretaries aptly dubbed her, the "Princess of Pettiness."

But until Nick Stewart spoke, it hadn't occurred to me to do so. Once he put it in my mind, I was certain I would. I had made occasional notes, but I had never kept a diary . However, I was blessed with an exceptional memory (until I was 30, I never recorded phone numbers; I memorized them)

I spent that summer,1976, one of the hottest on record, sitting in my bedroom, wearing only my pants, working on my recollections of my time at No.10, particularly the horrors that flowed from the tantrums of Lady Falkender and my dismay at the abuse of the Honours system as one after another of her friends were lined up to receive them. It is right to say that I left Downing Street on a down note. Graham Greene, chairman of Cape and a friend of Bernard Donoughue, was keen from the beginning to publish my book and was steadfast in resisting those who feared it would bring a host of libel writs down on his head. He trusted Bernard and if Bernard said it was true he accepted it. I also had a sworn afffidavit from Albert Murray testifying to the truthfulness of it.

When it was completed, I showed the typescript to Terry Lancaster and he showed it to Tony Miles, deputy chairman of the Mirror Group and Mike Molloy, the *Mirror's* editor. They were excited and offered me £65,000 for the serial rights (of which the Inland Revenue took 83 per cent, which left me with about £13,000). I happily agreed – having decided to expose what I deemed to be corrupt, I wanted the maximum publicity. The net sum I received was equivalent to the yearly salary I was earning and I did no other work for a year.

In that book, which I entitled *The Politics of Power,* I ruminated upon Harold Wilson's time as Prime Minister and Leader of the Opposition, which I carried forward in *Glimmers of Twilight* which was published in 2003 and I have continued to do so ever since and I do so again now, my final refinement and judgment. I do so still inhibited by matters to which I was sworn to secrecy. They may influence my verdict but they do not, I think, distort it.

* * * * * * * * *

The working class have only twice provided a Prime Minister of the United Kingdom. Ramsay Macdonald was one and he did them no credit, and James Callaghan was the other, but as the son of a Chief Petty Officer he would probably rank as lower middle-class. But James Harold Wilson, son of a Yorkshire middle-class family, had a closer affinity to the working class than any other, not least because his father, a chemist, suffered two long periods of unemployment as he was growing up. All of the other post-war premiers, except Callaghan, were London Metropolitan or South of England, either by habitat or constituency. True, some, like Harold Macmillan (Stockton) and Tony Blair won their seats in the North of England but they were at heart Southerners, even though Blair was born in Scotland. Clement Attlee (Limehouse) could not have had a more working-class constituency, but he had compassion, not affinity. The hostility to Wilson came from Fleet Street, the BBC and political opponents, not from ordinary voters.

His kind of background, upbringing and education was a world apart from many of his political contemporaries but he was fascinated by politics, as I was, even before he reached his 'teens. He wrote an essay at his grammar school in 1928, envisaging himself 25 years hence, about introducing his first Budget as Chancellor of the Exchequer. But the grim reality of those years was that his father was out of work for four of them, shameful for middle-class families in those days. He was not a great sportsman, though he played a bit of rugby, league and union, at his schools. Perhaps appropriately for his future career, he shone at athletics as a long distance runner. He was still a schoolboy when he met Gladys (later known as Mary) Baldwin, a shorthand typist at Lever Brothers, and then they played tennis together. She was his one and only serious girl friend and later became his wife.

Wilson won a scholarship to take him to Jesus College, Oxford, not regarded as one in the elite class, like Balliol (Roy Jenkins's college). It was not the place for a student looking for fun, but then he wasn't. Riotous party-going groups like the Bullingdon Club would have been anathema to him. He went to Oxford to learn and was no doubt regarded by the more louche undergraduates as a swot. When he left, showered with degrees and prizes he went to work, at no pay, for Sir William Beveridge, the social reformer who left an indelible mark on British public life. It was the start of a career which was to lead him to be the youngest member of the Attlee Government at 29 and then the youngest member of the Cabinet at 32.

It wasn't all smooth going. Fellow MPs thought him a dull stick as President of the Board of Trade but he made a name for himself by proclaiming "a bonfire of controls," a welcome promise to a country still over-burdened by a wartime legacy of them. In 1951 came Attlee's greatest crisis – the resignation of Aneurin Bevan creator of the National Health, Wilson and John Freeman, a junior minister. The difference between Bevan's resignation and Wilson's was crucial. Bevan resigned on principle against the decision of the Chancellor, Hugh Gaitskell, to impose charges on the NHS. Wilson resigned on more complex and pragmatic grounds: the money to be spent on defence was unrealistic and couldn't be spent and if it were not spent the NHS charges would not be necessary.

Before I started writing this book, I asked old friends who knew him well – and there were not many - how they regarded him today. Janet Hewlett-Davies said he had a "terrific brain" and understanding. "No one since has had his quality of intellect. A political giant." Others referred first to his sense of humour and his complete lack of pomposity or "side." That is right, too. All said he was kind and there were plenty of instances that that was so. He would treat anyone who argued with him as an equal, even though in intellect or status they were not. I found I could disagree with him without being afraid of rebuke. He could win an argument but never seek to humiliate the loser. I once did something that he had asked me to do and so I did it. When I reported back to him he looked at me in genuine astonishment: "But you said you disagreed with me," he said. "You are the Prime Minister," I replied, "and I'm your press secretary. The day I'm right more often than you, I should be Prime Minister and you my press secretary."

He would listen seriously and reply seriously and respect your point of view. He once refused to see me and Bernard Donoughue on the grounds that we were neurotic about the subject we wanted to raise. But when he saw us he was not dismissive. When he finally accepted we were right and he was wrong, it was a ready acceptance.

Jim Callaghan was known to remind an aide of his position; Wilson would have regarded that as taking an unfair advantage. He had an extraordinary academic record at Oxford and never boasted of it in private. Unlike Roy Jenkins, whose educational record was not so good, he never affected an accent or a superior position. He didn't tell jokes but he was extremely funny and quick-witted. He understood politics more than any other politician I ever met. I never heard him say anything derogatory about the voters (unlike, say, Gordon Brown, who notoriously called an elderly lady "a bigot." I wouldn't say Brown was wrong, but it wasn't the right thing to say during an election campaign). All these things were right about Wilson. It was impossible to dislike him as a person and very easy to admire or even idolise him. And yet, and yet...

There was a flaw, another side, a witch in the room. My appraisal is naturally subjective but I have to admit it. When Lord Goodman said that "but for that woman he would have been the greatest of our Prime Ministers" I thought he went too far in praise of Wilson but, on reflection, I believe his words were intended to be a condemnation of "that woman" rather than a final judgment on the prime minister. But how are we to judge greatness? By a comparison of flaws and failures or by a comparison of achievements? Or by both? By comparison with his immediate predecessors or with his successors? By the changes he made to his country or by those he didn't make? By overcoming failure or by his contribution to that failure? Is a general defeated in battle more than once thus a bad general? Rommel, for example, after his early successes or the early Wellington before his successes? And how does one judge what is success or failure? Is Mrs Thatcher to be praised for her destruction of the miners' union and its disastrous leader, Arthur Scargill, or is she to be condemned for what she did to some of the finest men who ever adorned the working class scene? Success, like beauty, is in the eye of the beholder, the voter in the first instance and then the historian.

I can only answer the question of his greatness or otherwise, of his place in history, by splitting his career into three: from 1963 when he became leader of the Opposition before becoming Prime Minister in 1964; from 1970, when he became the leader of the Opposition again; and from 1974 when he became Prime Minister once more until his retirement in 1976.

In 1964 when there was a demand for change in Britain Wilson epitomized that demand. The scandal-ridden Macmillan Government had ended in a cloud of sleaze. He was old and looking older, he was tired, he had left the Conservative party in disarray as they fought over his succession. He had virtually imposed a new Prime Minister upon them when a cancer scare caused him to resign. He rejected his colleagues in the Commons and chose the Earl of Home, who had quickly to rid himself of his hereditary peerage and win a by-election to return to the Commons, where he had once sat as Lord Dunglass, in the guise of Sir Alec Douglas-Home. The party accepted Sir Alec because they needed a new face; there was no such practice then as a democratic election for leader. But he was not a fresh face. He was impeccably free of sexual or financial taint. But he was an appeaser, a man who went with Neville Chamberlain to Munich to meet Adolf Hitler, a man who stood behind Chamberlain as he waved a piece of paper and proclaimed, "peace in our time." So, of course, was R.A. Butler an appeaser, a minister in the pre-war Government and opposed to Churchill becoming Prime Minister in 1940. Home was merely a parliamentary private secretary, the lowest of the low in ministerial terms, Butler a senior minister. In the event, Home did remarkably well as Prime Minister, in that he hauled the Tory party back from the brink of catastrophe and took them within a few seats of retaining power. But he was an aristocrat, scion of a past age, wealthy and as remote as a man can be with a telephone number of Coldstream 1 and a habit of taking a taxi from the Scottish borders to Westminster.

Wilson was the fresh face, the new kid on the block, ready to throw off the shackles of the past and become part of what he had described as "the white heat of the technological revolution." He dispelled the doubts about his political honesty. He attacked on all fronts. As the Tories reacted to the last assault he was up and away and mounting another. He virtually won that general election single-handed.

There were problems. Anti-immigration feeling was on the rise. Labour lost their seat at Smethwick in that 1964 election to a Conservative candidate, Peter Griffiths, who played the race card shamelessly. But Wilson laid out a programme of social change which led him to a further victory, by 100 seats, in March, 1966. He was just 50, historically young for a Prime Minister winning his second term of office. I have written above of what went wrong, the seamen's strike, the industrial unrest, Rhodesia, South African arms, devaluation, wage control, inflation, the failure to get Britain into the European Common Market, rebellious colleagues, the attempts by the old right and some on the new left to unseat him. They were all rooted in a party and a Cabinet who did not realise change was necessary but nonetheless was taking place. But could anyone else have overcome them? For the first time in his political career he felt secure, on top, in charge. It didn't last long.

The failures he suffered were honourable failures. But his government's achievements were substantial. The Open University was the source of his greatest pride, resisted by colleagues like Roy Jenkins who had had the best of education themselves but thanked by the hundreds of thousands of students who passed through its metaphorical doors and gained the degrees and the education that were otherwise beyond their reach. More houses were built than by any succeeding prime minister. Capital punishment was abolished, the start began of the greatest social liberation programme this country has ever seen. You don't have to agree with all of it to accept that the achievement was undeniable. That was a record to be proud of. It wasn't enough to win him the 1970 election but it places him head and shoulders above his contemporaries. For that period, he deserves Lord Goodman's description without the caveat of "that woman."

But that caveat was there increasingly in subsequent years. Marcia Williams was already a powerful influence behind the scenes and, for much of the time, an apparently constructive one. I was working with her for 18 months before I saw her true nature and it was violent and coincided with the aftermath of the 1970 defeat. For that campaign she had advocated a presidential-style programme for Wilson, which was begun and, as I have written elsewhere, quickly abandoned by him. She brought in a quirky publicist, Will Camp, whose purpose was to sideline me. There was no evidence that he wanted to play that game. I never met anyone so lacking in the energy and 24-hour commitment that a general election demanded. He offered nothing but disruption to the campaign and seemed more interested in influencing the *New Statesman* – which supported us, anyway - than the mass circulation newspapers and leaked like a sieve. Nothing ever felt right, not even the polls which made us the winners.

With the defeat came the inevitable Resignation Honours List. Wilson proposed to make me a CBE. Perhaps puritanically, prudishly or even pompously I turned it down on the simple grounds that I hadn't been there long enough, or done enough, to deserve it. What I didn't realise was that he had offered the same honour to Marcia and she had accepted it. Whether my refusal was the cause or not but she refused to go to the Palace to receive it and afterwards complained that they had sent it to her in a brown paper bag.

Shortly afterwards, Marcia, in a raging temper had demanded my sacking for having tea and cake with a departing secretary – who was leaving because she couldn't stand Marcia's ways and consequently didn't invite her to a little party - and *instructed* Wilson that I was to have nothing to do with writing his book – unknown to her I had already written the first chapter, which had to be scrapped – the "Mirror, mirror on the wall" syndrome was unleashed. Nobody was to have influence with Wilson bar her. She condemned me for being disloyal in fraternising with the secretaries. I pleaded guilty, which only infuriated her the more. Threats to resign were frequent. As I have said, I didn't know she had given birth to two children in less than a year which could have led to some of her ill temper, but not all of it. My wife scolded me for not noticing she was pregnant, but she wore what was known as an Empire line coat whenever she was in the office and I didn't think to see beyond or underneath it. I have no doubt that the children changed her whole life, which was not surprising. The trouble was that they changed other lives, too.

The temper, the tantrums, the rages, symbolised her insecurity and she fed the insecurity of Wilson: it is us against the world, she was saying; trust no-one but me. When all others fail you I will be there, and in a sense she was right. She abused him, humiliated him, swore at him, called him "Walter Mitty" and "little man", "king rat" and hurled other insults at him accompanied by threats to destroy him, but she never abandoned him. Her demands were more than unreasonable; they were fantasies; the demand that Wilson leave a party conference at Brighton and return to London to visit her because she was feeling ill was only one example.

Demands for a private flat at another conference, costing Wilson a considerable sum, were met by him, and Albert Murray scoured Blackpool for something suitable for her, keeping up the pretence that if he got it she would come. He got it and she didn't come. Wilson's taxpayer-funded car was not available to him when she wanted it for chauffeur-driven shopping. Her behaviour ranged from the outlandish to the bizarre. Copies of Wilson's draft conference speech at Blackpool one year had to be ferried to London by her secretary on expensive train journeys so that she could make her negligible contribution. I could put up with that; it was far better than when she was there. But we couldn't make progress until her copy was ferried back.

After I wrote *Glimmers of Twilight*, a Liverpool academic, Denis Kavanagh, with no personal knowledge of Wilson, Marcia or me wrote that I was "bitter." Difficult for him, a stranger, to understand, but I was not bitter. I was outraged. Nor was I jealous of her influence, which was incontestable. I deplored it. I hated her peerage, but not because I hated her. I didn't. I just hated what she did and I hated the gross misuse of the Honours system which sent her to be an unspeaking expenses-paid appendage to the House of Lords. I wasn't envious of the honour. When the opportunity of a peerage came to me I refused it. But I resented the system and Wilson's name being tarnished. Above all else, I was outraged, deplored, hated what she did to Harold Wilson, damaging his premiership and his reputation. And all this during a time when I had begun to worry about his health, physical and mental.

Why she did it, I cannot say. What personal devils drove her on, why she needed to dominate, always to be pre-eminent, to scorn, to humiliate, to despise all perceived rivals and try to banish them, to be the one and only, to possess the trophy yet to diminish it in the eyes of others. I have no expertise in the field of human psychology. But I know others were equally shocked. I made no attempt to influence Bernard Donoughue when he arrived to join us. I didn't need to. One day, soon after we went to No.10, when he was in Wilson's study, Marcia phoned. Wilson told Bernard to tell her he was not there and scurried off to his lavatory.

When Bernard spoke to her she shouted: "I know he is there. Get the King Rat to come and speak to me. I'll ruin him. I'll destroy him."

There are some who have doubted the version of events described by Bernard Donoughue and myself. Matthew Parris, the former Tory MP and now a newspaper columnist, once did so in a book about parliamentary scandals. But without personal knowledge how are they to know? It is difficult for a reasonable man to understand unreasonable behavior.

It was Harold Wilson himself who told me, immediately after it happened, how Marcia called Mary Wilson to her house at Wyndham Mews on January 12, 1972, to tell her that she had slept with Wilson six times in 1956 "and it was not satisfactory." Why did she do it? Ostensibly, because Wilson had taken his wife out for lunch that day, her birthday, without first telling Marcia. Insecurity again, on her side this time.

That was the story he told me after being called back by his wife to his home from his office in the Commons where we had been working. Nothing she ever said or did was to me more outrageous than that. Accept that Wilson was telling the truth (why would he lie about it, how would any man fabricate such a story about his personal life and tell it to another man?) and accept that it is not a story that I made up in some insane way to damage her and that my conversation with Wilson that evening did take place, accept that Wilson said to me, as he did, "she has dropped her atomic bomb at last, she can't hurt me any more," accept all that, then what other conceivable emotion can there be but utter outrage? Everything else she said and did, from scorning him daily to calling him a c*** for leaving a House of Lords party which she had demanded he should attend, is secondary but falls into place. That she was a woman who knew no bounds in trying to control the foremost politician of him time and, sadly, succeeding.

Wilson handled well the always difficult task of opposition after losing the 1970 general election. The party, generally, was hostile to joining the Common Market but the PLP never officially opposed it. Wilson, as he told me he intended to do, "ducked and weaved" in order to keep the party from officially opposing. Harold Lever, a passionate European, who said he had vomited in the division lobby when opposing the Government on one aspect of Europe, reluctantly accepted his word. When his vomiting was raised at a lobby meeting and I said that made Lever "the sick man of Europe" that was promptly reported back to him. He didn't complain, as his informants had hoped. He laughed.

Roy Jenkins, who so disliked Wilson that he would never believe a word he said, resigned as deputy leader. Wilson survived the odd plot against him by anti-marketeers and, compared to the Tories, was in good shape when the general election came in 1974 and Labour scraped home. This period of his leadership, out of office, doesn't technically qualify for judgment of "the greatest Prime Minister" but it was an interregnum which had its effect on the final period of his leadership and premiership.

Winning the first general election of 1974 gave Wilson the shot of adrenalin that he needed. He was looking in better health the day after Polling Day than he did a month earlier. The flurry of activity that followed gave him a new zest. The miners' strike had to be settled on terms very favourable to the miners, but that was what the country wanted. He pushed ahead with the plans for the next election in October and at first all went well. Even the fractured relationship between Marcia and me and then Bernard Donoughue and Marcia held out for a few weeks. And then the old, tiresome, exhausting, distracting tempo of her personal affairs began to rise again. The shine she took to Bernard rapidly wore off, though Wilson used him as a shield against her when she was in one of her rages, even asking him one night to go to her home and pull out the wires of her telephone to stop her ringing the Press Association (which she wouldn't have done).

Her relationship with Walter Terry, the father of her children, was not going well. I was in her house one evening, playing with one of her sons, when Walter came in. She treated him like a footman, instructing him to "go and sit in the corner." Visibly shocked at seeing me with his son – I don't think he realized that I knew - he did as he was told. One of the finest journalists of his time got the same disparaging scorn that she meted out to the

Prime Minister. Wilson complained to me that Terry had only given Marcia £500 towards the upbringing of his children. He told me it was £5,000 and I believed him.

On several occasions Marcia, during her frequent losses of temper, would shout, almost scream, "I will destroy him," meaning Wilson , and tap her handbag as if there were something inside it which was documentary evidence that would bring him down. Other times she repeated her threat to "ruin " him. Always the threat was unspecified, but always it was to bring him down. Often, it was in relation to an issue which had little or nothing to do with him. She did this in front of me, Bernard and Albert Murray and, I haven't a doubt, Lord Goodman and Joe Stone, and probably led to him toying with the idea of making a future prescription for her a fatal one. Twice, once in the spring and once in the summer of 1974, she said to Donoughue that Wilson was a rat "a King Rat," and she would ruin him, accompanied by the tapping of her handbag.

It has puzzled us for years how would, how could, she ruin or destroy him? And it still does. There are plausible theories but no facts. If there is or was documentary evidence of a kind that would destroy or ruin him then it would have to be something that went beyond an affair or affairs. Rumours about an affair between them were spread first in 1964 by Tory MPs in what Andrew Roth said was a deliberate smear campaign. Would it have done so, though, even then? After all, Hugh Gaitskell's affair with the wife of the novelist, Ian Fleming, had been an open secret at Westminster for a long time. Harold Macmillan was a knowing if unwilling cuckold with his adored wife for many years the mistress of Bob (later Lord) Boothby, as unsavoury an MP as I ever met, a friend and, according to some, a more intimate worse with the notoriously criminal Kray Brothers, or one of them. Perhaps after the Profumo affair which darkened Macmillan's last days, it would have been very damaging in 1964 but in 1974? It never made sense to think that it might have "ruined" him nearly 20 years after the supposed events she described to Mary Wilson – which she later denied she had ever said - and 10 years after he became Prime Minister.

It has been suggested to me that the answer was always staring us in the face and we didn't see it. What would have ruined him or destroyed his reputation was something criminal or treacherous and no one had ever thought to accuse him of that, except Peter Wright, the right-wing Secret Service man who was obsessive about Wilson and his links with Russia. But in 1967 he sued the Paris-based New York *Herald Tribune* for libel after one its columnists had alleged an affair between him and the then Marcia Williams . If that involved the swearing of an affidavit, which is usually a document of the court, then that could ruin him. But it would ruin her, too. Did something happen in the Soviet Union during his visits in the 1950s on behalf of Montague Meyer, that would have damaged him? Had he received other monies, similar to the Brayley money, which would have brought condemnation? These, like other explanations for the handbag-tapping, can only be speculation, but whatever it was clearly had crucial importance in Marcia's mind and we were meant to understand it as such. She is the only person who can clear it up because only she can know what is or was in her handbag. It is one of the last great stories about Wilson which remains untold, unless to ease her perennial money worries she chooses to cash in.

Wilson still conducted his last Government with skill but he was tired and lacking will. The Wilson of the 1960s would have done so much more, including my own pet scheme, developed by Donoughue's Policy Unit, for the sale of council houses which he said "could be historic." It was, but under Mrs Thatcher and significantly different from and worse than we had advocated. I proposed that the money raised in selling the houses should be devoted to building new council houses. Mrs Thatcher expressly forbade it.

The toll on his health became more evident as the months of 1975 passed. His drinking increased. He grew to hate Prime Minister's Question Time where he had once dominated. Even when he had a particularly successful day she burst into his room behind the Speaker's chair and sneered, "I suppose you think you are clever," in a room full of his civil servants and advisers. She was telling us, "He is my man and I control him, not you."

He wanted to get out of Downing Street and while his staff, principally Marcia, delayed his first intentions (for good reasons as explained above), nothing could stop him. Paradoxically, in those last months he seemed happier than he had been for years. But still he was forced to twist and turn and submit to ridiculous demands, ending in the final humiliation of his Resignation Honours List. It was a depressing ending to a period in Britain's political history which was remarkable by any standard. He had achieved what he had set out to achieve: to make Labour a natural party of Government.

It has had good times and bad times since. It survived Militant but has succumbed to Momentum. It thrived under Tony Blair and collapsed under Gordon Brown. It changed its rules about electing its leader twice and twice came up with the wrong answers: Ed Milliband and Jeremy Corbyn, but as long as there is a Conservative party in Britain there will be a Labour party, of some kind, to oppose and occasionally defeat it. And those who remember Harold Wilson will be able to claim some of the credit on his behalf. His manifesto was more left-wing than Blair's or Brown's or anything that Jeremy Corbyn has drawn up but he was swift to recognise when a policy was failing and to change it. But for that final signing off of the Honours List and for the dubious and downright criminal people he allowed himself to be associated with, his reputation today would not need to be defended For that, he has Lady Falkender to thank. He *was* great, but for only part of the time.

* * * * * * *

Maxwell and the Mirror

My book was serialised by the *Mirror* for a week and dominated most of the other national newspapers as well. "Marcia: the Truth" shrieked the *Mirror* and reporters from other papers bombarded my home with phone calls and occasional door-stepping, without luck. Had they known, I was staying at the Howard Hotel, in Arundel Street off the Strand, where once Herbert Morrison, Clement Attlee's deputy dallied with his mistress, Ellen Wilkinson, and I walked every morning from there down Fleet Street and Fetter Lane to Holborn Circus, the *Mirror* Group headquarters, and was never recognised. The best way to hide is in the open.

The furore was slightly greater than I expected, but that's the skill of tabloid newspapers. I was only disturbed when I heard the tearful widow of Henry Kerby, a Tory MP, denying on the radio that her husband had ever colluded with Wilson to betray his party. The secret help Kerby offered had gone on for some years. I assumed she knew all about it. Clearly, she didn't. I was hurt that she was so hurt. Frankly, it had never entered my mind that she would be. Though it wasn't relevant, I considered resigning from the Royal Commission on Legal Services, to which Wilson's successor, James Callaghan, had appointed me, until my wife asked me, simply: "Why?" and I didn't know why.

Apart from that, it was great fun. Mike Molloy, the *Mirror's* youthful editor may have thought it "dull", as he wrote many years later, but the *Sunday Times* bought a chapter of the book about the Treasury from the *Mirror* (for £2,000) and *The Guardian,* typically, informed us that they were going to print the chapter about Northern Ireland, without payment or consultation. The *Mirror* lawyers quickly disabused them. The *Daily Mail* printed too copiously from my book and had to pay a very large sum, indeed, to compensate, which they freely did. It was always ahead of its rivals in spotting the news value of it, largely because I had given its political reporter, Gordon Greig, a copy of the book two weeks beforehand. He was a good and close friend and never disclosed that he had it, but it gave him a head start. Meanwhile, Lady Falkender denied everything and Harold Wilson, half-heartedly and without conviction deplored rather than denied what he, better than anyone, knew was true

At the end of that week, Mike Molloy, who had spent it in a state of excitement, asked me to write a reply to my critics, who, sadly for me, included the paper's Keith Waterhouse, who I regarded as the best writer of his generation. But I picked on the less reputable, like Peter Lovell-Davies, whom I had frustrated in 1975 when Lady Falkender tried to push him into my job. "I have read this book," proclaimed Lovell-Davies, "and it is the politics of trivia." I pointed out that he had not read the book because it hadn't yet been published or sent out for review and advised him: "Next time, Peter, look before you creep."

Molloy told me that that sentence induced him to offer me a job on the *Mirror*, at £8,000 a year, about 40 per cent less than I was getting in Downing Street but with £50 a week expenses which I didn't need to justify plus £300 cash in hand for newspapers, both free of tax. (It was not uncommon to see fellow journalists coming into the office to read their own paper because they didn't buy one at home). Many years later, he said of the adaptation (by Terry Lancaster) of my book that it was so boring that he had to ask the women's editor, Joyce Hopkirk, to write a more readable version. In fact, Lancaster rewrote his version and it was that was used, not Hopkirk's. She was a fine journalist but politically naïve, like Molloy.

But if the book was so boring to him he concealed it very well. The rest of Fleet Street had shown him that they would have liked to be bored by it, too, but Mike had a spiteful side to his nature. Many years after the serialisation, he wrote an agonised, self-pitying article for the *Daily Mail* in which he explained why he had changed from voting Labour to voting Conservative and I wrote a rebuke reminding him of what the *Mirror* said in the 1983 general election when he was editor and Michael Foot was leader of a Labour party doomed to defeat: That while Labour was often wrong, its heart was in the right place, and while the Conservative party was sometimes right, its heart was in the wrong place. Mike condemned my book after that.

146

The BBC's *Panorama* programme spent a whole edition on *The Politics of Power* with Robin Day, then the best of political interviewers and a former failed Liberal candidate himself, interrogating me with his usual forensic scepticism. Just as I was entering the studio, Margaret Douglas, herself a producer of the programme, whispered to me: "He is going to try to make you lose your temper." I was grateful for the tip. He baited me for writing about economic matters when I wasn't an economist (and nor was he) and poured scorn on the power which I claimed Lady Falkender had. "Well," I said, "she could have made you director-general of the BBC." The television crew laughed loudly, though their laughter wasn't picked up by the studio microphones. Robin Day's ambition to take the top post at the Corporation was well known. For a moment, he was rattled.

Despite what many people believed, a job at the *Mirror* had never been part of the deal to serialise the book. I had been offered other jobs, including one from Harold Evans, editor of *The Sunday Times,* but I was never interested in working for a paper that published only once a week. I had worked every day, with intensity, for years and I needed more. I quickly found that being a feature writer on the *Mirror* was not enough, either.

Molloy ran a relaxed ship, accepted the absurd and tyrannical constraints placed on his job by the Fleet Street unions, the closest bodies to institutionalised corruption existing outside the gang bosses of south and east London, and he and the paper's executives were rarely tempted to take them on. They were a fact of journalistic life, like chains on a slave's ankles. On a turnover of £400,000,000 the group would be lucky to make £500,000 profit. It was never going to be able to continue; the unions were simply and suicidally paving the way for Robert Maxwell and Rupert Murdoch.

After a few weeks as a feature writer, I was fed up. No one was expected to do anything - or were rebuked if they did nothing - except the regular columnists like Waterhouse and Marge Proops. I wrote several features, but each was no more than a short day's work. Other writers contributed even less. John Pilger, still living on the reputation he made during the war against

Vietnam and consumed by a hatred of America, would disappear for weeks, write about an issue that concerned him and then disappear again. His copy was inviolable. No sub-editor was allowed to touch it. Later in my career there, when I was an assistant editor, I saw an article by him which said, in a long anti-American diatribe, that Richard Nixon, the Watergate President, had been arrested. I told the sub-editor dealing with the copy to strike it out. He protested that he couldn't. "Mr Pilger's copy is not to be touched," he said. I insisted that it was inaccurate and out it came.

Another inactive writer, Eric Wainwright, was a kindly, friendly man for whom one felt an instant affection on the occasions, once a month, when he came in to collect his expenses. But he never wrote anything in the 13 years I was at the paper. I once asked why he was able to live this non-working life and was told that he had done "great things for the paper in Cyprus."

Good luck to him. There were others on the paper that did little more for less reason. An attempt was made once while I was there to get Eric back into print. He happily agreed and went to his desk in the Features Department which had been unused for many years. He reached it and said, "Good God, someone's pinched my typewriter" - the chain holding it to the desk had been severed, possibly months or years earlier. That ended any likelihood of him resuming an active career and Eric toddled off to resume his monthly visits until he formally retired.

We had a dartboard in the Features room with which we would while the time away between lunch and evening departure. The then Features editor, Roy Harris, who seemed permanently harassed, paid us a rare visit one day, saw the board and wrote a letter to us (!) demanding that it be taken down and not used again. We pinned it to the dartboard and competed to see how many times we could hit it. Paul Callan, a bow-tied, elegantly dressed reporter, who specialised in covering important funerals and claimed to have been educated at Eton (the managing editor, Neil Bentley, investigated Callan and said that for "Eton" we should read "Norwood Grammar"), bet me £1 he could get nearer to the bull's eye than I. When he lost, he doubled the money. And again. And again. When his debt reached £254, I called a halt and we settled for him giving me £100 for a youth club in Bermondsey. That was the hard-drinking, swift-moving, dare-devil, rip-roaring, dangerous glamorous world of Fleet Street in the 1970s when journalists thrived on surviving perilous situations. You were always in danger of entering the room and being hit by a wayward dart.

I had just decided I had had enough of not working when the leader-writer, David Tattersall, went on holiday and I was asked to fill in for him. I was happy to: it gave me something to do every day. Unfortunately, Molloy and/or Tony Miles, the mercurial deputy chairman, a brilliant writer who hated writing, decided they wanted to keep me in the post. David threw a cup of tea at a clock on the wall when he heard the news. I was sorry about it because I liked David but the sloth was driving me mad. The change gave me a room of my own.

One day, *Panorama* wanted to film another lengthy interview with me in that room. I sought the necessary permissions, which included one from the Electricians' Union because of the possibility that extra lighting would have to be used by the BBC's electricians. The *Mirror's* ETU were agreeable – provided that the BBC gave them 10 days' notice. They were trying it on. When told them their demand was ridiculous and that *Panorama* was a news programme not a monthly magazine, they generously agreed to give permission, provided two of their members were in attendance throughout. So two electricians sat in the corridor outside my room for two hours on double time while the broadcast took place. Their services were never required or requested. The next time the BBC wanted to interview me they booked a room in the Charing Cross Hotel. It was cheaper and without fuss.

Union leaders have asked me, deeply pained, why they always received a bad press. That was a small instance why, together with countless other examples of Spanish practices, as their restrictions were known. Journalists, for example, at that time – 1977! – were on a four-day week with six weeks' holiday a year, got a month's sabbatical every four years, were muttering about asking for a month's paternity leave and got days off in lieu of working bank holidays, Easter and Christmas. I worked out that if a wife had two children in a year (it is done – Lady Falkender had two in 10 months) then a journalist need work only 132 days in his sabbatical year of double parenthood. The printing unions schemes for earning more money for less work were more ingenious, less open, more scandalous and verged on the criminal (demanding money with menaces). That is why the press were generally hostile. Even the most liberal minded executives, like Sydney Jacobson, had no sympathy for them. You can be afraid of a bully but never sorry for him.

Despite the intrigues and blackmail of the unions, the journalists were fantastically loyal to the paper, even if many of them were sceptical of editors and the executives around them. Bosses came and went, the paper was permanent. Over the years I have had the same attitude towards leaders of the Labour party. But it was hard for journalists when a big story broke to find that the only edition published that day was the early one for Wales and they couldn't get their news in the paper. More seriously for its future, London football supporters of, say, Arsenal, Chelsea, Tottenham or Millwall (me) did not wat to read of the exploits of Newport County over their breakfast. It was a tribute to the loyalty of the readers that the *Mirror* was still selling well over 3,00,000 copies a day and when my book was serialised, along with other big serialisations shortly afterwards it crept back over the 4,000,000 mark.

The paper jogged along and industrial disputes came and went but still the paper thrived until, politically, in 1978, we had a disaster affecting our reputation. Early in August, Terry Lancaster received a call from Tom McNally, Prime Minister Jim Callaghan's chief political adviser, asking for him and me to travel to Rye, in Sussex, where he was on holiday and meet him for lunch (we paying, of course). Callaghan's Government was in trouble. It had no majority and had been propped up for a couple of years by an understanding with David Steel's Liberal party which kept them in office. An election had to be held by October, 1979, and the outlook for success was poor. However, things had brightened during that summer and the prospects were improving. There was at least a chance that if an election was held that year we might win again.

McNally's news was exciting: Callaghan had secretly decided to call a general election in the second week of October, he said, naming the exact date. McNally was clear and definite. We could publish the news as long as we kept secret his involvement. The *Mirror* splashed Lancaster's story. Most political correspondents were on holiday and the rest of Fleet Street took the news cautiously. But it was the *Mirror* saying it and we were the paper closest to the Government as well as its principal, if only, newspaper supporter. We repeated the "fact" at every opportunity with the greatest confidence. After all, our source was impeccable.

There were phone calls between Lancaster and McNally and we saw him again at the TUC's Brighton conference early in September. He was emphatic: the general election was going ahead. What is more, he said, he had booked Harold Wilson and David Basnett, general secretary of the Municipal and General Workers' Union, to speak at his own eve of poll meeting at Stockport, where he was to be the Labour candidate. A warning bell might have rung at that moment but it was too distant for us to hear it. But I was concerned that neither Tom McCaffrey, Callaghan's Press Secretary, nor Bernard Donoughue, his chief policy adviser, knew anything at all about Callaghan's plans and they told me so.

I put the doubt out of my mind. Callaghan was notoriously secretive and operated on a need to know basis. I once had a covert meeting with the leader of the Portuguese opposition, Mario Suarez, before the dictator, President Salazar, was ousted and reported back to a meeting of officials with Callaghan in the chair. I had only spoken a sentence or two when Callaghan abruptly interrupted me and said the meeting was over. After the others had left, he explained to me that what I was saying was too sensitive and should not be known beyond himself.

Stories about the election were now widespread and Michael Foot was said to be urging Callaghan not to go. Callaghan himself had teased the TUC conference with a mystifying rendering of "There was I Waiting at the Church" and no one knew what he meant. (No. 10 asked me who had sung it; I told them Vesta Tilley, but his speechwriter thought that Marie Lloyd was better known and attributed it to her instead. Amateurs!) Then, after the conference came the expected call to Lancaster from Downing Street and he left with high expectations to meet the Prime Minister..

He returned grey and shocked. There was to be no election. Callaghan said he had never intended to have one and whoever Lancaster's informant was, was wrong. Lancaster was devastated and the *Mirror* was in a pit of McNally's making.

I urged Terry that he was no longer bound by our promise of secrecy and that he should write the whole story of McNally's lies and expose him. He thought he was still bound not to name him. I disagreed and still do, which is why I am writing this now. Lancaster and the *Mirror* were the victims of fake news. Donald Trump didn't invent the concept.

We had to run the story big, of course, and we did so under a headline I suggested: "Jim Unfixes It," leaving the reader to infer (wrongly) that he had fixed it in the first place. The effect on Lancaster was profound. He thought his reputation had been damaged, and it had, and I don't think he ever fully recovered from McNally's betrayal. He grew increasingly reluctant to write his column, though he handled the subsequent election in 1979 and Mrs Thatcher's victory with admirable professionalism. Apart from the mental hurt of McNally's lying he had begun to suffer from rheumatoid-arthritis and it hurt him physically.

Years later, in his retirement, Callaghan asked me about our general election story and why we had run it with such certainty. I told him. He stated emphatically that he had never said anything to McNally to give him the idea of an early election and dismissed him, irritatingly, saying "he was only thinking of himself and his safe seat." But Callaghan hadn't helped. He teased the TUC and he teased trade union leaders with whom he lunched. He could have killed the story but never did. McNally never blamed Callaghan, nor did he ever apologise, either to Lancaster or to me.

It was almost unbelievable that more than 30 years later, McNally, having scuttled to the Liberal Democrats via the Social Democratic party and reached the House of Lords and membership of the David Cameron Government – typifying his transferable loyalty – and after he had finally admitted his guilt, should be one of the parliamentarians who set up, under royal charter, the body to choose a panel to regulate the press, which led to the Max Mosley-funded body, Impress, which every newspaper boycotted. A sense of decent shame should have led him to excuse himself from that role.

McNally had betrayed Lancaster, in particular, and me but when the election came in 1979 there was another betrayal, this time of Callaghan, which was unknown at the time and little noticed since and concerning someone we both knew exceptionally well, Lady Falkender. Charles Moore, the biographer of Margaret Thatcher, discovered she had approach Gordon Reese, Thatcher's PR adviser and, Alistair McAlpine, treasurer of the Conservative party, offering to help to defeat Callaghan. She was a Labour peeress taking the Labour whip and Callaghan's secretary before she joined Wilson. How she got away with it without being expelled from the party is still a mystery.

After that election, Lancaster remained sore. The Labour party saw a resurgence of its latent left-wing activism and elected Michael Foot as its leaders. I'm not being wise after the event: I wrote at the time that Foot - a delightful, highly intelligent and genuinely amusing man, unlike most figures on the left – would be a disaster and so he proved. An attempt by Tony Benn, a left-winger with many of the attributes of Foot but who had lost his sense of humour, to become deputy leader caused a major crisis in the Labour party and a minor one between me and Lancaster. Benn opposed Denis Healey, a robust intellectual, physically and mentally who would not call a man a fool without a preceding adjective. He was fitted mentally to be a Prime Minister, especially in wartime.

Terry Lancaster knew very few of the younger people in the party and, what's more, didn't want to and announced he was going to stay in his hotel bedroom while the deputy leadership votes were being counted in the Brighton party conference centre. I promised to return to him with the result so that he could write the story. That, because of the party's chosen timetable, was going to come very close to the first edition printing of the national newspapers. The party went to extraordinary lengths to keep the secrecy of the ballot result. All the tellers at the count were to remain in the room while the count was conducted and had to stay there until after it had been announced. No method of communication with the outside world was allowed. Tellers were only to be allowed to leave the room for an urgent call of nature and then only if accompanied by a party official. Under no circumstances were they allowed to speak, wink or gesture to any of the reporters outside. And that was the flaw in their security. I arranged with one of the tellers, a good friend, that if Healey was the winner she would ask to go to the toilet. If she did, that was all I wanted. No signals. She walked past us, with escort, without raising her eyes or looking at anyone, and I ran all the way back to the hotel to Lancaster's room and told him Healey had won. He said he had been caught like that before (McNally) and he wasn't going to write it until it had been officially announced.

And I wasn't going to waste the careful arrangements I had made with his knowledge and then miss the story. I decided to bypass Lancaster and telephoned Mike Molloy and gave him the result. There was just time to get it into the paper on the front page. That deepened the rift between us and I wasn't in the least apologetic, though I cursed McNally once more. When the election date was finally decided Tom McCaffrey told me when it would be. I passed it on to Lancaster. He told me he didn't believe McCaffrey or me.

It was our custom at the *Mirror* that each day, before the content of the day's leader was decided, we would discuss the possible subjects. One day, there was a big political story - which I have long forgotten - which Terry told me he would deal with in his column. So when the usual leader writer's conference was held – Molloy, Miles, Lancaster, Geoffrey Goodman and me – I suggested a different topic. Miles asked why I wasn't writing about the other issue. I said Terry was dealing with it in his column. Miles exploded, tactlessly: "The leader is more important than the column." Terry got up, said he was resigning and walked out. It wasn't my fault but our relationship worsened even more after that. He didn't go, though. He was at his desk the following day and nothing more was said.

The *Mirror* opposed the Falklands war. Miles, Molloy and I thought there were other ways to settle the dispute and that Britain's policy in that part of the world should not be determined by 1,600 descendants of Welsh farmers. Lancaster and Goodman, both former RAF officers, disagreed, but we all accepted that as soon as the fighting started we would drop our opposition. It wasn't a popular policy and we lost readership.

Journalists come and go, but our best recruit during this period was Paul Foot, scion of the famous Liberal/Labour family, a member of the extreme left Socialist Workers' Party, and, coincidentally, a friend of Kay Carmichael's. We were looking for a good investigative reporter and I suggested Paul to Molloy. Molloy knew him and jumped at it, but ran into a problem immediately: Paul rejected the offered salary of £15,000. He said it was too much. Molloy asked me to speak to him. I did and my line was simple: if he took less he was undercutting other journalists on similar salaries (like me), which was not a comradely thing to do. (In his star-struck autobiography, Molloy puts Foot's salary at £40,000 and my arguments to Paul become his arguments; for those who know us both, it depends on whom you think has the best memory). Paul saw the point and joined and was one of the *Mirror's* great successes until Robert Maxwell came along. I'm surprised at the £40,000 figure Molloy quoted. In those days that was close to an editor's salary: around the same time we could have had Alan Titchmarsh to write a gardening column for us for £15,000 a year and Molloy turned him down.

It was during my years at the *Sun* that I first met Robert Maxwell. I already knew of him by disrepute and observation from the Press Gallery. He was, according to a common consensus, bumptious, arrogant, rude, loud, vain, untrustworthy and insensitive to individuals and the mores and conventions of the House of Commons. A pirate rather than a buccaneer. An interloper. A foreigner. The kindest thing said about him was that he was like Horatio Bottomley, the jingoist proprietor of *John Bull* and MP during the First World War. He was a great entertainer but ended up in prison. Maxwell was as amusing, in a frightening kind of way and might well have ended up in prison as well but for his sudden death. The shortened summary of opinion then of Maxwell was that he was a crook, a sweeping allegation without specifics but a description I was to use when I opposed, at an emergency chapel (trade union members) meeting, his takeover of the *Mirror* group. He was, however, a Labour MP for the constituency of Buckingham - though he looked like a whale out of water - and as a political reporter I had to deal with him as such.

I was eventually to write a biography of Maxwell, as a result of a considerable change of mind on my part, which is not to say I never lost my suspicions. After all, even his name wasn't true. He was born Ludvik Hoch, eldest son of a Ruthenian Jewish labourer in the small village of Solotvino in the foothills of the Carpathians in Eastern Czechoslovakia. His mother, father, three sisters, a brother and his grandfather died in Auschwitz concentration camp. Two other siblings died in infancy. Maxwell (as Hoch) fled Czechoslovakia when the Germans were threatening it in early 1939, made his way to the Lebanon and joined the French Foreign Legion at the age of 16. Transported to France in 1940, when he was still only 17, he had barely arrived in Marseilles before he was evacuated to England, not speaking a word of English.

He decided to adopt an English name, however, toying with several before choosing du Maurier, which he had seen on a cigarette packet. I joked once that it was lucky he hadn't first seen a packet of Bisto. To those who were disrespectful about his foreignness, he had a short, irrefutable answer: "You are British by an accident of birth. I chose to be British." He eventually discarded du Maurier for the more English, or Scottish, Maxwell. It was symbolic of his attitude towards facts. If he didn't like them, he changed them.

He had a chequered history, no pun intended, winning a Military Cross with a recklessness he was later to bring to his business affairs (his commanding officer told him he would either get killed or be court-martialled when he announced he was going to attack a house held by the Germans with British prisoners inside it; rescuing them, he narrowly missing being killed by a British rifleman who heard his accent and thought he was German). About the same time, he shot the mayor of a German town who had approached under the shelter of a white flag to surrender. His reason was that the German SS had fired on members of his battalion when they were protected by a white flag.

Victor Sassie, the celebrated Birkenhead-born Hungarian proprietor of the Gay Hussar restaurant in Soho, seemed to have a close but mysterious acquaintance with Maxwell in his early days. Sassie, like Maxwell, was abroad when war broke out but returned to this country in 1940. He claimed to know a lot about Maxwell's military record. He says that it was not only the mayor that Maxwell shot but several other German civilians; he also claimed that Maxwell promised to wipe out a troublesome German machine gun-post, provided his commanding officer recommended him for a VC if he succeeded. According to Sassie, the CO made that promise and Maxwell destroyed the machine-gun nest, but he didn't get the ultimate military honour for bravery. One of those instances where if you ask you don't get. Strangely, on several occasions when I raised his friendship with Sassie with him Maxwell refused to discuss it and changed the subject. He refused even to confirm what Sassie had told me, that he and Sassie used to sell goods from the back of a car in London's most notorious street market, Petticoat Lane. I often went to the Lane in my 'teens. They would not have been out of place there..

I discovered the white flag episode in going through his archive with his outstanding archivist, Wendy Whitworth. When he realised that I was intending to use this in my biography of him he was agitated and asked me to remove it. I refused, saying that it displayed an essential part of his character. "I might be regarded as a war criminal," he said. I replied that no one was going to prosecute a Jewish officer in the British army who family had perished in Auschwitz for shooting a German civilian in 1944. I did not know at that point that there may have been other victims as well.

Twenty years after the war, having first made a fortune and acquired the ability to speak 10 languages, Maxwell became a Labour MP. Victor Sassie was a life-long socialist, which suggests another connection between them. Petticoat Lane then was a long way from the Gay Hussar which Victor started in 1953 and the international publishing empire Maxwell was still building until it collapsed in such spectacular fashion. They were a couple of outstanding, if unusual, socialist entrepreneurs.

Our first meeting was an occasion for stimulating my dislike. Maxwell was chairman of the House of Commons Catering Committee and had caused outrage among long-serving MPs by determining that the House's restaurants and cafes should pay their way, partly by selling off a very fine wine cellar whose contents were being sold for a song at the MPs' dinner tables. In an inept charm offensive he invited me and two other political reporters, plus an attractive young woman whose name, occupation and purpose I never discovered, to lunch at the Commons (including fine wine) to explain what he was doing. He was impressive if boastful, spoke a lot and listened impatiently, but we were near-persuaded of his intentions to modernise what was, in effect, an old buffers' dining club enjoying valuable wines sold cheaply. When the young woman said she had to leave, Maxwell courteously rose to show her out of the building. Discourteously, he never returned to us, though we waited 45 minutes for him. The charm offensive had failed. He had, as the cliché has it, snatched defeat from the jaws of victory. Not for the only time in his career.

Early in May, 1984, Roy Hattersley, deputy leader of the Labour party and no friend of the "bouncing Czech" as Maxwell was already known, warned me that the businessman was intending to take over the *Mirror* group. An occasional lunch party consisting of the leader-writing committee and Bob Edwards, editor of the *Sunday Mirror,* was about to meet and eat and I told them about it. Shock! Horror! Surprise? Not in the least.

Molloy was mildly alarmed, Miles brushed it aside, understandably so because he had been guaranteed more than once by Sir Alex Jarrett, chairman of Reed International, owners of the group, that it would never, ever, be sold to Maxwell. Edwards laughed, but didn't explain why, Lancaster said nothing and only Goodman shared my consternation. If Miles was naïve in trusting Jarrett, I was doubly so in trusting some of my colleagues

Shortly afterwards I heard from Hattersley again. He had now been told by a friend of Maxwell, presumably the same person who had told him in the first place, that he had lost all interest in the papers and would not be bidding. In the light of what subsequently happened, I have no doubt that Maxwell had been told about the lunch and my contribution to it and decided to deny any interest in case it scuppered his plans. My doubts were briefly, but only briefly, erased. Maxwell had been trying to crash into Fleet Street for many years and news that he was circling began to spread again and he was not going to give up easily.

Suddenly, in early July, the rumours began to gain substance. Reed's still maintained that they wouldn't sell to Maxwell, even for the £105,000,000 he was said to be offering. But they didn't say it with the same conviction. He was overshadowing every conversation in the News Room and an emergency chapel meeting was called on the afternoon of July 12, 1984, to discuss what attitude they would take. I totally misread my colleagues, not for the only time. I thought they would be ready to strike to stop Maxwell. Not in the least. They were all say and no do.

I made an impassioned speech warning that the only way to stop a takeover was to prevent Maxwell from ever entering the building. Once he was in, I said, the fight would be lost. I forecast that there would be 3,000 redundancies within six weeks and I called him a "crook." I did not mean, and nobody took me to mean, that I had evidence of criminality because if I had I would have reported it to the police and stopped him. Anything I could do. My meaning was absolutely clear: by "crook" I meant he was not to be trusted. Paul Foot and John Pilger, our two renowned left-wingers, were there but said nothing, though Pilger said a lot afterwards, much of it inaccurate, and Foot deliberately antagonised Maxwell so that he would sack him, a kind of heroic resignation. For political reasons, he preferred to be sacked and the paper lost the best investigative reporter it ever had. David Thompson, the father of the chapel, supported me and said if

Maxwell came in the front door he would go out of the back. Freddie Wills, the diplomatic correspondent, and David Seymour, my occasional deputy as leader writer, did the same. But Paul Callan spoke up for the craven. "Let us at least give the man a chance," he said, in probably the most obtuse sentence of his career. The chapel, with some abstentions, supported him with only five votes against to support me. They had thrown in the towel before the fight started. Those who voted for Maxwell at that meeting bore a huge responsibility for what happened afterwards but never admitted it.

All this is relevant to the Maxwell and the *Mirror* story and what happened later. Despite its promises, Reed's had sold out, saying it was an offer they couldn't refuse and Maxwell was the new owner. Ominously, for those who were superstitious, Maxwell entered the building the next day, Friday the Thirteenth of July. It was my day off but I telephoned early to find out what time the next chapel meeting would be held. There wasn't to be one, so I went raspberry picking with my wife, instead. That simply confirmed their surrender and determined my attitude for the future.

Clive Thornton, who had been installed by Reed's as the chairman of the papers, was a modest man who had lost a leg in a childhood accident. He had successfully run a building society, but he was completely at a loss among journalists. He did not like their culture, seeming to him to be one of heavy drinking and lavish lunches, all paid for by generous expenses, and generally louche behaviour. Why he was chosen, reputedly on Tony Miles's recommendation, was a mystery. His new employees were not the sort of people he might unhesitatingly have extended a mortgage to in his previous occupation. For some reason, he took to coming down to my room and consulting me about the papers and their workers, but I was never able to make him understand the journalistic ethos. He was memorably described by Paddy O'Gara, a genius in newspaper make-up and not unknown in the office pub, the Stab in the Back: "In the land of the legless, the one-legged man is king." He made one symbolic gesture towards moderation in the short time he was there. The very large chairman's room occupied by Cecil King, once a legend, now forgotten, was divided by him into two. Thornton, a small man, was uncomfortable with its original size and opulence. Maxwell's first instruction when he moved in was to have the wall destroyed. Size and opulence were what he was about.

My wife and I talked seriously about what would likely happen when I went into the office that Sunday. In view of my opposition to him, I expected the sack. It would not have been unreasonable. But that turned out not to be Maxwell's way: he embraced his enemies the better to control them. The front page of the *Mirror* on the Saturday was full of a message from Maxwell about the future of Britain and the future of his papers (his purchase also included the *Sunday People*), written by Terry Lancaster. I wasn't asked, thankfully; I couldn't have done it. Maxwell, although he spoke 10 languages, did not easily command written English. In any case, why bark when you have a whole kennel to do it for you?

I hadn't been in the building for long that Sunday when the inevitable message came from Maxwell: he wanted to see me in his office on the ninth floor. Everyone knew I had been summoned. It was a moment of high tension for me and general interest among the others. A public execution was expected.

When I got to his office, work had already begun to dismantle the wall dividing his office. Maxwell didn't like to hang about; he was chronically impatient about everything and with me he got straight to the point: "I have been telling Mike and Tony" (Molloy and Miles, both of whom were with him, with Molloy giving me an encouraging smile and Miles standing stone-faced) "about my plans for the paper, which I will willingly tell you , but you have not said you are staying."

At that point, no one had asked me if I was leaving, either, but clearly someone had been talking; who, I found out much later.

There was no point beating about the bush for either of us. I said: "I will stay if you will agree to my conditions." "And they are?" asked Maxwell. "That the *Mirror* remains committed to supporting the Labour party, that you do not tell me what to write and you do not interfere with anything I have written," I replied.

I had under-estimated him; like many others, I was outsmarted by him. "I agree," he said and I had walked into a trap of my own making. I had laid down my conditions for staying and he had accepted them. I could hardly then have told him that was not good enough. Therefore, I was committed to staying. That settled that. "There is one further thing," said Maxwell. "Mike wants me to make you an assistant editor." Molloy nodded. It was my turn to accept and I did. No extra pay was involved – I was already being paid the rate for an assistant editor; it just gave me an additional authority. And it was clearly Molloy's decision. Or so it seemed. But I was too hasty and regretted it afterwards. It looked as if I had been bought.

When I returned to the News Room groups of colleagues were waiting to question me. "Have you resigned on principle? one reporter asked. It was a day for one-liners. "I am not going to resign on principle to a man who hasn't got any," I replied. Another reporter asked: "Is you job secure?" "So secure," I replied, "that I'm going to buy a weekly season ticket." The personal crisis seemed to be over. Later that day, Maxwell invited me to the first of a series of lunches he was intending to hold each Tuesday. He listed the others who would be present: the editors and Geoffrey Goodman. I asked about Lancaster. He said he wasn't inviting him, an ominous note. I told him I couldn't attend unless Lancaster was present and he readily changed his mind. I didn't know that he and Bob Edwards had already discussed Lancaster's presence and deliberately decided to omit him.

The lunch was jolly on the surface, if on edge and mutually suspicious underneath. Halfway through it, Maxwell banged on the table for attention and said: "I think you ought to know this: Joe feels so secure in his job that he has bought a weekly season ticket." Everyone laughed or smiled, which they would have done even if they hadn't found it funny, and I was appalled. A private conversation I had had with fellow journalists had swiftly and treacherously been repeated to Maxwell. I asked him later how he had heard. "Two or three different sources," he replied. He may have been lying, but one was enough so far as I was concerned. On the Friday of that week, my remark about not resigning on principle to a man who didn't have any appeared in *The Spectator,* the Tory magazine. Someone, a colleague, a fellow-reporter who thought I should have resigned at Maxwell's coming (no one else did, by the way, except Tony Miles) was trying to engineer my departure by other means. A mass resignation would have been one thing and I would have joined it, but a symbolic resignation, by me alone, was another. I needed to work and pay my mortgage as they did. The brilliant Keith Waterhouse, who dubbed Maxwell Cap't Bob, resigned much later, another sad loss, but it wasn't only because of Maxwell.

It didn't take long before Maxwell broke his promise about not interfering with what I had written. It was my practice to circulate my leading article to the chairman, editor, the News Editor (for the chief sub-editor) and Lancaster, and to show it to Goodman if the article was on industrial affairs. A week after his arrival, the copy sent to Maxwell returned heavily altered, in wording, clarity and meaning. I promptly went to all the recipients and told them to take my name off the leader and insert Maxwell's. I then asked the editor to tell Maxwell that if anything like that ever happened again I would this time resign. It never did. I believe Maxwell was trying out my resolve.

Maxwell's sheer size, over 6ft tall and weighing at least 250lbs, intimidated his staff, and not only the journalists. His bombast terrified those who knew him until then only by reputation. He required immediate answers, immediate solutions and instant attention with the threat, sometimes implicit, sometimes explicit, of the sack if he didn't get it. He took to asking my advice on almost everything, to my surprise, and frequently turned up in the News Room asking for me instead of calling me up to his room. Given what I had said about him, it was embarrassing. I didn't understand then why he was treating me with such respect. Bob Edwards was to show me one reason why. Another, deeper, reason was to emerge much later.

Edwards was the great survivor of Fleet Street, his own words. Elegant, handsome, with an easy charm and persuasive voice, he loved the comparison of his looks with that of a a Hollywood star, Joseph Cotten, and frequently made it himself. He had worked for

Lord Beaverbrook, a self-made Canadian terrorist of an employer, held to his left-wing opinions, refused to write leaders in support of the Suez invasion, which was far-seeing and courageous, edited the *Daily Express* when it was the giant of the popular press, and *The People* and at the time of Maxwell's arrival, was editor of the *Sunday Mirror.* He retained his friendship with the left of the Labour party, particularly Michael Foot, and fitted easily into the Left attitudes of the group. He was also an obsessive intriguer and renowned escapologist, a British Houdini, from tricky situations in Fleet Street.

In his autobiography, *Goodbye to Fleet Street*, probably the most literate by any former editor, Edwards was frank. He and Maxwell had known each other for 20 years. They exchanged Christmas cards (at that level, Christmas cards are an investment, not a seasonal greeting). Maxwell phoned him regularly at the *Sunday Mirror* to see what was in the other Sundays' first editions and he phoned Edwards, two days before his takeover, telling him he was bidding for the *Mirror* group. What Edwards didn't reveal in his book was that he was in touch with Maxwell before that call and the bid and, in order not to be overheard, used to get his driver to take him out of the Holborn area so that he could speak to Maxwell from a public call-box. He had no hesitation on the Wednesday before Friday the Thirteenth in offering Maxwell his advice on how to succeed in his bid, even though it had yet to be agreed with his employers whose public position was that they would not accept it.

"Whatever you do," Edwards said, "don't attack the *Mirror* papers. Say they are first-class with good editors." It was unnecessary for him to add that he was one of those editors, but vanity would have compelled it. Maxwell did as he suggested. If he had rejected the advice, Edwards said, Maxwell would have had all the editors against him – including Edwards, who hadn't at that point thought to consult his editor-colleagues, including those in Scotland, either about Maxwell's imminent arrival or the terms on which they might accept him.

Edwards's detailed recounting of the manoeuvres among the Board's directors and senior executives are a brilliant insight into what went on at executive level. The reaction of some at Maxwell's coming was craven, except for Tony Miles. He retained his fury at Reed's betrayal and left soon afterwards. But I was more concerned to discover what Edwards said about me (without ever telling me, of course). Maxwell told him he wanted to run some campaigns and Edwards said: "The one person you must have if you are to run good campaigns is a brilliant leader writer. Joe Haines is possibly the best in the country." Edwards, with his ineffable immodesty, added: "(Since for some years some people thought I was, I did not wish to concede entirely.)" He added to Maxwell: "He loathes you, told the chapel you were a crook [correct] and said that if you walked through the front door he would go out the back [incorrect, that was Thompson] But he's the one."

The plot thickened. Maxwell instructed Edwards to invite me to the editors' lunch to be held the following Tuesday. "Certainly," replied Edwards but he said at that point that Terry Lancaster would have to be invited, too. He had brought me into the company, was my boss and the paper's political chief. According to Edwards, Maxell replied, "No, I don't want Terry. I want to please Joe. *Terry's an old friend of mine.*" (my italics). When I read this passage, things began to fall into place and I wondered how I had been so gullible.

When at that lunch Maxwell mentioned my joke about buying a weekly season ticket, Edwards said I told Maxwell "with his[my] icy smile": You are on probation." That remark would have astonished Maxwell's managers in his other businesses, said Edwards, who would have regarded such bravado as the equivalent of diving into a water tub from the top of the Empire State Building. All very flattering to my ego, but I had decided I would go on as I had begun on the previous Sunday. What I didn't know was that Maxwell had decided the same and wasn't to be deflected by defiance. It's a pity Edwards didn't report my further remark, that I would not accept from Maxwell, a backbencher, what I did not accept from a Prime Minister, Harold Wilson. Anyway, at my insistence, Lancaster was there and he attended every lunch until Maxwell decided to sack him later in the year.

I wrote a furious letter to Edwards when I read his version of events and he was genuinely astonished at my reaction. But I regarded his behaviour as treacherous. I think I over-reacted. He did pay me one final compliment: "Without him, the strong, consistent editorial policy and powerful advocacy that had been handed down from the Cudlipp era would have been lost." Perhaps, perhaps not. Molloy could always have asked Joyce Hopkirk to do it.

Maxwell couldn't leave his new toy alone. He had the very mistaken idea that a slavish readership would follow whatever Fleet Street instructed them to do. Politicians and newspaper proprietors should never under-estimate the intelligence of their voters or readers, yet they do so, at every general election or newspaper takeover. However, it is difficult to over-estimate a proprietor's ambition, either. Like a true man of money, Maxwell thought he could increase the circulation of his papers by expensive give-away schemes like a £1million bingo prize. The papers were full of these, week after week, but I, fortunately, never had anything to do with them. Looking back, I'm surprised he never thought of giving the papers away. That might have been amazingly successful. He also decided that *Mirror* writers would tour the country to meet the readers. I went in a party, including Marge Proops, by train to Manchester but didn't meet any readers except two Northern executives of the paper whom our night editor, with me as his partner, challenged to play snooker for money. We won comfortably, despite his deliberately throwing away the first of a match of three frames and then doubling the stakes. . He was a friend of and played with Alex "Hurricane" Higgins, at the time probably the best player in the country, not a fact he mentioned to our Northern colleagues.

More seriously, Maxwell decided he was the one to end the miners' strike, which had begun the final decline of the miners' union. He, Bob Edwards, John Pilger and I went to talk about so doing with Arthur Scargill in Sheffield. Predictably, it got nowhere. Two massive egos locked horns like stags and it was a day wasted, a conclusion already reached by Pilger who watched sourly and said nothing. Maxwell's heart was often in the right place, like the

Labour party's, but he got his decisions wrong. It was a hot day and we returned to London by helicopter. Maxwell sat in the front with the pilot and Edwards and I in the back. Maxwell, a man who suffered from the heat, opened the window and put his hand out, deflecting the rush of air to us in the back, so we suffered a draught all the way to London, having achieved absolutely nothing.

He also decided he wanted a platform for his ideas which none of us, me included, was willing to provide under our own name, so he revived a pseudonym once used by Hugh Cudlipp and Lancaster and Goodman wrote articles for him under the name of Charles Wilberforce. Edwards thought I largely ghosted them. I didn't. That was part of my agreement with Maxwell. I was not to be told what to write. Edwards praised as "brilliant" a full page article attacking the *Sun,* at Maxwell's command, but got his dates mixed up - it appeared 18 months before Maxwell arrived on the scene.

During this time, Maxwell, for whatever reason, could not have been kinder to me personally and it would be curmudgeonly not to say so. He asked to see me every day on one thing or another; when my wife was taken ill by an obscure affliction I had never heard of (Bornholm's disease, named after a Scandinavian island where it first appeared) Maxwell knew of it, and offered to send down "my surgeon" to attend her and then offered us a three-week holiday in Portugal, all on his credit card, while she recovered. We turned down both offers: the first because it would have been embarrassing, the second because, as my wife said, we would have been beholden to him. It was a clear sign that he wanted friendship and was prepared to buy it and I slowly realised that he had no friends. It was, in many ways, a gap in his life which was to have disastrous consequences.

In essence, he was a lonely man surrounded by people, metaphorically tugging their forelocks and saying, "Yessir" or "Nossir" when the occasion demanded. He actually enjoyed someone disagreeing with him, provided that, in the end, he got his way. Most times. He wanted loyalty but not blind obedience. He wanted admiration but not subservience. He hated the establishment but longed to be accepted by them for his achievements. He resented Rupert Murdoch for the way he eventually gained acceptance in British society and couldn't understand it was his fault that he wasn't .

In April, 1987, I bought a new house with a wooded garden of over an acre, fulfilling a long-term ambition. In that October, a hurricane laid waste to much of southern England, especially Kent. In Sevenoaks, the eponymous trees were all destroyed. More important to me, I woke to find 38 mature trees in my garden wrecked and a Cedar of Lebanon, believed to have been planted in 1642 (the area was once owned by Elizabeth I and other royals before and after her) was so severely damaged it had, eventually, to be taken down. But for the immediate crisis I had no solution. I told no one at the office except my deputy, David Thompson – and he told Maxwell. He phoned me on the Tuesday, saying he was sending down his head gardener – an Irish viscount, no less - and a team of six men to clear the debris. It took them two weeks, driving from Oxford each morning, to complete the job and remove the timber by lorry or by bonfire. I thanked him; he never mentioned it again.

To digress, while my wife was in hospital I collaborated with a Channel 4 TV producer who said my leader-writing was similar to writing a speech (which I had done regularly for years for Harold Wilson) and he believed in the "theory of three" where the use of using three different ways all at once to say the same thing (for example, "fair, right and just") in a speech strengthened its impact. He wanted to judge that impact in a public arena and his chosen subject to carry out the experiment was the wife of a London taxi driver who was attending the Social and Democratic Party's annual conference.

The TV team brought her to my home so that I could hear her views and make a speech out of them. What she was doing in the SDP was beyond me; her outlook on politics was similar to many taxi drivers I had encountered. She would have done better on the right-wing of the Conservative party. She was in favour of grammar schools – which the chairman of the conference, Shirley Williams, and most of her party, were against – in favour of public schools (ditto) and against immigration. She was reluctant to let go of her ideas but we persuaded her she had to for the sake of the programme. Instead, I wrote a speech mocking all her listeners in the hall for being middle-class *Guardian* readers and leaving plenty of pauses for applause. There is nothing such an audience likes better than to be rebuked by a working-class sister, as long as she is not their sister-in-law. They loved her. The applause and laughter came repeatedly, in what was only a four-minute speech. We had even calculated how much time that applause would take up and decided the length of the speech accordingly.

Robin Day, the prime TV interviewer of the age, ordered BBC staff to "get hold of her" and bring her to his studio for interview but it was whispered to him, confidentially, that the whole thing was a hoax. No one told the *Guardian* leader writer, however, and with its usual senatorial pomposity the paper singled out two speeches at the conference: the first, it said, carefully crafted over weeks before, was by the leader of the SDP, David Owen; the second, more spontaneous, was by the wife of the London taxi driver. In fact, had they but known it, her speech was even more craftily calculated than Owen's. It wouldn't have made the *Guardian* feel any better about me when they found out eventually, but it made me feel better about the *Guardian*. To use the theory of three, you could say they had been caught hook, line and sinker. It paid them back for the semi-vendetta they had carried on against me during the Wilson years. And it was welcome fun away from the *Mirror*.

* * * * * *

In the autumn of 1984, Maxwell told me he intended to sack his "old friend" Terry Lancaster and replace him as political editor with me. I had discovered, as journalists eventually do, that before Maxwell's overt move to buy the papers, Lancaster had twice written to him urging him to do so. Maxwell attached a great deal to loyalty. It was one thing to collaborate with Bob Edwards because Maxwell had initiated it and Edwards was made vice-chairman of MGN. It was another to contact Maxwell unasked, which is what Terry had done and I believe that was a deciding factor in getting rid of him, apart from what I later decided was an effort to please me.

Maxwell was not to be deterred from ending Lancaster's time at the *Mirror*, though I tried. It was his prerogative to hire and fire and to appoint. As he was to say in a double-edged declaration about his policy: "My editors have the freedom to publish what they choose and I have the freedom to sack my editors." They were, he was pointing out, his papers. But I told him I could not take the job unless he treated Terry generously. I asked him to pay Terry his full salary until the end of the year and to give him the pension he would have got had he stayed until he was 65. He agreed and I accepted. (I didn't appreciate, though I'm sure Maxwell did, that under the terms of the pension Lancaster was on, he was entitled to the full pension anyway). Then he sent for Terry. When Terry left him, Maxwell phoned to tell me that he was on his way down and that he had urged Maxwell not to appoint me in his place. He had long intended, at least since the McNally episode, that Chris Buckland, a cheerful and irreverent former *Mirror* reporter and reformed alcoholic, should replace him. Chris could have done a good job, but wouldn't have lasted five minutes with Maxwell. But the job was not in Terry's gift and would not have been even if Maxwell had not existed. The refusal of his advice, however, was perceived as another insult to him. He refused a leaving party which Maxwell offered him and asked instead for two first-class air tickets to the US, which he got.

I did not want to make immediate changes to the parliamentary staff. I was not a football manager. The reporters knew what the paper wanted and they provided it, with one exception. One of them occasionally began his stories, "In the House of Commons last night...." which was about the laziest method of writing I could imagine. In addition, he was putting in expenses which I knew he hadn't incurred. It was the practice of the major political parties to deliver as many "week-end speeches" as they could drum up and deposit them in the Press Gallery on a Friday afternoon; I had received them for years when I worked there. No one was supposed to check that these speeches had ever been made but we all suspected that many of them were not. When he put in expenses for a trip to Chelmsford to report a Friday night speech by Norman St. John Stevas, a minister in Mrs Thatcher's government, he crossed a red line. He should have known that I knew the speech was contained in a distributed hand-out and he was asking me to be complicit in his fraud and I told Molloy I didn't want him any more. In true Fleet Street fashion, Molloy solved the problem by promoting him. That didn't stop the Father of the Chapel from telling me, bluntly, that I could not change any journalist's post without his, the journalist's, consent and it would not be forthcoming. It was another example of the absurd power the union had over the bosses. I said that in that case, he could stay in the job but I did not want him to do any work and therefore he would be unable to claim any expenses for anything. He decided to accept the promotion.

According to Edwards, Maxwell cut the workforce of MGN (as it was now known, with a roaring lion in its logo, a straight pinch from Hollywood) from 6,000 to 4,000 in three months which was more or less as I had forecast at the ill-fated Chapel meeting. But not journalists. He had a soft spot for them, "Management on tap, journalists on top" was his slogan and he kept to it in his own way. But his indulgence didn't extend to his printers. He had one great advantage over them: he knew as much about printing as they did and he could have written or dictated, a book on their Spanish practices. Foolishly, the printing unions decided to take him on.

A succession of disputes, all calculated to win more money for less work, enraged him. In August, 1985, our papers were not printed for a fortnight. In Manchester, a dispute with the company which printed the papers, not MGN itself, for the North of England stopped work there and SOGAT 82, the printing union led by the late Brenda Dean (elevated to Baroness Dean, such is the Labour movement), refused to allow the London presses to print more to make up the losses. Maxwell had had enough. He decided to accept the challenge and defeat them, the first proprietor to do both. I was wholly in agreement with him and wrote a full-page leading article headed: "Fleet St. The party is over." At the foot of the leader, in large type, was a quotation from it:

"The gravy train has hit the buffers." I got nothing but congratulations from journalists, all fellow-trade unionists, when they read it. Journalists had had enough, too, of their livelihoods threatened by mass obstruction and systemic corruption. Maxwell was so pleased with it that he decide to sign it. That's the fate of any anonymous leader writer.

As the leader pointed out, the printers earned up to £25,000 a year, £3,000 more than the journalists whose work they were paid to print, for a four-day week and six weeks' holidays a year and that was in 1985; I didn't even mention the "blow" system they operated which meant 48 men were employed in two shifts of four hours in a department whose establishment was 24 men; when the four hours were up the first 24 men were told to "blow" (Cockney rhyming slang: scarper, Scapa Flow, go) -i.e., go home or wherever, so that the other shift could take over; nor the fact that shop stewards organised a sickness rota so that one man would be ordered to be off sick one week and a fellow-worker would do his job at double pay and when he came back it was the other worker's turn to feign illness. Nor the union leader who complained that his garage was full of cases of whisky and he wanted something more readily convertible (cash) next time there was a settlement. To put all these and other matters in and it would have taken several pages This corruption was killing all Fleet Street newspapers, not only MGN's. Of course, the unions tried to strike to stop the leader being published. But Maxwell himself went down to the print room and by a combination of knowledge and sheer bullying got 30,000 copies printed. Symbolic but potent. It was the real start of the revolution in Fleet Street, not Rupert Murdoch's later move to Wapping.

Maxwell was increasingly involving me with his industrial matters and when the strike which provoked the leader attack was about to be resolved, he took Molloy and me with him to settle the final details. When all was agreed, he suddenly threw in a demand which it was clear to us would not be acceptable to them and we left with the strike still unresolved. "Why did you do that?" Molloy asked as we walked away. "I decide when this newspaper is going to be published, not them," he replied.

The old Spanish ways (are Spaniards really so bad?) died slowly. Maxwell decided to cut the over-full printing staffs on the Sunday papers to give them a better profit margin. He insisted I went with him and negotiate with the trade unionists from *The People* while he dealt with the *Sunday Mirror*, though they were intimately connected. It wasn't a good idea. I struggled because if they were going under - and they knew they were – they wanted to go under to Maxwell himself, which would give them someone important to complain about, rather than me. I found out one thing, though, which helped to end it. The union's concern was that no "financial secretary" should lose his job in the cuts – they were prepared to give Maxwell what he was asking for in terms of job losses as long as this group were protected. I asked who the "financial secretaries" were – they were the shop stewards who collected the union subscriptions; ordinary members could go hang as long as the union officials were saved. So much for the comradeship and unity of the working classes. Maxwell could be cynical, too, and allowed the concession.

By the nature of the job, the Sunday paper workers were part-time casuals, most of them working just on the Saturday before publication. The overall leader of the men on our papers was known as the Imperial Father of the Chapel. It turned out that before he called the strike on our papers he had arranged for himself a shift working for the *Sunday Express*. As far as I could tell, no one minded.

Away from the self-promotion, which was often embarrassing, Maxwell was intent on making the MGN group papers the first to be in colour in Britain. The Eddie Shah new paper, *Today*, was actually the first but its quality was so poor it hardly counted. It was a massive miscalculation by Rupert Murdoch that colour would not be a success and he stayed with black and white until he saw the error of his ways. When he did, he did so with enthusiasm. But the staid, by English standards, *Daily Record* was so deeply upset at having to print its Page 3 nudes, a Murdoch innovation, of course, in colour that the management and editor protested to Maxwell that they were losing circulation, apparently on the basis of about 30 readers' letters. Why a nude figure in black and white was acceptable to Scots and one in colour was judge indecent baffled me then and still does. I suspected that a wife or two in management had protested. *The Bulletin* ladies of my younger days would have approved.

Maxwell then began to involve me with Scottish industrial matters, presumably because I had worked on Scottish papers for so many years. Their printers were as intransigent as any in the south, added to which they were not going to be seen giving way to an Englishman, either real (me) or adopted (Maxwell). He sent me to Glasgow to try to resolve a dispute with them and they turned out in force. They deliberately set out to wreck our meeting from the start, one of them having a loud conversation with his neighbour as I was trying to talk to them. I stopped, saying either I spoke or they interrupted but I wasn't having both and that I would be happy to return to London there and then. I then suggested that their committee should come and meet me in the quiet atmosphere of the ninth floor of the *Daily Record* building, where the executives' offices were. The management were appalled. Vic Horwood, the chief executive, exploded: "We never allow the unions up on the ninth floor!" I decided there and then that the problems in Glasgow were among the management as well as the labour force and more deep-rooted than I was likely to solve in a flying visit.

The printers' union official who had kept interrupting me was later found to have instructed two of his members to break the fast-running paper when the machines were printing the first edition. That could be easily done. All it needed was to flip a matchstick or a paper clip into the machine and the paper would rip. He either overlooked or didn't care about one thing: that it was industrial sabotage and a criminal offence. Two printers told Maxwell and he got them to swear affidavits to the effect that they had been told to wreck the print run. Maxwell then asked the general secretary of the union to see him and said that the union official concerned would be fired. The general secretary attempted to bluster but Maxwell produced the affidavits and said he would take action in the Scottish courts. The general secretary dropped all opposition to the firing but pleaded that the man concerned had a wife and family and would Maxwell pay him off, say £20,000? Maxwell told me later he would do so. I thought he was crazy. The sacked official then got a job at the *Glasgow Herald*, such was the power of the union.

Then I had to deal with the journalists. They weren't going to give up any of their privileges. They didn't like Maxwell, they didn't want him and they were not prepared to work for him. So they said. They talked a good fight but they over-reached themselves, like the printers. Maxwell gave me power to reach a settlement, even if it meant over-ruling the management, who I thought were being unnecessarily stiff-necked. The Father of the Chapel was the friend of a friend of mine, Helen Liddell, former general secretary of the Labour party in Scotland, later a director of the Scottish papers and later still a member of Tony Blair's Cabinet, and she arranged for me to meet him.

We met in strict secrecy in a hotel near the office. I told him that what I was about to say was strictly confidential because I would have later to broach it with the Scottish management. He agreed to keep it confidential. I then outlined a new offer which met some of the union's demands but not all. He said he would consider it. He then left the meeting and went straight to the *Daily Record* negotiator and told him what I had said. He may have thought it a clever thing to do to double cross Maxwell's man, but he was mistaken. I was not a lackey of the Scottish management nor part of the hated London management. I was a journalist who had worked for Scottish newspapers for more than 20 years. There was no better way of ensuring he lost in the end. In the meantime, it led to stalemate. It was clear that the management would never trust me again. It was also clear that I would never trust the union.

After a strike of about three weeks, Maxwell phoned me on a Saturday night saying he was in despair and did not know what to do. I said there was a simple answer if he had the nerve to do it: he should raise the stakes. He was an inveterate gambler and the idea appealed to him. He asked how he should do it. I told him to write a dignified letter to every journalist individually, that night, informing them, regretfully, that the papers would close on the following Friday because they had left him no other option; that he would not sell the titles but retain them; tell them that a further letter would be sent to them later in the week outlining their pension entitlements; and that meanwhile they were now free to seek jobs elsewhere. They would not, of course, be entitled to receive any compensation because the closure of the company was due to the strike.

I told Maxwell to ensure that the letters were delivered around lunchtime on Sunday, when the journalists and their wives would be at home and the wives would have something to say about it. Given a plan, Maxwell could carry it out, brilliantly. The letters were delivered, the journalists returned to work the next morning and the strike was over. Bluff is a game two can play and he had called theirs. The difference was that if the journalists had stayed out and called his bluff Maxwell would have closed the papers down. They shouldn't blame me or Maxwell but the Father of their Chapel.

MGN's papers were, of course, close to the Labour leadership which Neil Kinnock had assumed after Michael Foot's disastrous defeat in 1983. Maxwell never wavered in his support for the Labour party though his policy ideas were sometimes closer to Mrs Thatcher's. Kinnock came to lunch and Maxwell was clearly suspicious of him, particularly on nuclear disarmament and the use of Trident. Asked if the question was one of principle or pragmatism, Kinnock replied: "Pragmatism". That was good enough for Maxwell; any other answer would have committed the MGN papers to oppose him, vociferously, on the issue.

The *Mirror* had long been leading the fight against the Militant Tendency which was corroding the Labour party. The National Executive of the party had asked me to serve on a sub-committee investigating the structure of government in Britain but my appointment was revoked when I published a document exposing Militant's practices, which had been given to me by the party's then National Agent (now dead, so I can say so). The MP responsible for ejecting me from the committee was Eric Heffer, MP for Walton, Liverpool, a blusterer, a Bennite and, when it came to it, a coward. He hated me. When I was with Wilson,

I had drafted the letter telling him he was dismissed from his junior ministerial post if he delivered a speech in the Commons against membership of the Common Market.

I sat in the Press Gallery above where he was sitting. He knew I was there. He must have known why. The letter, signed by the Prime Minister, was in my pocket. He decided to speak, nevertheless. As soon as he finished, I dashed down to the members' lobby to give the letter to him. A policeman told me that "Mr Heffer has left the building,",. His office didn't know where he was. "Fled the building" would have been a better description. He couldn't be found anywhere. Wilson's driver finally put the letter through the door of his home at 10pm and I told the press he had been sacked. Next morning, he bitterly complained that the press had been told before he was and that made me the culprit. So later he got his own back by getting me removed from the sub-committee. He shot himself in the foot so many times it was a wonder he could walk.

During the best conference speech of his life, at Bournemouth, Kinnock destroyed the Militant Tendency's control of Liverpool, mocking the council leaders for dismissing their workers by redundancy notices around the city by taxi. Shouting and waving his arms, Heffer stormed out of the conference hall, losing his way en route and had to be guided out of the building by a Labour party press officer. If anyone followed him, I didn't see them. He never counted for anything again. It was sad, more than 20 years later, to see Militant resurgent again, rejoining the party and voting for Jeremy Corbyn.

I did have one brush with Kinnock and another with his dark shadow, Peter Mandelson. Kinnock asked me to serve on another committee, on the future of the party's newspaper, *Labour News,* which had some good journalists but no prospects, was making a heavy loss and in Kinnock's view had to close. It had to go, but I was astonished to find later that his deputy, Roy Hattersley, knew nothing about Kinnock's intention and wanted to keep the paper running. One evening, I had written a big story about the party just before I left for a crucial meeting on the *News* and couldn't see it into the paper. Unfortunately, the headline by the sub-editor was at variance with the story and I got a furious letter the next day from Kinnock blaming me for it.

I thought he was old enough and wise enough to know that reporters do not write the headlines. What's more, I was away doing the assassin's work on a party newspaper at his request. I wrote back, saying "This letter is marked 'confidential' which means you can leak it immediately..." as he was running the leakiest office I had ever known.

The brush with Mandelson was more serious. Kinnock had made a speech of some length which Mandelson thought was important and I didn't. It only got a half-column in the paper. Mandelson wrote a letter to Bob Maxwell complaining about me. People offended by a story can write to the editor complaining if they wish. Writing to the proprietor is below the belt – the only intention can be is to get the offender sacked. Editors care about how many people read their newspapers; proprietors care about who those people are. It is a crucial difference.

Peter Jay, a good friend, an outstanding columnist and economist, formerly British ambassador to the United States Jim Callaghan's son in law and lately appointed Maxwell's chief of staff, saw Mandelson's leter first and passed it to me before Maxwell could read it. By a happy but astonishing coincidence, I was reading it when Mandelson telephoned me to congratulate me on a leader I had written in that morning's *Mirror.*" Without hesitation, I called him a "hypocritical bastard" and put the phone down; unsurprisingly, he took offence and never spoke to me again for three years, which was totally unprofessional of him. Whatever he thought of me, the paper was Labour's only ally in Fleet Street apart from the occasional half-hearted support of the *Guardian..*

I got in another dispute on behalf of Kinnock at the time of the first Iraki war. Ken Follett, a writer of popular fiction and husband of, Barbara, later to become a Labour MP, had asked me to get Maxwell to under-write costs of a West End theatre show by leading actors, singers and comedians to raise money for the Labour party. The three of us had a pleasant, delightful (and expensive) lunch in which Barbara proudly told me that Ken had written her speech seeking nomination for the safe Labour seat of Dulwich and she had only lost it by the narrowest margin to Tessa Jowell, destined to be a cabinet minister under Tony Blair. It was not the appropriate moment to tell them that I had written Tessa's successful speech. It might have soured lunch.

However, I recommended to Maxwell to provide the sponsorship, at a possible but unlikely, cost of £15,000. I thought it was a sure-fire winner. Maxwell agreed to do it. Then the Iraki war broke out. Larry (now Lord) Whitty, general secretary of the party, phoned to ask me to withdraw the guarantee as it seemed likely that some of the performers would use the occasion to denounce British involvement in the fighting and Neil did not want the show to go ahead in those circumstances. It didn't. I told Follett that in view of what was likely to happen, the guarantee was withdrawn. Follett was apoplectic, furiously attacking me; people like me were the cause of the party's unpopularity, etc (not millionaires like him living in the more expensive part of Chelsea). I replied in similarly friendly terms. When I told Maxwell later, he shrugged and said he would have paid the money if I had asked. I couldn't always second guess him.

When Patricia Hewitt, Kinnock's press secretary asked me to get Maxwell to contribute to a new left-wing think tank that was being set up, The Institute for Public Policy Research, he agreed to give £25,000, which at the time was a substantial sum, to my mind. Not to Mrs Hewitt's. She thought he was "mean." I spoke to Kinnock about it; her approach to me was unknown to him and he didn't welcome it, he said. He was thinking of nominating Maxwell for a peerage and he couldn't do it if Maxwell was seen to be a substantial donor. I suspect Maxwell wouldn't have taken it if the offer had been made, for which their Lordships should be thankful: His acceptance would have been akin to planting a volcano amid the courts of Wimbledon.

On the whole, Maxwell kept his promise to keep the journalists on top and the management on tap, except that as he was the management he thought it his prerogative to move the editors around. Molloy, who had been *Mirror* editor for nearly 10 years was promoted to editor in chief of all the paper in

1985 and replaced by by Richard Stott, an aggressively irreverent journalist who was just what the paper needed. He was an antidote to Maxwell, determined to show his independence, sometimes shockingly so. His attitude was good for staff morale.

At one of Maxwell's Tuesday lunches, Bob Edwards suddenly tapped his wine glass and said he wanted to offer a toast and, then, turning to Maxwell, said: "To you, Bob, you are a genius," and it was drunk to, with varying degrees of enthusiasm. Richard Stott then raised his glass and, turning to Edwards, said: "To you, Bob, you are a fucking creep," which must rank high in the annals of daring insults, even in Fleet Street. Maxwell neither laughed nor scowled but, as I thought at the time, took note. Richard later capped it, though, when Maxwell recounted an incident in which he had lost out. "Made you look a right c---, didn't it, Bob?" said Richard. There was a stunned silence. Again, Maxwell said nothing, but I think both remarks would have been in Maxwell's mind when he made the disastrous decision to switch Richard to edit *The People* and replace him with Roy Greenslade, a reputed Maoist-Marxist-Leninist and full of gloom about the future of the mass-circulation tabloids.

He was totally unsuited to work with Maxwell. For a start, he thought he could make new expensive appointments, such as columnists, without consulting Maxwell. I never met the first; he committed suicide shortly afterwards. The second was John Diamond, a brilliant writer and husband of Nigella Lawson, a celebrity cook. I was asked to have lunch with him and I happily agreed. Maxwell had already shown his hostility. Deleting the expletives, he had asked me why "Greenslime" as he had taken to calling Greenslade, was spending his money and taking on new columnists without asking him first. I tried to explain to Diamond that the objection to the appointment was not to him personally but to the way he had been appointed. I didn't succeed. Neither he nor Greenslade believed me.

Greenslade also refused to have a Women's Editor for the paper, which was a mistake. Marge Proops didn't like him and he didn't seek to assuage her, which was another mistake. Then he went missing one evening when Maxwell urgently wanted to consult him. Journalists may not have been expected to be on tap except when Maxwell wanted them to be, and he couldn't be found. An agitated Night News Editor, Tom Hendry, came to me and told me Maxwell had fired him for his failure and asking what he should do. "Ignore him," I said, cheerfully. "But he's fired me!" said Hendry. "Pay no attention," I said, and he went back to his work, uncertain whether he should do it. Maxwell never mentioned it again. Then Greenslade decided to cut the space given to my weekly column and to reduce the size of the font on the bogus excuse that there was too much news to go into the paper. In a previous column I had attacked a protest march by the National Union of Journalists, among others, and he didn't like what I was writing. I didn't like the left-wing extremists he supported. I threatened to resign and he should have sacked me. Instead, he did it again. But promised not to repeat it when I made it clear I wasn't bluffing. It was weak editorship.

Maxwell eventually did the right thing and brought Stott back to edit the paper. Richard didn't change at all. When Maxwell finally got round to reducing journalistic staffs, he re-asserted his independence by refusing a pay rise.

There was a worrying tendency on Maxwell's part to spend big abroad and save money at home. He hit on an idea that was novel to me: low-producing journalists were to be allowed to work at home on full pay. The saving came from the fact that if they were working from home they had no claim on expenses or office space.

But the *Mirror* had a better look about it. Columnists like Marge Proops, Anne Robinson, Paul Foot and I provided regular features although we missed Keith Waterhouse; Maxwell had a particular regard for Anne, who had been treated badly under the Reed regime. Molloy had made her an assistant editor in those days and she was in charge of editing the paper occasionally, usually on a Sunday. One Sunday she consulted me about a story written by James Whitaker, the paper's Royal correspondent, sensationally reporting that Princess Diana was suffering from the eating disease, bulimia, which suggested other, more deep-rooted problems. This was to be the beginning of the saga which led to disaster and the death of the Princess in Paris. Knowing the uproar it would cause, Anne was understandably cautious. She asked me if I thought she should run it, though I think she had already made up her mind to do so. The detail of the story was flimsy, but Anne was convinced of its accuracy. My opinion was that she should go ahead.

The uproar was in our office. "The Palace," I was told, had complained to Sir Alex Jarrett, the chairman of Reed's and Jarrett had instructed Tony Miles that Anne was not to edit the paper again: that's the problem of proprietors, as I wrote above. They are concerned about who reads the paper, and how important they are, and not how many readers it has or whether a story is accurate. I was told that the decision was strictly confidential to be imparted to no-one. I told Anne because I thought it was a disgraceful decision and it was right that she should know, especially as she was considering leaving the newspaper industry and embarking on a TV career (I should add that in one of the most disastrous pieces of advice I ever offered anyone, I was to tell her later not to try for the latter because she was too old. The BBC only want dolly-birds, I said. She was still signing new contracts when she was in her seventies). In her autobiographical memoir detailing her battle with alcoholism she tells a markedly different version. I'm being kind in suggesting it was a lapse of memory.

As my influence with Maxwell seemed to grow as he thrust more and more upon me outside my proper job, colleagues began to ask me for favours. I wasn't easy about it because I didn't want the responsibility, but as the favours usually involved asking Maxwell to spend more of his money, I did it. The first to ask was Anne Robinson. She came to my office one day and asked if I could get her a pay increase. She told me she was getting £30,000 a year, which wasn't much. We discussed how to do it. I asked if she had ever received an offer to join the *Sun*. Vaguely, she said. That was good enough. I told Maxwell she *had* received an offer and he raised her salary to £40,000. Her version was that I couldn't keep anything to myself and had told Maxwell of the offer, which in truth was one that I had concocted with her.

The next was a bright and talented young reporter, Anton Antonowicz. He described me as his "mentor" in a history of the *Mirror* written by Bill Hagerty, a journalist Maxwell persistently and foolishly under-rated. Anton was seriously considering leaving and I thought he would be a loss. He was not rated as highly by Richard Stott as he was by me. I spoke to Maxwell and Anton's salary went up. I didn't know at the time that Richard had refused him one, but I should not have interfered: it was the editor's job, not mine. Anton paid for it. On the day when the big story was the final end to the months'-long miners' strike, the paper devoted a large part of its edition to a story about Maxwell – by-lined Anton Antonowicz and I assumed he was embarrassed by it.

A third request came from the Sports Editor, Keith Fisher: he wanted me to ask Maxwell to lend him £180,000 as a bridging loan for a new house he was buying. That was a favour too far and I refused. That had nothing to do with the success of the paper. I don't recall that he ever spoke to me again. One of our industrial correspondents, Alan Law, however, wanted to borrow money for a similar purpose and approached Maxwell directly and got it.

I liked Alan. We were occasional snooker partners even though he had a habit of recklessly wrecking the triangle of reds as soon as a frame started but we got on. I wanted Maxwell to choose him to replace Geoffrey Goodman when Goodman retired, but Maxwell chose Terry Pattinson, as short and surly as Law was tall and cheerful, because he was Father of the journalists' chapel and Maxwell thought the appointment was a good investment. Pattinson checkmated him by resigning from his chapel post as soon as he was officially made Industrial Editor, so Maxwell had the worst of both worlds. Pattinson knew I didn't think he was up to the task and tried to take his revenge later.

A greater difficulty and well within my sphere of interest came when Alistair Campbell, by then Political Editor of the *Sunday Mirror*, came one evening to tell me he was thinking of resigning because he didn't feel his job was safe under Maxwell. I said it was, but to prove it I would go to Maxwell's office in Finsbury

Square and get a guarantee from him. I went. I got it. And when
I came back Alistair had already resigned, taking a job on the
Night News Desk of the new paper, *Today*. I told him it was a
mistake and so it proved to be. After a nervous breakdown, he
was offered a job by Richard Stott and he gladly took it and never
looked back on his rise to be Tony Blair's press secretary and the
man the *Daily Mail* loved to hate, and still does.

He was to have one major clash with Maxwell, however,
which threatened his career, at least at the *Mirror*. On the late
evening before Mrs Thatcher's resignation, Alastair phoned me.
He had Greenslade with him. Maxwell had phoned him saying
that Mrs Thatcher was about to resign after a Cabinet revolt. His
story was full of lurid details most of which were wrong, though
the main point was right, and he demanded that Alastair write the
story. Alastair asked Maxwell to tell him the source of the story
and a bad-tempered Maxwell had refused; Alastair was reluctant
to swallow it whole without knowing where it had come from.
I said to him that if he didn't believe the story he shouldn't write it,
but hope that Maxwell was wrong. Alastair wrote a cautious
story for the final editions, which in the circumstances was the
best to be done. A furious Maxwell was on to me early the next
morning saying he was going to sack Alastair. "Do you know
what he said to me?" he demanded. "He wanted to know the
source of the story. He didn't trust me!"

I told him I would have done the same. "You don't trust me
either!" he exclaimed. "It is not a question of trusting you, Bob,
it's a question of trusting your source," I replied. "Alastair had to
make his judgment on that. Anyway, who was it?" I had to ask
him again until he replied, "Norman Lamont." I haven't the
faintest idea whether he was telling the truth or just plucking a
name out of his memory, the first one that he thought of. But
I suppose he was right in one respect. Neither of us trusted him.

Maxwell once told me : "If a gentleman in the City offers you
his word or his bond, take his bond." However, he didn't regard
that dictum to applying to himself. During one of his frequent
quarrels with the printing unions, he asked me to settle it with
Brenda Dean, general secretary of SOGAT82. It was the time of a

Labour party conference and I met her at the Grand Hotel in Brighton. I offered her a solution to whatever the problem was and she accepted it. Then she added: "I want it in writing." "He won't do that," I told her. "You've got to take his word." She wouldn't and was adamant, he was offended and immovable. There was no agreement.

My name or fame (largely erroneous) as someone who could tame the untameable spread within Maxwell's empire. He appointed a new deputy chairman at the British Printing Corporation, a small man totally unsuited to working with him. After five weeks he came to see me with a routine that was becoming monotonous: "Joe, will you do me a favour?" which was a bit much to ask seeing I didn't know him. His problem, he said, was that Bob Maxwell was being rude to him and would I stop it? No, I said, that is up to you (Anyway, why should he be the exception?). His remedy was disastrous. He invited Bob and me to lunch with him at the Savoy Grill. The head waiter was all over him. Clearly, he ate there often.

He led us to a favoured table, addressed the head waiter completely to the exclusion of me and an exasperated Maxwell who was marking his deputy's card minute by minute. When he said he would choose the wine (which Maxwell always took upon himself) he sealed his fate. After all, the lunch was on his expenses, which meant Maxwell was paying for it. It was the last meal of a doomed man. I never saw him or heard of him again after he was sacked.

There was one area where I had no influence at all with Maxwell, and that was his propensity for taking legal action. He successfully sued *Private Eye* after I had urged him not to. If the *Eye* had called the right witnesses he might not have won. It was a perjured verdict. He also took another printing union, the National Graphical Union, to court for contempt. On that occasion I had to go into the witness box in the High Court because the leader of that union had spent some time on the phone to me in the early morning at the Labour conference in Blackpool over the issue. He was belligerent about it and I had warned him that his intentions were liable to be held in contempt. He paid no attention. His QC asked me a question about that morning and repeated my answer, totally twisting it to give a different meaning. I protested that I had said exactly the opposite of the words he was putting into my mouth. The judge rebuked him, saying: "Mr Haines did not say that" and he retreated.

Then another QC, Mr James Goudie, rose and started to approach me. I prayed that he would ask me the same question because, in a flash, I knew what I would reply. Unfortunately, he changed his mind. Pity. If he had asked me what I was doing that morning I would have replied that I spent most of it in my bedroom with his wife, Mary. Absolutely true, with no improper connotations whatsoever. Mary (now Baroness) Goudie worked for Roy Hattersley, deputy leader of the Labour party, and she was outlining a speech Hattersley was going to make later that day and urging its merits upon me. The judge might have warned me about my flippancy but it would have lightened an otherwise dull day in court.

Maxwell's insatiable demand for self-publicity spread to the football league with the purchase of lowly Oxford United. When they won the Milk Cup at Wembley he celebrated on the pitch. And when they won what was then the Third Division he called up Molloy and me and the then Sports Editor, Ted Graham, to his room to celebrate. He couldn't resist the chance to show off and asked Graham what price he could get on Oxford winning the Second Division in the coming season. Graham phoned a bookmaker: "100-6" he reported. "Put £12,000 on them for me," he instructed. "What if they come second?" Graham reported much lower odds. "Put £6,000 on," said Maxwell.

I forgot all about it until the following year when Maxwell called me to see him. His two sons, Kevin and Ian, were standing dutifully in front of his desk. "Get out," he said to them in his usual brusque way, "I want to talk to Joe." Denizens of Fleet Street were seldom shocked but I was disturbed by his blatant bullying of his sons. They loved him in their way but they were also afraid of him. They simply turned away and left. I stayed and sat down, determined not to be dutiful and he threw a cheque across to me: "Look at that," he said. £223,000, I think from

William Hills. It was his winnings from the previous year's bets. I asked him what he was going to do with it and he shrugged his shoulders. It was the achievement that was important, not the sum or its destination.

Having made a calamitous mistake in advising Anne Robinson about her career, I then made a comparable mistake in advising Maxwell. He told me he had been offered a million pounds by Liverpool for Oxford's centre-forward, John Aldridge who, he said, was 28 (in fact, I think he was only 27 and a year is a crucial difference in the life of a footballer) and what should he do? I said if he could get that money for a player of that age in a lower division he should take it, and he did. It was the best bargain Liverpool ever got and one of the worst Maxwell ever made. The expert should stick to his last. In similar circumstances today, more than 30 years later, £50million would not be too much for Aldridge. I did, however, tell Maxwell he was wrong to raise the salary of Jim Smith, the club's manager, by only £1,000 a year after he had won promotion. An indignant Smith left, so I was right about that. After all, he had only banked the £223,000 as a result of Smith's efforts.

Maxwell took to inviting me to go to functions with him and I usually avoided them, but two I couldn't duck. One was to fly to Bavaria to meet Franz-Josef Strauss, the leading right-wing politician in Germany in his day – it yielded nothing, another instance of two giant egos sparring - and to go with him to a bank in Munich where he borrowed 150million deutschmarks at an interest rate of five per cent . When we got back to our hotel, part of it was on fire, though fortunately not our part. But something always happened when Maxwell was around. When we came out of the bank, I said, "Bob, how can you forgive the Germans after what they did to your family in the Holocaust" (10 of them died in concentration camps). "I can forget them but I can't forgive them," he replied. He told me the next day he had invested the money in London at 13 per cent.

The other visit was to Poland and General Jaruzelski, its communist dictator who was about to be dethroned. He was cold and unfriendly and I didn't see any point in the meeting, but that was usually the case with Maxwell's foreign visits. It was the 50th anniversary of the German attack on Poland in September, 1939, and I went to a ceremony in what was then Danzig and is now Gdansk. The air raid sirens and the playing of the recording of the German warships bombarding the city were eerie and moving. Maxwell, resplendent in the uniform of a British army captain (a new one; he had long outgrown the original) solemnly laid a wreath which he had stolen from someone else at the memorial to the dead.

He was courted and flattered by presidents and prime ministers, ranging from the United States to the Soviet Union. He went to see George W. Bush and showed him a copy of a leader I had written for a new newspaper, *The European* urging him to read it. He had access to Mikhail Gorbachov and took me and Noreen Taylor, Roy Greenslade's wife, with him: me to interview Gorbachov and Noreen to interview his wife. Neither interview happened. He also took me to see the editor and other senior officials of *Pravda* who wanted his advice. He bluntly told them, in effect and in Russian, that they didn't know how to produce a newspaper.

I travelled in an official car with him in Moscow with a Russian, a German and a Frenchman. Maxwell spoke to us all in our languages. Impressive piece of showing-off, I thought. Lech Walesa, leader of Solidarity and the first post-freedom Prime Minister of Poland, later wanted to see him in London and offered him the opportunity of buying the Polish TV and radio networks. Maxwell wasn't interested. Whatever these important people may have thought or said about him after he was dead, they were only too anxious to know him and his money when he was alive

He could not understand why I persistently refused his offer to provide me with an office car. The explanation that I couldn't drive and didn't want to learn was insufficient for him. My wife could use it to drive me to office functions or to by-elections, he argued. Yes, she could but she wanted her own car, not his. In the end, he got serious about it. I was about to leave the office for lunch one day when he telephoned from his Finsbury Square office to say he would be passing shortly and would pick me up. Once inside his Rolls, he reverted to the question of a car. He told me he took my attitude as a personal reflection upon him; I could have any car I wanted, including a Rolls. I told him I'd never get it into my garage but he wasn't going to be put off by flippancy. In the end, I conceded and chose a Mercedes because the local supplier was opposite the railway station. If it needed servicing my wife could take it in after she had dropped me off to catch my train. He was immensely pleased, stopped the Rolls so that I could get out and left me two-thirds of the way to the Czech embassy where he was having lunch and 45 minutes late for my own. And also provided a minor problem for the future, after his death.

He was also very fond of dogs and had a huge Weimeramer at his home at Headington Hill Hall in Oxford, but banished it to the garden when it came indoors and messed on his carpet. He was always asking me about our dog and one day handed me a stuffed toy as a present for my poodle and asked me to take a photograph of both for him. I did, and he placed it in a frame and kept it on his desk for months. I hadn't the heart to tell him that my real dog had systematically destroyed his stuffed one on the day she received it. He might have taken it personally.

He loved Headington Hill Hall (the Triple H ranch, as an American visitor called it), which he rented from Oxford City Council at a derisory rent, and on his 65th birthday had an enormous marquee erected for hundreds of guests for a white-tie and tails (or, in the Scottish Cabinet Minister's Malcolm Rikfind's case, white-tie, sporran and kilt) dinner and dance. I was hoping and expecting that my wife and I would be safe among the crowd. To our dismay, we found Maxwell had put us in charge of one of the tables. I sat at one end with Tam Dalyell, MP, who could talk his way through a five-course dinner without pausing to eat, and at the other end, to my wife's horror, she sat between possibly the two worst guests it could be imagined: the East German ambassador and his dour wife. You could have scoured the country to find anyone les appealing to my wife and not succeeded.

Maxwell gave every guest a gift, a toilet bag for men or a jewellery roll up case for women, but was indifferent to personal possessions himself. Senior editorial staff at the *Mirror*, including me, clubbed together and bought him a telescope for £180 but I doubt if he ever looked through it. David Frost, the television presenter, generously gave him a £500 bottle of wine which Maxwell had put into his wine cellar and which was soon used by his chef as a cooking ingredient. (No one ever told him it was special, he complained). Around this time, Maxwell took to wearing a Rolex which he had been given. It was on his wrist, of course, but I suppose he couldn't think of anywhere else to put it. Up till then, if he wanted to know the time he would ask one of his staff.

Maxwell was forever and increasingly restless, always wanting to buy or, less frequently, sell, eying acquisitions at home and abroad. His abortive efforts to pilot the *London Daily News* to success was doomed from the start. In the field of newspaper promotions he was an amateur among professionals. He could print them but he didn't know how to run them.

He called me up to Headington one Saturday lunchtime to consider the projection for the new paper. My wife got me there in 50 minutes from Tonbridge, Kent, which must have been close to a record, and he genuinely wondered what had kept us. Maybe I should have asked him for a helicopter rather than an office car. And as a present he gave her a sumptuous leather-bound copy of Mikhail Gorbachev's speeches and a presentation box of five apparently silver coins, probably Bulgarian, which had been given to him. If they are silver, they would be worth their meltdown value at least. If not silver, I imagine they are worthless, Bulgarian currency of the Soviet era not being in high demand;. The book remains unopened to this day and the "silver" coins are tucked away in an obscure drawer. I suppose the thought was the thing. As for the projection, it had been dreamed up in La La Land. I quickly saw that future predicted profits were based upon no increases in salary or production costs over the next three years. In the Fleet Street of that time, hell would have frozen over first. Maxwell generously returned it to its authors and told them to start again instead of telling them to get on their bikes. Eventually the paper was launched. It was to his new editor. Magnus Linklater, that Maxwell said, "My editors have the right to print what they like" and Linklater was visibly impressed, so much so that he may have missed the line that followed: "And I have the right to sack my editors." The paper never had a chance and folded after a few months, scuppered deliberately by the revival of a former London favourite, *The Evening News,* which, once it had done its job, was closed down again.

He publicly boasted of buying *Today* but he hadn't tied up the deal and Murdoch gazumped him. He saved the Edinburgh Commonwealth Games from financial collapse and emerged more disliked than liked for his efforts. He had fingers in pies I never knew existed. He appointed and he dis-appointed. He made me a director of the Daily Mirror, Ltd., approved by the "suits", led by Bob Edwards, with generous but not convincing applause. They were suspicious of journalists being a director of a newspaper produced by journalists. I took the post for one reason only: Maxwell had put a tight grip on spending and no one below directorial level could spend £500 without his authorisation, and £500 was no more than pocket money in Fleet Street. I had once, during the Reed regime, been offered the Cecil-Parkinson-Sarah Keays story – the affair, the illicit child – for £800 . In a curiously straitlaced way the *Mirror* didn't want it. Both the editor, Mike Molloy and Tony Miles knew of it but didn't want the paper to take the lead in exposing a Tory scandal. I heard *The Observer* turned it down for similar reasons. I wouldn't have hesitated but under Maxwell as political editor I would never have had the power to buy it without being a director.

He made me a director also of his Scottish publications, the *Daily Record* and the *Sunday Mail.* Their board's reception was less enthusiastic but more genuine. At least they knew I had worked for Scottish newspapers for 18 years. But they resented Maxwell. They resented English interference. They didn't want a Maxwell appointee. The daily had had an editor who drank too much and he was English. Maxwell offered me the editorship of the *Record* and I refused it. Even a Hugh Cudlipp would have been treated with hostility and I was no Hugh Cudlipp. Maxwell later appointed Helen Liddell to be a director and she is a Scot; but she is also a a woman and not clubbable, which was nearly as bad as being English. She also had great intelligence and ability, became an MP, a Cabinet Minister and Britain's High Commissioner in Australia and eventually a baroness. Not bad for someone who wasn't a man, but perhaps still not good enough for the closed world of Scottish newspaper management.

Maxwell announced at one of his lunches one day that he was appointing Henry to be editor of the *People*. "Henry who?" I asked innocently. Wendy Henry was the answer, which brought a gasp from others around the table. She was the daughter of a Jewish market trader, which might have aroused his sympathy, but she was also a member of the International Communist League and was once arrested for attempting to throw a carton of milk at Edward Heath, which was not the reputation suitable for a newspaper editor apart from the *Morning Star*. She didn't last long after a couple of tasteless photos of a seven-year-old Prince William peeing and a ghastly picture of Sammy Davis, Jnr, ravaged by throat cancer, Maxwell sacked her for one or other or both offences. He wasn't sure which.

On another lunch day he suddenly announced a new policy for his papers. In future, he said, IRA suspects should be lined up and shot. Without trial. In a country which had abolished capital punishment. If a pre-echo is possible, it was a pre-echo of Donald Trump. And we, radical, left-wing newspapers, were to advocate it. Nobody else said anything, but I felt I had to. "My typewriter won't write that, Bob," I said. He shrugged. "All right, if Joe won't write it, forget it." Peter Thompson, an Australian who was deputy editor of the *Mirror,* said to me afterwards: "I'm glad you spoke up. If you hadn't, I would have." He had a habit of being late with his bravery as I was to discover later. There are many men who might have been decorated for bravery on November 12, 1918, had it not been for the Armistice on November 11. Willingness to go over the top after peace had been declared smacked more of bravado than courage.

As I read of the antics of Donald Trump, I am frequently reminded of Bob Maxwell. He took the problem of Northern Ireland as something he could solve where everyone else had failed. One Thursday, he told me I was to write a leader calling for the immediate withdrawal of British troops from the province (thus breaking our agreement that he would never instruct me to write anything). I had enough dealings with Irish problems when I was at No. 10 to know that was ridiculous. He said he was serious about it. I said so was I. He then picked up his phone and asked Geoffrey Goodman to have lunch with him that day, a childish reaction to show I was out of favour.

When I left him, he said he would call me the following day (my day off) and see if I had changed my mind. He called and I hadn't. He said that we had a serious situation and I was to see him on Monday at noon. I phoned Molloy and told him. "Oh, God," he said. "I'm supposed to be in the South of France then; I suppose I'll have to come back." I told Peter Thompson, who was acting editor, about the problem on the Sunday and that I wouldn't change my mind and he assured me he would come with me to see Maxwell. At five minutes to midday I called at his office; he had an issue to deal with, he said, and if I went on alone, he would catch me up. He never did. When I walked into Maxwell's office, he was busy being filmed in a BBC interview. Melodramatically, he halted the interview and told the BBC, "This is a very important matter about Northern Ireland," and then he turned me and said: "Have you done it?" "No," I replied and I heard nothing about it again. He could hardly be caught on film sacking me, which had been his week-end threat. Or perhaps he realised the policy was nonsense as I said it was.

There was to be another explosion between us. He was increasingly going abroad in his private plane for which the company was charged an enormous sum. He returned one day, tired and angry with the British press which had been criticising him, as they routinely did. He called me up to his room and showed me a press notice he had written to be issued immediately. His press secretary, Janet Hewlett-Davies, who had been my deputy at No. 10, was there and clearly had not been able to talk him out of it. A friend of mine, Andrew Roth, an American who had made himself a British parliamentary expert and was a considerable amateur psychiatrist, had previously told me Maxwell was paranoid. This was part of the evidence. It became obvious for the world to see when it was revealed, more like Richard Nixon than Donald Trump, after his death that he had instructed a former police officer to install bugging devices in the offices of various people including his senior journalists. They may not have been on tap but he was putting them online. The conversations of Richard Stott, in particular, must have sent him steaming with rage. But why, given the example of Nixon and the Watergate tapes, did he ever do it? Paranoia seems the only answer.

The rant against the press which he was proposing to deliver was inaccurate, almost hysterical and bound to damage him publicly. I told him not to do it. He had asked for my opinion but that wasn't the opinion he wanted. He waved his hand dismissively at me and turned his back. I lost my temper. "You can do that to the poodles who run up and down outside your office," I said, "but you don't do that to me. You asked for my opinion and you've got it. If you don't want to accept it, that's your look-out," and I walked out of his office and went home. The press notice was not issued but I didn't hear from him for a week, which was unprecedented. I had no inclination or need to apologise and he wasn't able to, or not directly.

But I got a call from him on the Friday evening asking me to go to his office. I went in and faced a spread of smoked salmon sandwiches and a bottle of pink champagne. "I thought you might help me finish these," he said, though he hadn't started either. I did. That was his way of apologising without saying sorry and my way of being gracious without fawning. Normal service, if it could be called that, was resumed.

One deal he didn't want to do and eventually did with great reluctance was to end in disaster for all participants. The unions representing the Helicopter Pilots' Association, urged on by Clive Jenkins, the technicians' union leader, a man who had opinions on everything and nearly all of them wrong, came to Maxwell and urged him to buy a helicopter company serving the North Sea oil fields. Maxwell told them he didn't want to be involved. They, pleaded, they entreated him, they appealed to his emotions as a patriot and as a socialist businessman. And, against his better judgment, he gave in. The result was that when his crash came the pension fund of the pilots was wiped out. That was one theft for which he was largely blameless. I recalled that Jenkins was the principal union backer and intriguer for the election of Michael Foot as leader of the Labour party, which led to disaster, too. But worse was to come. Much worse. He turned his buyer's eye to America, specifically to New York.

By that time, I had actively turned to thoughts of retirement at 60. I had been working since I was 14. I thought that more than enough. In fact, I had asked the Pensions Manager at MGN, confidentially, how much I could expect in pension if I retired at 60. It wasn't much (£14,000 a year) but I thought it enough for my wife and me – we did not lead extravagant lives. Quite improperly, the Pensions Manager, whose terror of Maxwell was to have disastrous consequences, told him about my inquiry. Maxwell reacted swiftly and formally by letter.

To retire on £14,000, he wrote, was to retire in penury (in 1988, that was an exaggerated definition of penury, especially when the pension would increase by 5 per cent a year). He offered that if I would stay on until I was 62 and a half my pension would be increased to two-thirds of my final salary. That seemed to me a substantial offer and I accepted it. My wife is five years younger than me and it would give her added security and comfort after I had died. Do I regret accepting? Honestly, no. It was the sensible and right thing to do, even though I didn't relish it. However, it deeply involved me in the troubles that were to come and if I could have avoided those then almost any price would have been worth it. I did not realise at the time that the pension he was offering me was the pension paid to directors of the Scottish companies, of which I was one, and, presumably, directors of MGN and directors of the new company he was forming for flotation, of which I was to be a non-executive director because he wanted to retain my connection with the newspapers. Nor did I realise at the time that there were three levels of pension at MGN, unknown to the chapel: the one I was currently on, the lowest; another, more secret, for senior journalists like Geoffrey Goodman, Terry Lancaster and various other species of editors and departmental managers; and the upper tier, the two-thirds beneficiaries. In true Orwellian tradition, all were equal but some were more equal than others.

Comings and goings increased, as if he was searching for a man/woman elixir for success that didn't exist. He sacked the editor of the *People,* Ernie Burrington, who was the lowest-paid editor in Fleet Street (indeed, by that time I was earning more than he was) and only the intervention of Richard Stott and myself saved him from unemployment. We knew that Burrington had unwisely invested his money in a firm run by a friend of his which had crashed. He needed a job. We went to Maxwell and told him of Burrington's problems. "I'll keep him on," said Maxwell, "what can he do, what shall I call him?" "Make him Editorial Director," I said, putting past enmities aside. "It sounds good but doesn't mean anything." There are times when one can be too objective.

He reached for his phone and spoke to Burrington. "I know you are leaving the *People*" he said, (leaving because he had sacked him)"but you are too valuable to me to lose and I'm going to make you Editorial Director." That was Maxwell at his most magnanimous. It was also another of my mistakes.

Less magnanimously, he cut the editors' budgets, a sign that money was getting tight but also to put the papers in better shape for his intended flotation. Those journalists who had been "working from home" had to be dismissed and those who were barely working at all had to go, too. One of those - Richard Stott's choice, despite his belief that Maxwell had ordered it - was John Pilger. Richard tried hard to get in touch with him but couldn't discover where he was. So he went ahead with his sacking and it was general knowledge. Mike Molloy told us that Pilger had phoned him from Australia - he was German-Australian by birth – and said he had been told of his dismissal by a friend. He asked Molloy - in a reverse charge call, according to Molloy - to get him a good pay-off, higher than the limit Maxwell had set for anyone. Apparently, again according to Molloy, when Reed's had taken over IPC, the Mirror Group parent company, Pilger had declined to join the Reed pension scheme. If so, that was up to him, a short-term saving and a long-term loss for anyone. He left with a reported £73,000 and an unjustified grievance.

Maxwell asked me to take charge of the annual negotiations over journalists' salaries. I told him I would only do it if I had something to offer them. He certainly gave me something. Traditionally, the union's claim was submitted in July and endless meetings would go on until December when an agreement was finally reached. As usual at the start of negotiations the Father of the Chapel, Steve Turner, and his team came in to argue their case and eyeing me with suspicion. After all, I was supposed to be one of them. I told them immediately that I didn't want a repetition of past years, when they put in an impossible claim and the management countered with an unacceptable offer and the talks dragged on for months..

"Instead," I went on, "I'm going to make you my first and final offer and there will be no change in it." More bristling. Then I said: "I'm going to offer you 12 ½ percent," which was pretty generous, seeing they were only asking for 13 per cent. I didn't expect to be overwhelmed with thanks and I wasn't. What's the catch? was the reaction. Well, there was one but it didn't seem much of one to me. Eight per cent was payable immediately and not delayed until the end of the year and for those staff who signed a contract, a non-negotiable demand by Maxwell, by December there would be another 4 1/2 per cent. Any contracts signed before then would get the whole sum, back-dated to July. Those who didn't sign would only get the eight per cent. Only! That would seem beyond the wildest dream of any worker after the 2008 financial crash but in those days the unions talked in, and expected to get, telephone numbers. Although I didn't tell them, I had decided not to take the offer myself and I didn't sign a contract, so no one could afterwards say I was lining my own pocket.

Astonishingly to say, the offer was rejected and we started the long march to a December conclusion, after all, but this time with a difference. I was convinced that the journalists would be overwhelmingly in favour and so they were all informed of it. James Whitaker, the Royal correspondent led the way. "I'm taking it," he exclaimed, and others followed. By November,

I was able to tell Turner that a clear majority of his members had signed up to the contract and were receiving the money and that he was beaten. I tried to sweeten the pill, with further angry results. Another of the chapel's annual demands had been that any journalist dismissed after 20 years service or more should get a pay-off of six months' wages. I persuaded Maxwell that that was too little for such a long service and proposed it should be a year's pay. I told Turner that this would be in the agreement. He exploded: "That's what I mean about you," he shouted. "You take decisions without consultation!" He hollered at me and I shouted back and we could be heard at the bottom of the News Room, 50 yards away.

I told Norman Willis, general secretary of the TUC, about this incident and he, like me, found it hilarious and it was included in his after-dinner speeches for the next six months. I gave up any further union negotiations but when I left to go into retirement, the average journalistic salary, from the editor to the newest recruit, was £36,000 a year, which in 1990 put them among the elite earners. Plus expenses. I got no thanks, for it either. I'd moved from being one of us to one of them, though I hope some looked back on the good old days once David Montgomery, a right-wing Ulsterman, former *Mirror* employee and Rupert Murdoch editor and thoroughly disliked by those who had worked with him, took over as chairman and began to recruit journalists on pay in the low-level 'teens of thousands.

Maxwell appointed a Director of Human Resources named Gregory. He didn't understand journalists or journalism, and Maxwell liked cruelly to taunt him in front of us. On one occasion, after Gregory had offended us in some way with a bureaucratic directive of some kind, Maxwell asked a small group of us to hear Gregory's apology and then leave it up to us whether he should be dismissed. It was the kind of humiliation no man should be expected to accept, but he accepted it and we forgave him.

Whether it was down to Gregory's initiative or not I don't know, but Richard Stott and I, as directors of the company, both received letters asking us to sign agreements of confidentiality, or non-disclosure agreements as they came to be known . I wrote back saying that if I were fit to be a director my confidentiality could be assumed. If it could not be assumed, then I was not fit to be a director. Stott was more direct. He threw his letter into the wastepaper basket. Neither of us heard any more of it.

A good and reassuring appointment Maxwell made in 1988 was of my old friend and Downing Street colleague, Bernard Donoughue. Good, because I knew he wouldn't buckle before Maxwell. Apart from Richard Stott and Maxwell's superb, loyal and efficient secretary, Jean Baddeley, I knew no one else in the organisation of that calibre. The appointment didn't last two years. A full account is in his published diaries of the period, suffice to say that they were never going to get on. As Donoughue was to say to me later: "The Maxwells found me a nuisance." Maxwell told him he was dismissed. To make sure of the situation, Donoughue formally resigned.

I should have, but did not, take that as a warning sign of the collapse that was to come. Donoughue warned me, too, that Maxwell had paid too much for the purchase of Macmillan in the US and the Official Airlines Guide, but it was all above board as far as I or anyone else knew and not illegal.

With all the scrupulous procedures, the due diligence for flotation of 49 per cent of MGN went ahead. Every fact that we, as individuals, contributed to the details had to be meticulously checked, with warnings from the lawyers than any mistake could scupper the flotation and with possible dire consequences for ourselves. Some of the requirements were absurd, even for the City of London, like having to prove that the *Mirror* was a Labour-supporting newspaper; it was not sufficient to assert it, we had to prove it. .

Anne Robinson said to me that she was surprised to read in the draft prospectus that the editor of the *Sunday Mirror*, Eve Pollard, was only 39; she thought she was older. Because I was a director, I was duty bound to report this to Burrington, who was in charge of the exercise. After discussions between Pollard and Burrington, the age was dropped from the prospectus. That was typical of the small detail that had to be observed, but it had no importance compared with what was missed.

The Maxwell offices were flooded by the big names of the City of London and the lawyers which always followed in their wake, like the diseases that follow a natural catastrophe. Bees around a honeypot is too kind a way of putting it. They were costing millions. The blue-blooded financiers of the city had golden pockets, stuffed by their clients. Bankers fell over themselves to do business with Maxwell and advisers deluged him with advice and were, in return, deluged with his cash. Mystifyingly to me, the report of the further DTI inspectors appointed to investigate the 1991 collapse said he appointed advisers "of the highest reputation." Perhaps I confused "reputation" with "competence."

Let me quote here from what the Inspectors themselves said, in their report or post-mortem on the Maxwell empire, of the City of London men who wanted to lend to him so that he could increase the size of it: "In the course of this expansion, Mr Robert Maxwell was courted by many leading professional advisers and investment banks who were eager to lend money to him or advise on corporate acquisitions which provided them with significant fees. He entertained and was entertained by leading politicians and world statesmen. The fact that leading professional advisers and banks were prepared to act for him or do business with him was used by him further to re-establish his reputation."

For the flotation, those advisers included Samuel Montagu, Ltd., who collected fees of £8.5million for their expert advice. Their position was that what had happened 20 years' previously when a DTI report said that Maxwell, despite his acknowledged ability, "was not a person who can be relied on to exercise proper stewardship of a publicly quoted company," was no longer relevant, and they were aware of Maxwell's style of management when they agreed to advise him. Knowledge of Maxwell's "style of management" was a matter for which the inspectors later criticised me while excusing others whose knowledge was superior to mine. Everyone else seemed willing to put the past aside or forget it in their greedy pursuit of his money. Some may have persuaded themselves that his style of management had changed, too, though there was no evidence of it. As the inspectors said, Maxwell was courted by politicians and others seeking favours or to do business with him. Let bygones be bygones seemed to be their mantra.

Due diligence and complex financial affairs were not my field of expertise. Equally, newspapers, especially a Labour-supporting group like MGN, were clearly not within the experience of these advisers "of the highest reputation," and not the field of the City experts. Samuel Montagu suggested a list of non-executive directors for the new company when it was floated, including Sir Bernard Ingham, who had been Press Secretary to Mrs Margaret Thatcher when she was Prime Minister from 1979 until her forced resignation on November 22, 1990, just a few months earlier. Had Samuel Montagu had the slightest knowledge of the *Mirror's* politics they would have known that the paper had hounded Mrs Thatcher throughout her premiership. A few perfunctory inquiries would have shown that the political side of the paper, in which Maxwell would always have been involved, had been at daggers drawn with Ingham over several years.

When Mrs Thatcher went to Moscow in 1988, he refused to give me the facilities granted to almost every other journalist who went there, except, possibly, the *Guardian's*. He would not help with my getting a visa, always a problem when visiting Moscow for any journalist. He tried to prevent me attending his morning briefings in a Moscow hotel when he was speaking on behalf of Mrs Thatcher and only conceded after other journalists protested. He would not allocate me a place on her plane when she flew to Tbilisi, when there was no other way I could get there. When I taxed him about his attitude, his reply was: "I will only help my friends, the Lobby." When the Prime Minister had visited a monastery some 60 miles outside Moscow, there was no place for me on the official bus.

Fortunately, I could do without him and his pettiness. A young friend, Nicholas Luis, son of a KGB colonel, who I had met through Maxwell, owned the only Bentley in Moscow and he loaned it to me for the three days of the visit, together with a driver. So imposing was it, that we joined the official convoy to the monastery on the VIP road out of the capital and the Soviet police didn't stop us. When I ran into the usual obstruction of Soviet telephone operators (if you asked to put a call through to London you were met with a surly, "tomorrow") Nicholas fixed it. And when we had an evening free, Julia Langdon, then with another paper in the MGN group, and Gordon Greig of the *Daily Mail* went with me to a sumptuous dinner, with three servants, in Nicholas's splendid dacha in a forest outside the city. (Nicholas, incidentally, was educated at Balliol College, Oxford, and had a fine house at Box Hill in Surrey. His family were among the more equal than others variety, and he was a generous and cordial host). If it hadn't been for Ingham's intransigence we would never have been there in the dacha. But that was a bonus. It didn't excuse Ingham.

When I had done the job of Press Secretary to the Prime Minister, I was quite clear about my purpose: it was to help the Prime Minister, not the press. I didn't have a problem about journalists travelling in the Prime Minister's plane. I stopped that privilege altogether. But I didn't discriminate, taking some and not others. And Hill Samuel, apparently, knew none of this and were proposing Ingham to join the new board. If they had applied the due diligence to our political affairs as they were supposed to do for our financial ones they would never have suggested Ingham as a non-executive director. Maxwell, predictably, exploded with rage, and sacked Hill Samuel. And Ingham, I imagine, would have breathed a sigh of relief.

The whole episode probably prompted Maxwell to appoint me as one of the three non-executives. If a former Press Secretary was going to be offered the job, though he didn't like the idea of non-executives being on the board at all, he had one of his own, even though I had by then retired from the daily commute and the monthly pay and was living on my pension.

So I was mildly surprised when, at 11.30 pm one night in March, 1991, he phoned, just as I was getting into bed, and asked me the usual rhetorical question: would I do him a favour? Rhetorical, because he always assumed that the answer to any request he made to anyone would always be Yes. "You know I retired nine months ago, Bob?" I asked. "Yes, I know," he replied, "but this won't take long. I'd like you to attend a meeting for me." I told him it was extremely foggy and would make travel difficult, but asked: "Where and when?" "Tomorrow morning," he said. "In New York. At 11 am. I've booked you a seat on the Concorde leaving Heathrow at 9 o'clock. It will arrive at JFK at 9.30 and a car will be waiting to take you to the Macmillan Centre in New York. You'll be told what it's all about on the way. A car will pick you up at your home at 6.30." That's what I mean by saying he always expected Yes to be the answer. But I wasn't going to miss a long-held ambition to travel on Concorde, a plane whose eventual abandonment by the French and British Governments was a 20th century Luddite tragedy.

So I got through the fog, was thrilled by the plane and we were on our flight path to land at JFK when what seemed inevitable when dealing with Maxwell's affairs, something unexpected happened: a military plane preceding us had just crashed on the runway and we were to be diverted to Newark in New Jersey. That was the start of the problem. I had no visa, no US dollars, nothing but a vague idea where I was going, no contact phone numbers in New York and a suspicious US Customs official (they are all suspicious) in an otherwise empty Newark airport to smooth over. Reluctantly he let me through. I found a public call box and made a reverse charge call to London and explained to Maxwell's office what had happened.

Eventually, my car arrived from JFK, but by the time I reached New York (the driver didn't even know where the Macmillan Centre was and no adviser was with him), the meeting I was to attend, at the cost of more than £3,000 for the flight, was long over. I went instead to the offices of the *New York Daily News* which Maxwell was intent on buying to ask him to get a return flight booked for me. That didn't work, either. He had already inquired. Concorde was booked up for the next five days. He shrugged, "While you're here," he said, "I'd like you to attend another meeting for me in this building today." That at least was simple. It was with the representatives of the union whose members delivered the *Daily News* throughout the city. Each van had three workers. Maxwell wanted me to negotiate the number down to two, "What can I offer them?" I asked. "Nothing," he replied. "Say No to everything."

That was easy enough, until a senior *Daily News* executive took me aside and said, "Do you realise you'll be negotiating with the Mafia?" No, I didn't. The prospect of repeatedly saying No to the Mafia was a different matter from dealing with the unions back at home. The union, he explained, was only about 1,200 members strong but was one of the richest in America and was controlled by one of the five Mafia families in New York. He told me that a few days earlier a street seller of the paper had come in with a grievance: he had been told to take 20,000 extra copies of the paper to sell (for reasons of their own, the Mafia wanted the paper to make a profit; they didn't want it to close down). When he protested, the executive said, he had been told that it was either that or ending up on the bottom of the Hudson river. He had been made the traditional Mafia offer that he couldn't refuse, but he had been brave enough to come into the office to complain. I went to Maxwell and asked if he knew he was asking me to negotiate with the Mafia. "I don't want to know about it," he said. "Don't tell me."

The *Daily News* executive told me that the Mafia would agree to cut the van crew numbers from three to two provided that all the "routes" were maintained, including those that went the wrong way up one-way streets to which the New York Police Department turned a blind eye. The "routes" were used to distribute the numbers game (also run by the Mafia), of which I had heard but knew nothing. It was apparently highly profitable. We sat and talked, and mildly disagreed but the union representatives were affable and agreed to cut the numbers in the crews and I suggested no changes in the "routes." The only sinister aspect was a large, middle-aged man who unsmilingly came into the room every now and again, whispered something I couldn't hear and left. There was no doubt he was the boss and he wasn't a van driver.

Maxwell threw a party for all the New York notables he could round up to come aboard his yacht moored in the harbour, including the black Mayor of New York, who he told to take off his shoes before he walked on the yacht's cream carpet. I was glad to leave a few days later aboard an ordinary BA flight which took me back to retirement. I'm not complaining. I wouldn't have missed Concorde and the Mafia for the world.

Meanwhile, the flotation was going ahead fast. Four non-executive directors were appointed: me, Lord Williams of Elvel, Alan Clements, former Finance Director of ICI, one of Britain's largest and most solid firms, and Sir Robert Clark, then deputy chairman of the Trustee Savings Bank Group.

Clark was an old friend of Maxwell's and a former chairman of Hill Samuel. I had met him previously when Maxwell introduced us in the bar of the Grand Hotel in Eastbourne during a CBI conference in the mid-1980s. There was no one who would have queried their appointments. Clements was told by Hill Samuel that the events dealt with in the DTI reports of 1971/73 were in the past, though they did point out to him that, "if you let him Maxwell would proceed all over you" and Clark was told by his old firm that MGN was run dictatorially, which he knew anyway.

No doubt bruised by the Ingham affair, Hill Samuel at no time got in touch with me; perhaps they thought I knew of Maxwell's management style. As the inspectors appointed in June, 1992, to look into the affairs of MGN pointed out in their report, apart from two brief and formal board meetings in April, 1991, Clements and Clark did not take the opportunity to get to know any of the executive directors of MGN nor to attend any meetings concerned with the business or management of MGN before the flotation. Lord Williams had had several business dealings with Maxwell in the past and they were well known to each other. The inspectors rightly pointed out that I had little financial experience, especially in relation to the other three, but then Ingham didn't have either. I wasn't appointed for my knowledge of the City of London but for my knowledge of the *Mirror*. The inspectors added that I was given no briefing on my duties and responsibilities as a non-executive director. I suppose I was to make it up as I went along. If Hill Samuel thought I was a Maxell sycophant then they were fools, albeit rich fools. I am not excusing myself, because ignorance of the laws or guidance governing non-executives is no excuse now, but it seems with hindsight that that failure was yet another of many failures by these "advisers of the highest repute" during the whole process of the flotation. I had never regarded the City of London and its reputation with other than scepticism. Today, I would treat it with hilarity. It seems that all of us, advisers and colleagues alike, including all the non-executive directors , in the shrewd words of Donald Rumsfeld on another occasion, did not know what they did not know.

What was not disclosed, certainly not to me or to other members of the new Board as far as I knew, was that Maxwell had been borrowing heavily since the autumn of 1988 and the pension funds were lending shares to Maxwell's private companies as collateral for loans and that at the end of 1990 the private companies only survived through borrowings from pension funds and unauthorised overdrafts. And that was before work started on the flotation. At the time the MGN company was floated on April 30, 1991, Maxwell's private companies owed the pension funds £100million and was using £270million of their assets as collateral.

I attended my first board meeting and was flabbergasted. Before each of us were the minutes of the meeting which was about to take place, including the fact that the meeting adjourned halfway through so that the Remuneration Committee, of which I was apparently a member, could retire and consider the salary to be paid to the chief executive and chairman, Robert Maxwell. It was, I recall, £300,000 a year. Nothing of the sort happened. The minutes were approved. None of the financial experts there said a word. It seemed to be the way that City boards went about their business. It was all over in seconds and I was on record as having approved and recommended Maxwell's salary when in truth, I knew nothing about it and it was never discussed.

That summer, Maxwell continued to buy MCC shares through "offshore entities," the inspectors' phrase, in an attempt to shore up the share price and the cash-rich newspapers with their continual cash flow were providing money and the use of bank borrowings to support the private side share price. Why did the board do nothing about it?. What was to become clear after the crash was that at least some of the directors were suspicious that something wrong was happening throughout that summer and certainly by August. One of them was my old foe, Ernie Burrington. I was particularly aggrieved that during the Labour party conference that autumn, Burrington had a room in the same corridor as I in the hotel where the senior *Mirror* staff were staying. He had every opportunity over a few days to tell me of his suspicions and he never did so. He and Vic Horwood of the SDR group were co-equals and both, I was subsequently told, were worried that summer.

Non-executive directors are at the mercy of the executives and they were the ones who might have been able to do something. They rely upon the executive directors for their information. If they don't get it they remain in ignorance and I remained in ignorance. I had no access to the accounts. No knowledge of the pension fund borrowings. No realisation that the Pension Fund manager of MGN was worried. I did try to get the father of the *Mirror* chapel, Steve Turner to be a member of the Pension Fund committee but Maxwell refused me: I thought because of personal antipathy to Turner.

All I did realise was that Maxwell was very tired and very concerned. With hindsight, which Fleet Street was to possess in plenty after Maxwell died, all the Board, me included, should have been more suspicious. The sale of Pergamon Press, was the outstanding example. If he ever loved any business, Maxwell loved Pergamon. It was the publisher of scientific papers, was highly successful and he was adored by the scientists who saw their work published by it when there was no one else to do it. Its repurchase by Maxwell after the 1973 inspectors' report was the beginning of his global success. To sell it was astounding. The first I knew about it was when I read it in another newspaper. And then on another occasion, in one of his rare bouts of melancholy, he said, "I wish I were 10 years younger," and then added: "My mistake was that I never borrowed as much money as Rupert Murdoch. If I had, the banks would never have stopped helping me." He did ask me to invest my retirement lump sum in a new Hungarian Fund he was setting up. Given that he knew the trouble he was in, that was asking me to throw £50,000 into his bottomless pit. I was cautious enough to tell him I had already spent the money on my garden and I never heard of the Fund again.

He was also during this time in the midst of an old man's passion, perhaps, particularly, an old newspaper proprietor's passion. He was infatuated by his young and efficient secretary, Andrea Martin. It first became obvious to many of us when he took a number of senior *Mirror* staff to Rhodes at the same time as a meeting of EU leaders in an attempt to publicise his new newspaper, *The European*. We all went out to dinner one evening and invited Andrea, who, like me, was staying aboard a yacht Maxwell had hired for the occasion, to join us. She was happy to do so. Maxwell adamantly refused to let her go. The next day a string of dealers arrived on the quayside bringing clothes and other gifts from which Andrea could make her choice, if any. He bought her, reputedly, a car – an eponymous Aston Martin. He was said, also, to have bought her, or helped her to buy, a flat in the newly-fashionable Tooley Street, in Bermondsey, south of the river Thames, where once my childhood neighbours, uncles and cousins worked as dockers.

Newspaper offices were an ever-rich source of speculation and it ran riot, but apart from the Rhodes episode, though, he was discreet. However, his adoration was obvious, the distress of his wife Elizabeth, palpable. That he had a roving eye was undoubted but his fondness for Andrea was serious. What was less obvious was whether she returned his regard. Nevertheless, Maxwell was contemplating divorcing Elizabeth, as devoted a wife as any powerful man could expect. The trouble was, as also became obvious, that Andrea's desires were elsewhere, with the *Mirror's* Foreign editor, Nick Davies, who was more popular on the secretarial floor than on the editorial.

Richard Stott had to fire Davies after he severely embarrassed the paper when he was accused of gun-running in Ohio. He strenuously denied to Stott and me ever having been in that state and we stoutly defended him in our leader column. We knew he was a fantasist, but a Davies as a gun-runner seemed beyond belief. When photographs appeared in another newspaper of him in Cleveland, we challenged him again. He admitted he had been in Cleveland but said he didn't know it was in Ohio. And he was the paper's Foreign Editor! It was like saying he didn't know Marseilles was in France. Maxwell fought strenuously to keep him in his job, but Stott was determined he had to go and I supported him. Davies took us to an industrial tribunal for unfair dismissal but lost the case. I assume that Maxwell did as he did because Nick's departure would upset Andrea. Later, after Maxwell's death, she married Davies.

There was one final row with Maxwell and, subsequently, Burrington, before the roof fell in. The *Mirror* employed three drivers who were on call 24/7 for whatever sudden event might unfold. They naturally had to take their cars home with them because at a moment's notice they might be told to go anywhere. The Human Resources department returned these cars as office cars for personal use to the Revenue authorities and suddenly the drivers found they were having to pay considerable sums for the cars and the petrol they used, which was usually submitted as an expense. It was grossly unfair and Richard Stott and I went to see Maxwell about it. Burrington was with him. Maxwell asked him to leave and then we outlined our complaint on behalf of the drivers. He reluctantly agreed to meet their extra costs. He called Burrington back and told him what was to be done.

At the end of the next board meeting, Burrington, muttering as usual out of the corner of his mouth, said, "By the way, Maxwell has changed his mind about the drivers. He isn't going to do anything for them." "He promised us," I said. "What are you going to do about it?" "He promised *you*," replied Burrington. "He didn't promise *me*." I told him that he was responsible for looking after the staff and called him a coward. He then went to Maxwell and said I had abused him, which was fair enough. I had. His whining made no difference. Eventually, the drivers got paid but the money was taken from Stott's editorial budget. Another sign that things were getting tight.

Maxwell was seen less and less in the office, more and more he was either abroad or with bankers. Whatever was simmering was coming to the boil. At the Labour party conference in

Brighton in the autumn of 1990 we had what was the traditional *Mirror* hotel lunch for the leader of the Labour party, in this case, Neil Kinnock. Maxwell was sombre. Afterwards, he asked Alastair Campbell (who had become political editor of the paper after I retired and was later to be Tony Blair's press secretary) to step out onto a flat roof for a private chat. When Alastair came in Maxwell called me out. I was nervous from the start: Maxwell was sitting on the edge of a low parapet with nothing between him and the pavement several floors below except Eve Pollard, editor of the *Sunday Mirror*. Well proportioned though she was, there was no way she would break his fall if he went backwards. After I jokingly asked him to sit somewhere else for Eve's sake, he came to the point: "Joe, I am going to need your loyalty over the new few months," he said. "I hope I can rely on it." "Bob," I replied, "you know I will always give my loyalty to the *Mirror*." Whatever he was, he was no fool. "I mean loyalty to me," he went on. Once more, I dodged a straight answer. "You are the *Mirror*, Bob," I said, and he had to be satisfied with that.

I knew exactly what he wanted. Many years earlier I had been on a bus packed, seated and standing, with Millwall supporters. One of them ranted continuously about the team – lazy, useless, spent all their time at the greyhound track next door to the Old Den – and the manager – useless, crooked, and robbing the club of the money taken at the turnstiles. "Then why are you going down there?" asked an exasperated fan. "Why?" he replied indignantly. "Because their my team, that's why." And that was exactly the kind of loyalty he had in mind. Bob, right or wrong. Only Jean Baddeley, his devoted secretary for more than 25 years, was capable of giving him that kind of blind loyalty, plus his wife, Elizabeth, and his sons, Kevin and Ian. It meant being an accomplice in any activity, within and without the law. I couldn't do it. Whether he would have opened up a bit more if I had given the pledge of personal loyalty (come what may, was implied) that he wanted I will never know.

I know he felt I had let him down. That the various acts of friendship he had offered me had been spurned. But he was asking too much. To negotiate with the Mafia on his behalf was one thing. To adopt their code was another. That was at the beginning of October, 1991. I never saw or spoke to him again.. Two months later came the deluge

* * * * * * * * * * * * * *

Robert Maxwell disappeared from his yacht, the *Lady Ghislaine*, in the early hours of November 5, 1991, as it cruised the North Atlantic (not the Mediterranean as Molloy wrote in his autobiography). It was characteristic of him that he died on Guy Fawkes's Day. Fate couldn't have chosen a more appropriate day for it to happen. Did he jump, was he pushed, was he assassinated? Or did he, boringly, just fall? For my part, I haven't any doubt that he fell, a conviction shared by Jean Baddeley. After Maxwell's death she moved to Malaga, in Spain, where I last saw her in the summer of 2015 in a splendid restaurant overlooking the town. We had a long talk about her former boss as I tried to persuade her that she should write the definitive Maxwell biography. I had finished my version with the words, "To be continued," but I had never intended to be the one to continue it.

She knew and understood him better than anyone outside his family, and better than most of those. Politely but firmly she refused and insisted that I should complete what I had started. One thing she was certain of: "Bob would never have committed suicide." She said he had been in this kind of financial trouble before and got out of it and he would have got out of it again if he had lived. I was disappointed because she could have written a great book, albeit on Maxwell's side. What I didn't know at the time was that she had just been diagnosed with an aggressive cancer. That November, she married her partner, Mike, an ex-naval officer, and she died in April, 2016. In her day, she could be fearsome, on other days she was charming. She was always loyal and always efficient.. Maxwell relied on her more than any other and gave her a Porsche to celebrate 25 years of employment with him. Naturally, those administrating the bankruptcy proceedings after Maxwell's death tried to claim it back. Naturally, she resisted them and successfully.

The Press and TV are always reluctant to accept an obvious explanation for sudden death, especially of a character as lurid as Maxwell's. Malevolent causes are always a better story than natural. Some suggested suicide, but he was not the suicidal type. Others preferred murder. One former employee, who could not, by the nature of his job, have known Maxwell very well except at the end of a telephone, has regaled after-dinner audiences with colourful stories of how Mossad, the Israeli secret service agency, either pulled or threw him from his yacht in to the cold Atlantic waters and then let him drown. To believe that, one has to believe that in the dark of winter, at about 4.30 a.m., hundreds of miles from anywhere, Mossad operatives boarded the moving *Lady Ghislaine* quietly and unknown to the yacht's crew or with its co-operation and then made their escape, silently and unseen. Perhaps they had an invisible spaceship manned by aliens to help them. Any motive ascribed to Mossad has to be equally colourful and implausible, but it was one of the remarkable facts about the tycoon that people would believe almost anything about him, false or true in comparable measure. But he didn't drown; he died of heart failure.

On November 5 I was lunching at my favourite restaurant, the Gay Hussar, when I had an urgent call to go to the office in Holborn. No explanation was given but I was asked to go right away. I abandoned my lunch and my companions and did so. The editor, Richard Stott, told me that Maxwell had disappeared from his yacht. In other words, he was dead. The board of the company, or those who knew of it, had decided to keep it secret until after the markets closed. My job, in the greatest confidentiality, was to tell Neil Kinnock, as leader of the Labour party, and no one else.

I telephoned his office and spoke to Charles Clarke, his chief of staff and later to become Home secretary under Tony Blair. I asked to speak to Neil and he asked what it was all about. I said I couldn't tell him. He said that unless I did he wouldn't put me through. A ridiculous piece of protective management. (All advisers nowadays try to protect their principal from the press or even from their colleagues, as Theresa May found out after she became Prime Minister. They rarely consider that their boss got to where he or she was without their help and didn't need to be enveloped in swaddling clothes). I said that in that case, when Neil heard the news on TV and radio in the next few hours and asked why he hadn't been told , Clarke would tell him that I had tried but he had refused to put me through. He understood then that it was serious and I spoke to Neil, stressing the secrecy of it all until the markets closed.

Richard Stott was preparing the next day's paper later including the tributes that began to flood in. Some of the tears that flowed were of the crocodile variety. Many others were genuine. Lord (Arnold) Goodman, solicitor to the wealthy, said he could arrange a memorial service in St Paul's Cathedral – fitting really, seeing St Paul's was built on borrowed money from Westminster Abbey. All were shocked. His sons, Ian and Kevin walked around like zombies, neither seeing or hearing. And, did I but know it, there were bankers galore shivering in their hand-made boots and calculating the fall in their incomes and reputation.

The board continued routinely under the chairmanship of Ian Maxwell, who flourished under the responsibility, and he and Kevin continued to address financial institutions about the prosperity of the Maxwell Communications Corporation until a firm of City lawyers broke to us what until then seemed the impossible truth: Maxwell had, in effect, been stealing on a grand scale from every pension fund within reach, including MGN's. It was probably the biggest corporate theft on record at the time. The fearful prospect with which we were faced was that everyone employed in his companies, and former employees like me were going to lose their pension entitlement and the prospect of a comfortable old age was threatened. Sadly, that complete loss was true of the British Helicopter Pilots' Association and of all the staff of the Maxwell Communications Corporation. The inspectors only investigated Maxwell's affairs up until the time of his death, an incomprehensible decision to me. Had they investigated what happened in the period up to the disclosure of Maxwell's crimes they might have wondered why two of his senior executives had transferred their pensions from MCC to MGN, one of them only the day before the exposure, without any recriminations and only a cursory inquiry.

It would be tedious to try to summarise the inspectors' report, delayed for some years by the possibility of criminal conviction, which never materialized, against the Maxwell brothers. Among others, I was found to have had a "limited responsibility" attached to my name because I knew of Maxwell's "style of management." Everyone, especially his so-called expert advisers who prepared the flotation of the company, and those employees specifically excused from blame, knew of it. Only the inhabitant of a desert island without any form of communication would not have known of it. Or two Government inspectors. That's why he was so notorious. Suffice to say, I believe their findings in that respect are wrong. There are two massive volumes to be read by any financial historian who wishes, dispassionately but with scepticism, to bring an objective judgment on the whole scandal.

I was concerned with the immediate aftermath as it affected the journalists and affected me, the fundamentally wrong approach of the majority of the board, and with forming my final conclusions about Robert Maxwell.

MGN and its successor, Trinity Mirror and its successors should be eternally grateful to the journalists on the group's papers and Richard Stott in particular. He was the kind of obdurate, aggressive character without whom the papers might have dissolved in a fruitless and catastrophic strike. He deserves the credit for saving the *Mirror* especially. His death at a comparatively early age of pancreatic cancer left a gap which couldn't be filled in Fleet Street. He led the indictment against Maxwell, exposing the fact that there was an extensive Nixon-like bugging of senior employees. I decided to ignore the board's instructions that our discussions were confidential and to keep Stott fully informed; I broke the news to him late one evening of Maxwell's robberies, immediately after I had heard it. It must have been hard reading for all those politicians and others who had inundated us with tributes, genuine or fulsome, about Maxwell at the time of his death. They didn't know what he was up to, either.

The board interrogated various people who should have known, including auditors, the company secretary and, in particular, the manager of the MGN pension fund. "Why," he was asked, "did you agree to lend without proper documentation Maxwell shares that were owned by the pension fund?" He replied, simply, "I did raise it with him and he placed his hand on my shoulder and said, "Trust me." I wasn't angry with him but sympathized. Anyone who knew Maxwell would have known what a powerful effect that would have upon an honest but terrified employee. To condemn him afterwards was easy.

I was the particular target of criticism by journalists inside and outside the *Mirror*. The cannibalistic instincts of journalists whenever a rival or even a colleague is in trouble came into play. I don't excuse my mistakes any more than I defend the multiple mistakes of those more culpable, but I reject the inspectors' criticisms and I do not feel anything but contempt for some of the downright farcical or even wicked events that took place concerning me. *The Guardian,* sanctimonious as ever, published an anonymous letter allegedly from MGN journalists about me. That is an unforgivable action by a newspaper, only acceptable if it took place in a dictatorship. The *Daily Mail* published a six-paragraph story by their industrial reporter which was partially true in only one of them and false in the rest. He had telephoned my wife that afternoon and she had told him I was out but to ring back at 5 o'clock. He said he would but he never did, but his story next morning included a quote from me and a wholly false figure of my pension (not that I would have told him the true figure had he asked; it was a pension properly contributed to by me and payment had begun before Maxwell had committed his crimes and it was none of his business) *The Sunday Times* demanded to know why I had not exposed Maxwell in my biography of him, written in 1987, for the malpractices he carried out three years later. The simple answer was that I was a biographer, not a prophet. The *Daily Express* had me weeping in the *Mirror's* News Room, which was about the only laugh I had during a terrible month.

The worse came from inside our own paper. I received a letter from Her Majesty's Revenue Office in Edinburgh, curt and offensive, demanding to know why I had not disclosed in my income tax return the fees I had received over the previous five years for my directorship of the company controlling its papers before flotation, and why I had not disclosed the fact that Maxwell had sold to me my Mercedes office car for £1.

The answer to the first charge was I hadn't declared the payments because there weren't any. When I became an MGN director after flotation, my fee for that was properly declared and the tax paid. The answer to the second accusation was that I asked MGN when Maxwell died to charge me the correct amount for a three-year-old Mercedes. They consulted the trade magazine for second-hand cars and asked for £10,500 which I willingly paid. And I had the documentary proof to show them. Previously to that I had paid the tax charged to employees who used an office car. The "information" could only have come from inside the paper and I guessed from whom. I walked into his office, accused him of it and warned him if he ever did anything like that again concerning me he would be fired. He muttered a feeble half-apology, half-denial and I left.

I took the greatest offence, however, against Anton Antonowitz, the reporter who claimed me to be his mentor. A former *Mirror* reporter who had moved to the *Observer* and remained a friend of Anton's, asked him to find out whether it was true that I had moved my pension out of the MGN fund just before the crash. If I had done so, of course, that would have shown prior knowledge on my part of Maxwell's shenanigans and made me a possible accomplice if there had been a criminal act. It was a legitimate inquiry from the reporter; he was ill (and subsequently died) and I understood him asking Anton for help. But there was only one way Anton could have found out the truth or otherwise: he should have come to me. Instead, he approached my secretary, Gloria Sharp, and asked her if she could find out. I found that deceit impossible to accept or forgive from a friend and he ceased to be one from that moment.

Early on, I took the decision not to refute every lying story about me. In one sense that was a mistake. If you don't correct them, they remain on the record and become the accepted truth.

If you determined to correct them all, the day wasn't long enough. The *Guardian,* naturally, published a two-page spread about me written by Francis Wheen, with the usual disregard for facts of a *Private Eye* contributor. I decided it was useless to try to correct all the errors, innocent or malign in that piece, and I ignored it. My tiny revenge was that I decided never to buy the paper again and I haven't done so.

Ironically, many years later, in March, 2006, the BBC showed a docu-drama, *The Lavender List* purporting to show Lady Falkender's later career at 10 Downing Street. The BBC had telephoned me for permission to "read" my books about my time there and I said Yes; after all, anyone could "read" them. They, apparently, meant much more because they later sent me a cheque for £3,000. I heard nothing more from them but, shortly before it was due to be broadcast, the *Daily Telegraph* sent me a video and asked me to review it. I identified 54 mistakes, all of which I could have pointed out and thus avoided if only the script-writer had consulted me, as the BBC's lawyers frequently did when the writ came in from Lady Falkender's lawyers.

I told them that in my opinion she would not go to court but that I would not appear as a witness for them if she did. How could I? I would have had to list all the mistakes and would have been a hostile witness, in fact if not in name. Lord Donoughue said the same. Eventually, the chief BBC lawyer handling the case told me he had been instructed "from on high" to settle out of court. Lady Falkender received £75,000 from the BBC and her solicitors received £200,000, which is how the English legal system works. Refusing to go to court was not a vendetta on my part against the writer, but I hoped it would make Francis Wheen more careful in future about his facts.

Once Maxwell's robberies came to light, Sir Robert Clark and Alan Clements came to the fore. An attempt by Ian Maxwell to retain the chairmanship of MGN was soon and ruthlessly quashed by Clark. Ian decided to call each member of the board to his office and discuss his and the company's future and I was the first. Clark was waiting for me as I came out and he asked what Ian had said. I told him and he swiftly moved to stop any other board member from seeing Ian. Soon afterwards, Ian Maxwell resigned and Clark nominated Ernie Burrington to be the chairman. The field marshal's baton was handed to a corporal and an over-promoted corporal at that. Shortly after that, with the company mired deep in crisis, the new captain of the ship, to mix the metaphor, went off on a three-week holiday in the Pacific on the yacht of a friend. I never spoke to him again after that, though I occasionally saw his car with its showpiece number plate, MGN1, in the streets of Tonbridge. He only lived a couple of miles away.

The firm of investment bankers, Schroeders, were recruited to sort out MGN's problems, largely consisting of a sharply-suited young man of about 30 whose knowledge of the newspaper industry seemed limited. He duly delivered his solutions to the board, beginning with a 10 per cent cut in the papers' journalists, the very journalists who had kept them alive in the horrendous weeks after Robert Maxwell's death. I immediately said that if there were any attempt to implement such a plan I would go down to the News Room, tell the staff what the board had in mind and would personally lead a strike (if they would have me). The cut was not pursued at that point but another way was found.

I soon heard that the Board was seeking to recruit the former Murdoch editor, David Montgomery, to be chairman. That was the last straw for me and a predictable end for Stott, of which he was fully aware. I had not long before written an editorial in the *Mirror* calling Montgomery a liar and a thief, "the jackdaw of Fleet Street." He had worked for us before and the universal opinion of him was that he was detestable. Alistair McQueen, a burly Northern Irishman most of whose friends appeared to be in the SAS, had once flattened him to end an argument he could only disrupt the papers. I phoned Clark and asked if this report were true. He immediately started going off about leaks (what did he expect? It was a newspaper). I immediately resigned. Another mistake. Had I stayed, the boardroom vote would have been against employing Montgomery, though I have no doubt some other way would have been found to bring him in. That was the end of my connection with the Mirror. I never went into the office or wrote for it again. I just contemplated the effect of Maxwell's seven years of ownership.

The tributes flowed in after his death and not only from those who had courted him when he was alive. Fifty seven journalists asked to go to his funeral in Jerusalem but withdrew their request when they found there would not be an office aircraft and that they would have to pay their own fare and for their accommodation. Once his thefts were revealed cynicism took over and the excuse for the huge crowds at the funeral of Louis B. Mayer, the Hollywood tycoon, that they wanted to be sure he was dead, took over. But that was after the event. Geoffrey Goodman, with a left-wing record more authentic than anyone else's on the paper, said in some ways he was a kind man and with good reason; when Goodman reached retirement age Maxwell refused to extend his time at the paper but instead offered him £15,000 a year as a "consultant." Geoffrey accepted but Maxwell was irritated at seeing articles by him in other papers and nothing in the *Mirror* and stopped the payments after a year. But still Geoffrey had a kind word. Anne Robinson said he was her "friend." I said I was saddened by his death and so I was. A dangerous, unpredictable but fascinating flare had been extinguished.

If I were to reprint the praise he received from politicians there would be a widespread blush covering the whole of the Houses of Parliament. He had a magnetic appeal for them. Why else would Jeffrey Archer, for example, come to the top of the MGN building in Holborn to wave him off in his helicopter on a trip to Europe, the unity of which was his one passionate political cause? Why did so many politicians go to his dinner parties in Oxford? Why did the scientific community who owed so much to Pergamon Press still defend him after the pension scandal was exposed?

He appointed and dismissed employees without much thought. His best move was to bring in Peter Jay to run his office, supplanting Jean Baddeley among others. Peter did his work faithfully and efficiently and with great loyalty, but Maxwell never confided in him about his business affairs when Peter was perhaps the ablest person to guide him away from the course he was taking. He was generous towards journalists, both as a group and as individuals. He cared nothing for personal possessions, only for the convenience they brought him. He cared nothing and knew nothing about art. When he wanted to decorate a room with paintings he gave a large sum to Roy Greenslade's wife, Noreen Taylor, to buy some artworks for him and told her to buy one for herself. Never at any time did I enter a room where he was and heard music playing. He once went to Glyndebourne but that was only to please his wife.

He was sentimental about dogs and kind to children, but that could have been said about Hitler. I wrote a Christmas leader about the meaning of Jesus and showed it to him and his eyes filled with tears. It was embarrassing. He was a Hasidic Jew and followed some of its customs, such as bestowing gifts upon visitors (including the book of Gorbachov's speeches he gave my wife), though I suspect the one he followed most was the one that allowed him to forgive his own sins.

His business skills were acknowledged by all the inspectors who investigated him. His resilience was astounding. Cynics said you can't keep a bad man down. But for all his skills and his personal courage – apart from the Military Cross, he refused to give up his seat on a South American airline for a local politician and stayed in his seat. A soldier pointed a gun at his head and told him, "or else…" Maxwell told him to go ahead and shoot - and for his innumerable acts of kindness, there was something deeply and profoundly wrong with him which caused irreparable damage to thousands of lives

He was never convicted of anything except driving his car while shaving and for that he blamed the Tory agent in Buckingham for telling the police. But, in the general way I first used to describe him when he came to the *Mirror*, he was a crook. He was also specifically a crook, too. He stole millions of pounds which were to give a life of comfort to thousands of his employees. An MCC switchboard operator once told me that he had been good for her and her family for 25 years and she loved him. But he destroyed her and so many others by his pension thefts. All the favourable things that can be said about him melt away against the enormity of the harm he did.

He was not a crook in the sense that he lived a life of crime. He didn't despise the law. He was indifferent to it. He would abide by it unless it conflicted with his business ambitions when he would readily bend if not break it. By hook or by crook, as it were. He was amoral. When he stole the pension funds that was a crime. I believe he intended to put them back, but his borrowing was effectively a theft whatever subsequent restitution. He knew it but thought he could conceal it. Hence his remark that his trouble was that he hadn't borrowed as much as Rupert Murdoch, meaning that if he had the banks would still have supported him because they could do no less.

What caused him to be what he was and what he became? How did the son of a large family living in poverty in Ruthenia come to be a matter of interest for a president of the United States (George W. Bush), members of the British Royal family and political leaders throughout the Eastern and Western world? If his ambition was always clear, leaving Czechoslovakia at the age of 16 to join the French Foreign Legion seemed an odd way to go about fulfilling it. But he was then a politically and financial ignoramus. Joining the British Army in 1940 was not, on the face of it, the best career move available at the time to a 17-year-old who couldn't even speak the language, though it did make him, in Keith Waterhouse's memorable phrase, "Capt'n Bob."

My own conclusion from what I saw working for him over a period of seven years was the deciding factor in moulding his character was the Holocaust. To say so is not to make an excuse, for there are no excuses for his last years. But to lose your parents, siblings and grandparents in a Nazi death camp would be for any reasonably sane person an unimaginably horrible experience, which most people would not be able to overcome. The world sees the Holocaust as its greatest ever crime and so it was. But under German law it was legal. Perhaps that contributed to Maxwell's attitude towards the law in general. Curiously, I think Maxwell's attitude to others was also hardened by the death of his eldest son, Michael, after a motor accident. While Michael lay in a coma over many months, Maxwell could not bring himself to visit him in hospital, though his wife went every day. Michael was his favourite child and his intended successor. His death was a death too many for a man who had already known seen too much of it.

What drove him? Not money. Money was something to gamble with, in the City or in the casino. If he won more he could gamble the more. But gambling was only a distraction. The roulette table became the friend he couldn't find. To lose was something to be forgotten. His anger when Richard Stott mocked him for being gazumped over *Today* when he thought the purchase was all wrapped up was palpable. To win was to achieve something. He was always seeking a new peak of success, a new triumph in the business world, a new newspaper to wield influence, a new Kilimanjaro to climb before he finally conquered his Everest. He wanted to succeed and win respect, whether it was with a football team he owned or a strike he defeated, but he was like a mighty tank crushing the field he desired to reap, eventually risking all to win in the USA and Europe when the prizes weren't worth the cost. He would have loved to have friends because he was a lonely man, but he didn't know how to win friends and influence people, only how to make enemies and terrorise others. He tried to buy friends, hence his generosity to journalists, but he never realised true friends don't need to be bought.

He demanded loyalty when he could have earned it more easily. In his personal life he had the unwavering loyalty of his wife, Elizabeth, but was willing to betray it in the end for his love of a young secretary, Andrea Martin, who didn't love him, though she certainly accepted his favours. Had he ever listened to the Beatles he might have been warned by their Money Can't Buy You Love. He drove one son, Philip, away from the family circle, he bullied his beautiful daughter, Ghislaine, and his sons, Ian and Kevin. He was brutal towards them because he was a Victorian father who could not tolerate them not doing what they were told and living up to a standard which he decreed even if he did not necessarily follow it himself. He resolved not to leave any of them a penny, saying they had to make their own way as he had but when he died there was nothing to leave but the burden of his ultimate failure. He gave them the tools, the opportunity, but never trusted them to do the jobs he bestowed upon them.

His loneliness gave him an unsurpassed impatience. He sought gratification but once it was achieved it became meaningless. When he watched television, the remote control became a weapon in his hands against every programme on it and he would switch channels every few seconds. I was with him one afternoon when he was trying to settle (i.e., win) an industrial dispute. He was going nowhere and he slapped his hands on the table and said, "Right, we meet again the same time tomorrow." One of his listeners spoke for all of them and protested: "But tomorrow is Christmas Eve," the one day of the year when every newspaper in England and Wales was closed in all departments. Maxwell glared at him in astonishment, as though he didn't understand the point being made and he probably didn't. But they understood him and promptly gave in.

Janet Hewlett-Davies, my deputy at No 10 and for a short while press adviser to Maxwell, had a gift for summing up people (see the conclusion of my section about Harold Wilson) in a sentence. He was, she said, "a genius and a monster," which was, I think, about right. It is a combination which many men, from Genghis Khan up until the present day, have displayed, to the admiration of some and to the misery of many. It is for the evil they left behind them, rather any good they may have done, for which they are remembered. But for all that, there was a lot to be said for Robert Maxwell and very few willing to say it.

End

Epilogue

Marcia Williams, Lady Falkender as she became in 1975, was Harold Wilson's political secretary for more than 20 years. She was a powerful figure behind the scenes, perhaps the most powerful in post-war history. She exploited her role and seemed to have Wilson, as well as many others, under her thumb. She died in February, 2019, just when this book was going to the printers and it left me free to add to add this epilogue

For four decades or more, every person who has asked me about the relationship between Harold Wilson and Marcia Williams has also asked me at some point the same question: what hold did she have over him? All accepted that there was a hold of some kind, which was significant in itself; why else was she so dominant?. The only explanation seemed to be that there was some awful secret which she could she reveal, something dark and scandalous which would blacken his name and end his career if he didn't bend to her will. In short, blackmail. They looked to me to enlighten them. I couldn't answer except to tell the story to which Bernard Donoughue and Albert Murray, Joe Stone, Lord Goodman and I could all bear witness: that when she was frustrated or angry – and the anger could be monumental – she would tap her handbag and say, "I will ruin him," him being Harold Wilson. That was our principal evidence and I consider it again in this epilogue.

But her death without those revelations ever being made and after a long period of a severe shortage of money prompted a deep and immediate rethink. The problem had been with us too long without a convincing conclusion being reached. I couldn't leave it alone. When she was reduced to asking for money from fellow Labour peers and others, sometimes with the direct suggestion that they had only received an honour because of her and now they should pay for it, I had to ask myself why she hadn't sold the golden bullet, the story that would ruin him? Reticence was understandable while he was alive or while his wife, Mary, survived. But after they were both dead? After all, she had expected £30,000 from the auction in 2018 of the "Lavender List," which in the end didn't take place because of Cabinet Office objections; how much, much more might she have gained, even 50 years after the event, from at last "telling all?"

There was a powerful argument for the "all" to tell when Wilson phoned Donoughue one evening in 1974 and asked him to go to Marcia's home and "rip her phone out because she threatening to ring the press and tell all." That call still weighs heavily with Donoughue and leads him to believe that was something scandalous she could reveal. On this we do not agree.

Over the years, he and I, in particular, continued to speculate on what the hold could have been. Janet Hewlett-Davies,the former deputy Press Secretary under me and the only other one of the last three alive who really knew Marcia from daily experience over a number of years, had no idea, either, though she was more reluctant than us to believe the worst. Was it the straightforward, customary scandal, endemic among politicians, of an affair? But she had tried that when she told Mrs Mary Wilson on January 12, 1972 – Mary's birthday – that "I slept with your husband six times in 1956 and it wasn't satisfactory." Unless you believe that Harold Wilson was lying when he told me, that same evening, about what Marcia had said to Mary – and for what conceivable reason would he lie? – or that it was the product of my twisted and distorted mind, then that is a fact. After Wilson had related the conversation to me, he added, "She has dropped her atomic bomb at last. She can't hurt me any more." It was a wicked, vindictive, even evil act and intended to humiliate, for the trivial reason that she hadn't been told of the lunch in advance. The obvious explanation of her remarks to Mary Wilson was that the story was true, but it might not have been. And would it have ruined him? In 1964, perhaps, when he was trying to become Prime Minister it might have damaged his prospects. But in 1972 onwards? I think not.

She was to boast later that she had successfully sued the BBC for "repeating the libel "of an affair in a documentary drama entitled, "The Lavender List," which wasn't exactly true, either, but that added to the belief that an affair couldn't be the explanation of the hold she had because it would expose her to a charge of perjury if a jury eventually found the story was, in fact, true. She didn't "win" the case in court but outside it. She had issued a writ for libel on a "no win, no fee" basis – in other words, a firm of solicitors had taken up the case on the chance of success. She had nothing to lose with a chance of making a lot of money if the BBC settled out of court, which is exactly what they did.

The BBC lawyers contacted me when the writ was issued because the docu-drama had been loosely -very loosely – based on my book, "The Glimmers of Twilight." I had reviewed the programme, a slip-shod production if ever there were one, for *The Daily Telegraph* and wrote that I had identified 56 errors in it, which may have inspired her lawyers to suggest a writ should be issued. I could hardly appear as a witness for the BBC if the case came to court. Her Q.C. would have had great fun taking me through those 56 errors. Nevertheless, I strongly supported them and told them what Dr Joe Stone, her personal doctor as well as Wilson's, had told me, that she could never appear in a witness box without breaking down. He said he would have to "stuff her" with Purple Hearts if she attempted it in another, lesser, libel action she initiated and withdrew when the newspaper concerned showed a readiness to fight it, and added that she carried a supply of the pills in a locket she customarily wore.

It all ended when a BBC lawyer phoned to say, sorrowfully, that he had been willing to take the case to court but that he had been ordered "from on high" within the BBC to settle. The figures reported were that she had received £75,000 and her lawyers £200,000 in costs, that being the way the law works. In 2007 she issued writs against Bernard Donoughue and his publishers, Random House, for various allegations made in his *Downing Street Diaries*. After Donoughue's solicitors had replied in considerable and formidable detail to her solicitors, the writs were withdrawn. But, after endless talks with Bernard on the subject and from personal experience, I decided that an affair between her and Wilson couldn't be the "hold."

But if not an affair, what? There was always the Soviet connection, of course. Wilson, latterly accompanied by her, travelled more to the Soviet Union during the height of the Cold War in the 1950s and 1960s than any other British politician when he was representing the firm of Montague Meyer, the timber traders. He was on friendly terms with some of the most prominent Russian leaders of the day, including Kosygin and Gromyko. Where other British politicians were given the cold-shoulder he was made welcome. And he was undoubtedly seen as a possible useful agent by the Soviets. As Shadow Foreign Secretary he had refused to condemn the Soviet invasion of Hungary in 1956 but subsequently condemned the East German regime which led the Soviets to believe he would not be of use to them.. Nevertheless, the suspicions about him persisted, promoted by Peter Wright, an MI5 agent, who believed passionately that Wilson was a traitor.

But few people believed Wright. Wilson was his own worst enemy in this regard, with his alliances, detailed earlier in this book, with left-wingers in the Labour party and trade unions who were undoubtedly included among the Soviet's team of "useful idiots." But he was not alone in that respect among prominent Labour leaders. For myself, I never believed a word of the allegations. Matters weren't helped, however, when Marcia refused to be vetted by the security services in 1974 and Wilson had to sign a specific instruction excluding her from the interrogation. Mine lasted three weeks and stretched right back into my childhood acquaintances.

So if that was out, too, what next? Had he committed perjury in a libel writ against an American newspaper which had alleged an affair between him and Marcia? But she was a partner in the writ, so if he were guilty so was she. It carried a plausibility for a long time, but I eventually discarded it. Or a financial indiscretion, secretly making money on the Stock Exchange while condemning the activities of "the City?" But he had no money apart from his parliamentary salary after he left working for Montague Meyer. And he and Mary didn't live the life of luxury and excess, foreign holidays and grand dinner parties, which seem to be the purpose of making excessive sums these days. What is more, when he left No. 10 after his first spell as Prime Minister he was £14,000 in debt. Nothing there, either.

What else could it have been? As I said, we puzzled over it for decades without coming to an conclusive answer. After Marcia's death, my intense thinking led me to the firm decision about the contents of the handbag. It is a wonderfully Damascene conversion and a Holmesian solution: eliminating the impossible meant that the improbable was the truth.

There was nothing in the handbag at all. It was a gigantic bluff, successfully carried out over the years. We were all fooled.

In other words, the "hold" was not sexual impropriety, financial malpractice or treachery but psychological. And to reach that conclusion I have to go back to the origins of their relationship.

What is crucial to understanding Marcia's power over Wilson is to understand what kind of person she was. She was not particularly learned or academic, but she was highly intelligent and ambitious. She wanted control because control gave her power and she used that control and power to humiliate, not just Wilson and his wife but many others, too. She wanted power because that would lead her to the life she wanted to live and the wealth necessary for it. And for two decades she was successful.

She was at her most frightening in small groups. Matthew Parris, the former Tory MP and *Times* columnist, described her as "one of the most terrifying women I have ever met" when she challenged him, in the House of Lords restaurant, about a chapter he had written for a book of Parliamentary scandals. "I'll never forget her piercing eyes," he wrote, "...I departed suspecting this sort of browbeating was, for her, perfectly routine." The headline on his piece read, "Meeting Marcia left me weak at the knees." One man, one meeting, one experience which summed up the impact she could and did make on so many. He was lucky, or unlucky. She didn't have many face-to-face encounters with outsiders.

She was always going to make her mark. After an apparently rebellious time at her school in Northampton and a degree in history at London University, she worked at the Labour party headquarters at Transport House at Smith Square near the Houses of Parliament. For a while, she was secretary to Morgan Phillips, perhaps the most famous of the general secretaries of the party, and in 1956 was appointed to take a shorthand note of the speeches at what became a notorious dinner given by Hugh Gaitskell, the Labour leader, for Prime Minister Bulganin and First Secretary Nikita Kruschev of the Soviet Union who were visiting Britain at Gaitskell's invitation. It was a private dinner which broke down in bitter acrimony. When Kruschev threatened to publish his version of the speeches and questioning at the dinner table, Gaitskell retaliated by saying Labour would publish its own verbatim record. And that record, at least in part, was presumably, in Marcia's shorthand. Kruschev didn't publish.

About this time she made a decision which amounted to a stroke of genius. She decided that Harold Wilson, distrusted and suspected by many senior figures at Transport House and in the Parliamentary Labour party was going to be the star to whom she should hitch her wagon and, perhaps intuitively, she understood the way to do it.

There are various versions about how they first met and neither of them seemed to remember which was correct. One was that they first spoke at the Bulganin-Kruschev dinner. Another was that they were introduced by Arthur Skeffington, MP, who knew Harold was looking for a secretary, the third was that he saw her at a bus stop on the way from Hampstead to the Commons, recognised her from the dinner and gave her a lift into town. That is the one I favour, though conceivably all are true in part. She was a tall, striking blonde and if she were at a bus stop waiting to catch his eye, she would have been at the front of the queue.

Around that time in 1956 Wilson had been receiving anonymous letters from someone in Transport House warning him of a conspiracy against him in the party headquarters. No one was more vulnerable to receiving news of such an allegation than Wilson. Despite his successes, he was a man of profound insecurity. He knew he wasn't trusted and he couldn't understand why. He knew he was considerably more able than most of them but not regarded at that stage as a future leader. The letters confirmed that there was a plot to bring him down and during that car journey Marcia confessed that she had written them. The rest is history at its beginning. She became his secretary.

At that stage in their lives it was an ideal match. She had a keen political mind and she learned from him. . It was in that year, 1956, according to the story she told Mary Wilson in January, 1972, that she slept with Wilson on six occasions. He told me of the conversation; she denied it. But what was undoubtedly true is that she was seen as a figure of significance, especially after he challenged Hugh Gaitskell for the leadership of the party in 1960. Roy Jenkins admired her for one. And she changed Wilson's style of politics. He had been a dull speaker but suddenly he was bright. He had been unfunny but suddenly he was amusing. Political opponents became afraid of his waspish tongue, and his political friends of the Labour benches had someone other than Aneurin Bevan that they could laugh with and cheer. And then a cartoon appeared in the *Daily Mail* comparing him with Mort Sahl, an American comedian. The humour was switched off as suddenly as it began. I learned later that it was Marcia's decision. Unbecoming to a Prime Minister.

I didn't know Wilson in those days; I was working for Scottish newspapers, which didn't have the same attraction for rising politicians as the nationals and only met him once or twice. But I did have the opportunity to watch him. After he became leader of the Labour party and I joined the left-inclined *Sun* I got to know him and Marcia better. She paid rare visits to the Press Gallery in the late 1960s, usually with Walter Terry of the *Daily Mail*. She was bright and cheerful, though a wary mixer among journalists. I was asked by Terry's wife, Mavis, what I thought of Marcia and I was generous in my praise of her. It was another of the landmark mistakes in my career.

I followed Wilson when he was Prime Minister on visits to Russia and the United States and covered his 1966 general election tour and I accurately forecast the by-election result in Hull in early 1966 which Labour won against the odds, causing Wilson to call a general election in March . I must have impressed her because at the start of 1968 I was asked to become his deputy press secretary and he wouldn't have made that offer without her approval. I refused it, but the offer was renewed at the end of the year and I accepted it on the terms I outlined earlier in this book. I was welcomed generously by her, clearly as an ally against the civil service. Just one thing disturbed me when I took over as press secretary in June: she chose my secretary and I wasn't consulted. She was making a civil service appointment which strictly was nothing to do with her. But the secretary, Miriam, was great and I got praise for appointing the first black woman to work in No.10.

Still, everything on the whole went swimmingly. I attended the political meetings of the tight circle around Wilson, which included Gerald Kaufman, whose later political career was crowned by being Father of the House of Commons, but who jumped whenever Marcia said jump. He was completely her creature and was protected by her when he offended Wilson and, in particular, when he offended me by throwing a glass of whisky over me. She leaped in and saved his face, literally, as I stood over him in Wilson's study and was threatening to alter the shape of it. She failed to attend the party conference that year because she was "indisposed." That was acceptable if, as I thought then, regrettable. Actually, she had given birth, though I didn't know it and the father was my old friend, Walter Terry, and I didn't know that, either. But her demand that Wilson return to London to see her because she was ill was alarming. It showed she had power I hadn't realised she possessed. More so, because Wilson was preparing to go until I forcibly objected.

The doubts grew when Wilson convened a meeting of his circle to decide when he would call a general election. We all said yea or nay and I was in reluctant agreement for a poll in June, 1970. Marcia was asked by Wilson for her decision, which we all understood would be decisive. "I am in favour if we are going to win," she proclaimed, "but not if we are going to lose." For a Marcia interpreter, which I was rapidly becoming, that meant she was not to be blamed if we lost. We opted for June and we lost. And on the dismal Friday morning when we waited for Wilson to return from his constituency at Huyton. I met him at the door of No. 10. "Well," he said, "Marcia was right. She said we shouldn't have gone." That was too much for me. "She backed both horses in a two-horse race, that's why she was right," I said. The tide of my opinion was turning.

Breakfast that morning was a wake. Marcia laid into Joe Kagan, the Gannex manufacturer whose coats Wilson always boringly wore, demanded that he provided a lorry to move the office equipment and files and treated him in a frighteningly abusive manner. Most frightening, however, was the way he submissively accepted her tirade. She organised our departure from No.10, saw the Wilsons off to Chequers for a last week-end, demanded that the office of Leader of the Opposition in the Commons be cleared out immediately when the Tories wanted to wait until Monday and stared at the crowd who gathered to boo us in Downing Street. It was all rather magnificent in its way, but entirely without sympathy or emotion for those who had lost a job and a Prime Minister. No hugs for Harold and Mary Wilson. No show of affection for anyone. It was almost sinister. She had been thwarted and it was time to start again.

Out of office, unprotected by civil servants, things soon on a different hue. Lord Goodman quickly arranged the publication of Wilson's record of the 1964-70 Government, with serialisation rights sold to the *Sunday Times* for a sum of about £240,000, plus extras. The extra included the payment of £5,000 to me for a year's work writing or rewriting the book and payment to Marcia's sister, Peggy, to type it at a time when we were already employing nine secretaries. If I were to write the book I didn't need a typist; I'd do it myself. I also slowly gathered that Marcia, who, like me, was not even mentioned in the book, was to get a substantial part of the paper's money, probably £60,000. Why? Why? Why? She contributed nothing to the book.

Then, after I had already written the first chapter, the first explosion occurred and I saw how terrifyingly angry she could get. It was over the trivial matter of my attending a secretary's leaving party to which she had not been invited. She burst into the room where Wilson and I were working on his book screaming at Wilson that I was "disloyal" and should be sacked and shouting that I was to have nothing to do with the book. She said that she was resigning and going to live a normal life and ran out. "What do we do now?" I asked Wilson. "Don't worry," he said, "She will be back."

But the anger and the screaming were deliberate. She achieved her purpose. I wasn't sacked but I was removed from the production on the book, except surreptitiously, because the next day Wilson told me he had decided to write the book himself. Meanwhile, the *Sunday Times* paid my salary. When that ran out, I had evidence of what I was beginning to suspect had been happening for a long time: Wilson paid me himself, in £50 notes, each month. I was not on the office payroll which was controlled by Marcia. I paid my own insurance stamp. The money came from a parcel of banknotes which Sir (later Lord, don't bother to ask why) Desmond Brayley, an East End of London industrialist who was later to die while awaiting trial at the Old Bailey for fraud, had given to Mary Wilson one morning when he arrived, unannounced, at the Wilsons' house. Mary, startled, naively asked Wilson's driver, the street-wise Bill Housden, what she should do with it; should she take it to the bank? "No, no," exclaimed Housden. Parliamentary scrutiny of an MP's income was much easier in those days, but even so that would have been a risk too much to take.

Marcia returned to the office and reduced it to chaos. Her sister, Peggy, dutifully typed Wilson's incredible output of small hand- writing , and I saw how completely subservient she was to her sister. She was totally under her control. A few years later Peg had a budding romance with a hospital registrar which was destroyed when Marcia had him investigated by the police and found he was not what he claimed.

John Schofield-Allen, an importunate freeloader who was once mooted as Marcia's second husband, was brought in to work in the Opposition offices. He, too, was terrified of her and didn't last after he abandoned work for the day for lunch at the Reform Club and never returned. Ken Peay, a wealthy man willing to work for nothing, came in to run the office, saw how inefficient it was, and advised Wilson that the only way to cure the fault was to sack Marcia. That was suicidal and he left. She remained in control.

Albert Murray, former MP for Gravesend and an old friend of mine, was then appointed to take charge of the day-to-day running of the office. I was amazed that she accepted my suggestion but not surprised when Wilson told me it was her idea. At first, all was well, but she turned cruelly against him when she discovered how close a friend of mine he was and how close a friend of Bernard Donoughue's he became. She complained to Wilson of his heavy drinking after I had seen her plying him with gin and tonics one lunchtime. One evening, Albert's wife, Ann, phoned me at home in tears. He had just arrived home and gone straight to bed, clearly in distress... She eventually got the truth from him: Marcia had deliberately withheld his salary after a minor dispute. Their house was new, the mortgage had to be paid and without his pay he couldn't do it. She deliberately humiliated him because she had the power to do so.

It was 10pm. I immediately phoned Wilson and told him what had happened. He was appalled but blamed Albert. He had made a mistake, Wilson said, she wouldn't do a thing like that, a risible excuse and he knew it because he promptly told me to tell Albert to see him first thing in the morning and he would give him his personal cheque. Again, it was all about control. Marcia knew about the new house, knew Albert was short of money and hit him where it would most hurt.

After that she sought to humiliate him again. When the donor she adored, Eric Miller, invited Albert to his son's barmitzvah in Jerusalem, she forbade it. When the traditional drinks party was held at No. 10 for Trooping the Colour she prevented his wife from attending, though other staff members were able to bring family members. And she forbade Albert from attending Wilson's count at 1974's second election for no other reason that she could.

When we returned to No. 10 after the 1974 election her behaviour had grown worse. Her own staff were completely dominated, as usual, but I saw how she would contest the civil service and win, especially over his diary. All official appointments had to be cleared by her. Appointments were made by her, however, without anyone being told. Wilson reacted against a meeting she made for him with Peter Walker, the former City of London financier and Tory Cabinet Minister, and Jimmy Goldsmith, the billionaire financier. "I can't see those," he told me. "I've spent my life attacking their kind." Shortly afterwards, she arranged a lunch with Goldsmith and David Frost. Wilson cancelled that, too. Finally, she arranged a meeting with Goldsmith alone, ostensibly to discuss France's planning regulation system and Wilson told me how knowledgeable Goldsmith was. She had won in the end. She had regained control and she had gained a friend in Goldsmith, who was to pay for her two children to attend the expensive Westminster School and, coincidentally (!) receive a knighthood in the Resignation Honours List, despite Wilson saying to Donoughue and me: "Why should I give him anything, I hardly know him?" Because Marcia promised him an honour, that was why. She had control.

Let me not mince words. That control – and there are numerous other examples which I could give - was used corruptly and criminally. Honours were given for monetary favours. Kagan and Miller helped her directly to live a life-style that meant she owned two expensive houses in a West End mews. In return they gained access to the top of the political world. That control enabled her to employ five servants. That ensured she used the Prime Minister's power to obtain a speedy visa for one of them. That gave her a house in the country and two cars. That allowed her to use the Prime Minister's car and civil service driver to do her shopping or take her to Harrod's to get her hair done, about which other drivers complained to me when they had to stand in for Housden's absence. That forced a British diplomat in one Arab state to hand over a letter of commendation for her brother, Tony's business to an Arab sheik.

She used that power and control to gain entrance to the film and theatrical world that she longed for so much. She only became genuinely distraught when issues arose which she couldn't control, such as when she faced a demand from the Inland Revenue for £20,000 capital gains tax on the profit made from slag heaps in Ince-in-Makerfield which she shared with her brother, Tony. She panicked in front of me, crying and moaning that she was going to be sent to prison because she didn't have the money to pay it. Lord Goodman was called in and I have detailed in this book how Wilson tried to get a Cabinet colleague to pay it for her.

It was at this time that Dr Stone proposed to me and, separately, to Bernard Donoughue, and then jointly to us that he should "dispose" of her – murder her, to put it more brutally - and we rejected it out of hand. Perhaps we should have questioned him more closely why he thought it was necessary. I believe, now, that he recognised a medical condition for which death was the only cure. Nevertheless, it was going much too far.

Throughout our last two years at Downing Street, life with Marcia was a constant burden. Wilson told Donoughue that he received letters every week from her demanding that I be sacked. He also told Donoughue to watch out for her attempting to "control" him, as she had done with Gerald Kaufman "and other wimps." As I have detailed, she tried repeatedly to get Donoughue out of Downing Street. She fought remorselessly to keep Wilson in office, although he was clearly unwell. In the end, he defied her but not before awarding her the peerage which did so much damage to his reputation.

When the story of the Resignation Honours List leaked, she took fright. Desperate attempts were made to get more "respectable" people into it and the publication of the list was delayed because of the press and public outcry.

After Wilson ceased to be Prime Minister, her control and added income continued, though much diminished. She had secretly arranged a TV series with David Frost and Yorkshire TV and was a "consultant" to the series. She was appointed to the board of one of Goldsmith's subsidiary companies and to a small South London building society. She attended the House of Lords regularly and claimed her fees for doing so; she was a member for 44 years and never made a speech or sat on one of its committees.

Albert Murray, made Lord Murray in *the* List, worked in Wilson's office for a while after he left office but played an active part in the House of Lords. He collapsed and died in the directors' box at his beloved Millwall football club. His friends blamed the stress of working under Marcia for several years. Before he left the office, Albert gave me about a dozen Christmas cards which had been sent to Wilson and which, in a temper, she had thrown into the wastepaper basket. They had some historical and small monetary value. The cards from the Soviet President, Podgorny, and the Soviet Prime Minister, Kosygin, were falling apart and stained where tea cups had been placed upon them. Others included, in good condition, were from the King of Norway, the King and Queen of Belgium, Indira Gandhi, Chou en Lai, the Dalai Llama, Eric Honecker, the Austrian politician, Waldheim, "Field Marshal Idi Amin, VC" (both the title and the honour were bogus) and Mrs Bandaraniaka, Prime Minister of Sri Lanka.

As Wilson's health faded she formed a closer friendship with the woman she had once held in contempt, Mary Wilson. They were both at his bedside when he died. She used to invite Lady Wilson to lunch at the House of Lords but I am told by someone who knew them both well that Lady Wilson stopped going because Marcia was so late so often in arriving that she felt "humiliated."

And that had become the story of her life: Humiliation. Power. Control. Avarice. Not her handbag.

Index

Lightning Source UK Ltd.
Milton Keynes UK
UKHW011308290519
343529UK00001B/104/P